D0618965

Themes and Debates

in Early Childhood

Edited by
Mary Wild and Alison Street

Belongs to:

~~[scribbled out]~~   ~~[scribbled out]~~

IF FOUND : ~~[scribbled out]~~

Bought in 2019 - This shouldnt
ebay.

be sold.

Themes and Debates

in Early Childhood

Edited by
Mary Wild and Alison Street

Los Angeles | London | New Delhi
Singapore | Washington DC

Learning Matters
An imprint of SAGE Publications Ltd
1 Oliver's Yard
55 City Road
London EC1Y 1SP

SAGE Publications Inc
2455 Teller Road
Thousand Oaks, California 91320

SAGE Publications India Pvt Ltd
B 1/I 1 Mohan Cooperative Industrial Area
Mathura Road
New Delhi 11 0 044

SAGE Publications Asia-Pacific Pte Ltd
3 Church Street
#10–04 Samsung Hub
Singapore 049483

Editor: Amy Thornton
Development editor: Geoff Barker
Production controller: Chris Marke
Project management: Deer Park Productions
Marketing manager: Catherine Slinn
Cover design: Wendy Scott
Typeset by: Pantek Media, Maidstone, Kent
Printed by: MPG Books Group, Bodmin, Cornwall

Library of Congress Control Number: 2012953310

British Library Cataloguing in Publication Data

A catalogue record for this book is available from the British Library

ISBN: 978 1 44625 635 0 (hbk)
ISBN: 978 1 44625 636 7 (pbk)

Contents

Contributors

Mary Wild is a Principal Lecturer in Child Development and Education, and has previously led the Early Childhood Studies degree at Oxford Brookes University. She teaches across a range of courses for practitioners and professionals in Early Years, including the MA Childhood Studies. Mary is a qualified teacher with experience in both the primary and Early Years sectors. Her research interests include: early childhood literacy; children's thinking; professional development within the Early Years workforce; and parenting. Mary is a member of the British Psychological Society and the British Educational Research Association (BERA). She is a member of the Strategy Group of the Early Childhood Studies Degrees Network, which brings together course leaders of the ECS degrees from across the UK.

Alison Street has spent 30 years in community music education, focusing on day-to-day musicality in families with young children. She composed and compiled all musical materials for the PEEP (Parents Early Education Partnership) Learning Together programme, which supports parents with their children's early learning. Her doctoral research (2006) explored singing in mother–infant interactions and mothers' perceptions of their roles. Project management and research include: *Music One-to-One* with parents with children under two; *Musical Babies* with practitioners in urban settings; and *Time to Play* (2008–9) in creative play with Muslim families. She works as a consultant and associate lecturer at Oxford Brookes University and on the Masters Programme in Early Childhood music, which is accredited by Birmingham City University. She is co-author, with Linda Bance, of *Voiceplay* (2006), published by Oxford University Press.

Catharine Gilson is a Senior Lecturer in Early Years at Oxford Brookes University. She is Subject Coordinator for the Early Childhood Studies degree and teaches across a range of courses in the Early Years strand of the PGCE, the Foundation Degree in Early Years and the BA in primary teacher education. She has previously worked as a teacher and as a local authority Early Years advisory teacher. Her current doctoral studies are focused on the professional development of teachers and practitioners within the Early Years.

Ingram Lloyd has worked as Programme Manager for Early Years Professional Status and as a Senior Lecturer in the Early Childhood Studies department at Oxford Brookes University. She is a qualified teacher and has worked mainly with 3–8 year-old children in the maintained and independent sectors, latterly as a head teacher. She trained at the Froebel Institute, Roehampton, and has an MA in education. Her specialism is outdoor play, risk taking and how the associated issues of outdoor play and risk taking affect the views of children, parents and staff alike.

Helena Mitchell is Head of the School of Education at Oxford Brookes University, one of the largest education departments in the country. Between 2000 and 2008, Helena was involved in the development of a range of courses focused on early years at Oxford Brookes University, liaising with the local authority on these developments. She also led on the establishment of the Early Childhood Studies degree at Oxford Brookes in 2000. Prior to working at Oxford Brookes, she worked as a teacher and deputy head teacher of a large nursery and infants' school in inner London. Her research work has focused on Early Years topics, including early literacy, student employability, and also workforce development especially for Early Years practitioners. She is a member of the British Educational Research Association (BERA) and the Strategy Group of the Early Childhood Studies Degrees Network, which brings together course leaders of the ECS degrees from across the UK.

Nick Swarbrick works as a Programme Lead in the School of Education, Oxford Brookes University, with responsibility for Early Childhood Studies and the Early Years Foundation Degree. His teaching centres on modules on Play and Pedagogy, Outdoor Learning in the Early Years, and Children's Spirituality. He also teaches on the Primary PGCE. Before joining Oxford Brookes, he was head teacher of a nursery school in Oxford. Nick's current research interests focus on young children's literature and the outdoors.

Rachel Friedman and **Carolyn Silberfield** also contributed to an earlier edition of this book (first published in 2007 by Learning Matters), originally entitled *Early Childhood Studies Reflective Reader*.

Acknowledgements

Every effort has been made to trace the copyright holders and to obtain their permission for the use of copyright material. The publisher and author will gladly receive any information enabling them to rectify any error or omission in subsequent editions.

Chapter 1

Extract 1

The Marmot Review (2010) Fair Society, Healthy Lives. Strategic Review of Health Inequalities Section 2.6.1 Early Years and Health Status, pp60–2

Extract 2

Vandenbroeck, M., in *European Early Childhood Education Research Journal*, 17(2), June 2009: pp165–7

Chapter 2

Extract 1

Alderson, P. (2008) (2nd edition) *Young Children's Rights: Exploring beliefs, principles and practice.* London: Jessica Kingsley Publishers

Extract 2

Freeman, M. (1993) Laws, Conventions and Rights. *Children and Society*, 7(1): pp37–48 and articles 3 and 12 of the UNCRC (wording of original version)

Chapter 3

Extract 1

Clough, P. and Nutbrown, C. (2005) Inclusion and development in the Early Years: Making inclusion conventional? *Child Care in Practice*, 11(2): pp99–102

Extract 2

Siraj-Blatchford, I. (2010) Diversity, inclusion and learning in the Early Years, chapter 11 in G. Pugh, and B. Duffy (eds) *Contemporary Issues in the Early Years* (5th edition) pp153–4. London: Sage

Chapter 4

Extract 1

Vygotsky, L.S. (2004) Imagination and creativity in childhood. *Journal of Russian and East European Psychology*, 42(1): pp11–12

Extract 2

Rogoff, B. Mistry, J. Göncü, and Mosier, C. (1993) Guided participation in cultural activity by toddlers and caregivers. *Monographs of the Society for Research in Child Development* serial nos 236, 58(7): pp5–6

Chapter 5

Extract 1

Bruce, T. (1991) Free-flow play and its features, in *Time to Play in Early Childhood Education*. London: Hodder and Stoughton, pp59–60

Extract 2

Rogers, S. (2010) Powerful pedagogies and playful resistance, in L. Brooker and S. Edwards (eds) *Engaging Play*. Maidenhead: Open University Press, p161

Chapter 6

Extract 1

Gerhardt, S. (2004) *Why Love Matters. How affection shapes a baby's brain*. London: Routledge, pp214–217

Extract 2

New, R., Mardell, B. and Robinson, D. (2005) Early childhood education as risky business: Going beyond what's 'Safe' to discovering what's possible. *Early Childhood Research and Practice*, 7(2) Fall: pp1–15

Chapter 7

Extract 1

Edward C. Melhuish, Phan, M.B., Sylva, K., Sammons, P., Siraj-Blatchford, I. and Taggart, B. (2008) Effects of the home learning environment and preschool center experience upon literacy and numeracy development in early primary school. *Journal of Social Issues*, 64(1): pp108–9

Extract 2

Brooker, L. (2010) Constructing the triangle of care: Power and professionalism in practitioner/parent relationships. *British Journal of Educational Studies*, 58(2): p183, p184

Chapter 8

Extract 1

Organisation for Economic Co-operation and Development (OECD) (2006) *Starting Strong II*, pp166–7. OECD Publishing

Extract 2

Moss, P. (2007) Structures, understandings and discourses: Possibilities for re-envisioning the early childhood worker. *Contemporary Issues in Early Childhood*, 7(1), 2006: pp31–4

Chapter 9

Extract 1

Wenger, E. (1998) *Communities of Practice Learning, Meaning and Identity*. Cambridge: Cambridge University Press, pp252–3

Extract 2

Glenny, G. and Roaf, C. (2008) *Multiprofessional Communication: Making Systems Work for Children*, pp95–7. Maidenhead: Open University Press

Foreword

Helen Moylett

In 1999 as we were about to enter the twenty-first century, Professor Tina Bruce, who has spent many years exploring early childhood as a parent, teacher and researcher (see Extract 1, Chapter 5 of this book for Bruce's definition of play) wrote about her own memories of early education and her fondly remembered favourite teachers.

> *These teachers ... seemed to create a feeling of calm, an anchored feeling, a settled feeling in a group which felt like a real community, and yet they seemed to do this in order to jolt you and make you rethink or think anew in quantum leaps. It was exciting to learn with them. You had a sense you would never be the same again, and you weren't! ... These were not quick fix, get there early, get good outcomes, good SATS results, League Table teachers. These were help-you-to-be-long-term-forever-learner kinds of teacher.*

(Bruce, 1999, p36)

Now, more than ever, all adults working with young children need to be that kind of teacher. (This holds good whether or not you have, or aspire to, qualified teacher status – all Early Years practitioners are involved in teaching young children through the positive relationships and enabling environments they provide.) Several years into the century, research and practice have confirmed John Holt's (1964) claim that since we cannot know what knowledge will be most needed in the future, it is senseless to try to teach it in advance. *Instead, we should try to turn out people who love learning so much and learn so well that they will be able to learn whatever needs to be learned*.

This is a book which recognises both the powerful learning capacities of young children and the need for practitioners to see themselves as learners too – to be like the inspiring women that Bruce praises and thanks for her own lifelong interest in learning. These were the sort of practitioners who listened to the voice of the child because they valued those children and knew that, as Gussin Paley (2004:8) says, *It is in the development of their themes and characters and plots that children explain their thinking and enable us to wonder who we might become as their teachers*.

This book is written by authors who believe in learning power both for students and those already in practice. It is informed by passion and commitment to children's entitlements to have the best provision whatever their personal or family circumstances. The writers have high expectations both for children and for student and practitioner readers. They also continue to wonder about their own practice as a community of university teachers and researchers. This is not, therefore, a quick read providing a collection of top tips. There are plenty of other books like that and they have their place, but this book goes beyond them into fundamental issues that inform and shape practice. Nonetheless it is easy to read because the authors use clear accessible language, but it is designed to provoke thought and it takes time to respond to the challenges presented.

The authors' mission is to engage the reader, whether student or practitioner, in exploring a range of issues which inform and shape Early Years pedagogy. Effective pedagogy rests on an understanding of both how children develop and learn, and the practices through which practitioners can support and extend that learning. Developing effective pedagogy therefore requires deep understanding about children and where they are in their lifelong learning journey, as well as willingness to be self-critical and aware of one's own impact. This in turn depends on the recognition that everyone's practice is rooted in their values, beliefs and knowledge and supported by theory and experience as well as the social and cultural context in which they work. Being a good Early Years practitioner requires self-knowledge and the ability to de-centre and stand in others' shoes. In other words, being an effective practitioner can be complex and demanding. It can also, of course, be life affirming and wonderful and it is in the small everyday interactions in settings that we see all facets of theory in action.

What Early Years practitioners do is intensely practical and may seem unrelated to theory when it's happening. But we all have beliefs and values that inform everyday practice. An example might be the way we praise children. Most, if not all, Early Years practitioners believe that praise is important in motivating children and recognising achievement, but have you thought about how and what you praise?

Let's look at an everyday example. A child is standing beside her picture looking pleased. Practitioner A smiles and says *Good girl, I love your picture*. This may sound supportive but think again about the hidden message the child may be hearing after the glow of recognition has worn off. Maybe it's *I am a good person when you love what I do*.

Practitioner B takes a different approach. She smiles and says *You really thought about the colours you used; which part of the picture do you like best?* Again the child will get a glow from being praised but the underlying message she is hearing is *My thought process is valued and I can evaluate the finished result*. In other words, she has control and her motivation can come from within, rather than being dependent on external rewards.

Such small everyday interactions are where learning happens for children and where they begin to become lifelong learners. They need and deserve adults who have really thought about the questions that Mary Wild and Alison Street pose in the Introduction: *Why do I believe what I believe?* and *Why do I do what I do?* Otherwise they get practitioners who are minding rather than teaching, boring rather than inspiring. Tina Bruce's teachers were not fettered by routine and they were inspiring because they were learners themselves who saw the children and themselves as part of a community. They were in love with learning and understood that the way to get children to be good learners was to share that love. In order to do that of course you have to see yourself as a thinker. As Lilian Katz says: *If teachers want their young pupils to have robust dispositions to investigate, hypothesize, experiment, conjecture and so forth, they might consider making their own such intellectual dispositions more visible to the children* (Katz 1995, p65).

This book helps to guide the reader into some fruitful avenues for thought. It provides some readings to provoke ideas and then unpacks possibilities for further thought and action while leaving plenty of routes for further exploration and discovery. The key themes which recur throughout the book and link the sections together are:

- identities;

- learning and well-being;

- professionalism.

The first section on identities really unpacks some of the taken-for-granted language of inclusion and exclusion. It may also feel very personal, as we all have personal and professional identities which are shaped by our own experience. There are no easy answers to some of the questions raised, but in relation to young children this section reminded me of the wise words of Maria Robinson (2003):

> *In order for professionals to work effectively with babies, young children and their parents, their first duty is to recognise themselves for who they are, what they believe and why. The emotions we see in infants and young children do not only belong to them, they belong to us. We have all been helpless infants, we all carry with us our history including that of being parented and therefore, consciously or unconsciously, we know what children are going through.*

The second theme of learning is, of course, tied up with identity. Who we are and who we might become as a learner inform our reactions to other people and the environment. The second section of the book explores how our habits of mind are formed as our brains develop and we come to understand ourselves as learners. The role of adults in this process is key. It is through the active intervention, guidance and support of a skilled adult that children make the most progress in their learning. As this section illustrates, this does not mean pushing children too far or too fast, but instead meeting children where they are emotionally and intellectually, showing them the next open door, and helping them to walk through it. It means providing secure attachment relationships and being a partner with children, enjoying with them the power of their play and exploration, and the thrill of finding out what they can do.

The emphasis in education has moved away from giving information and towards supporting learning skills – what Guy Claxton has called *building learning power*. Learning to learn has been identified as crucial for personal success and participation as citizens in an inclusive society (Education Council of the European Union, 2006) and many projects all over the world are focusing on the learner as a whole person.

And, despite all this ongoing interest and activity, we have too many children whose capacities to be citizens of the twenty-first century are being wasted like Emily's, a 15-year-old GCSE student.

> *I guess I could call myself smart. I mean I can usually get good grades. Sometimes I worry though that I'm not equipped to achieve what I want, that I'm just a tape recorder repeating back what I've heard. I worry that once I'm out of school and people don't keep handing me information with questions ... I'll be lost.*

> (Claxton, 2004, p1)

As Claxton puts it, *Emily sees herself as ready for a life of tests, but not the tests of life.*

Emily appears to have no sense of agency as a learner and to be sadly aware of her learned helplessness – what Carol Dweck (2006) calls a *fixed mindset*. The dangers of concentrating on short-term fixes at the expense of deep learning have been amply demonstrated by one of the strongest sources of evidence we have about the long-lasting effects of how we are encouraged to learn when we are young – the High Scope Perry Pre-School evaluations. The heart of the High Scope approach is social constructivist (see section 2, Chapter 4), supporting children to plan, carry out and review their own learning, motivated by their own ideas and interests and supported by skilled practitioners as appropriate. The original High Scope project has been the subject of a rigorous longitudinal study following children who took part in the programme until they were over 40 years old. One strand of the research compared children who had been in the project with those who attended 'direct instruction' (behaviourist/formal, practitioner-led) pre-schools.

Children who had attended direct instruction settings showed early achievement gains in English and maths, but as the children got older that advantage disappeared and the balance shifted. By the age of 15 children from the direct instruction group were half as likely to read books, twice as likely to have committed 'delinquent acts' and were far more likely to be socially and emotionally troubled than children from High Scope and traditional nursery schools. By the age of 23, the direct instruction group were almost four times more likely to have been arrested and had almost eight times the rate of emotional impairments. They were about half as likely to have graduated from college.

When, at age 40, the High Scope group were compared with children who did not go to any pre-school provision it was found that they exhibited less anti-social and criminal behaviour and were less likely to be drug users. They were far more likely to be doing voluntary work in the community, have stable marriages and higher earnings. It is significant that these High Scope children were all born in poverty and had been identified as at risk of academic failure. In other words, social disadvantage does not have to be a life sentence – good quality Early Years settings can make a difference, particularly if they work in partnership with parents.

Both High Scope in the US and the Effective Provision of Pre-School Education (EPPE) in the UK focused on children in provision for 3 to 4 year olds. Other studies have linked babies' persistence at various ages with parenting style and toddler outcomes. For example, one study compared babies' persistence at 6 and 14 months with their mothers' 'teaching style' They found that mothers who provide access to stimulating objects, are sensitive and responsive to children's emotions and support children's behaviours just above their current level, may foster both persistent behaviour and advanced cognitive development in the future. They suggest that practitioners should work with at-risk children and families to develop strategies that support the development of persistence as early as possible (Banerjee and Tamis-LeMonda, 2007).

These findings are supported by some recent research (McClelland et al., 2012) which interestingly compares the long-term effects of early persistence with the long-term effects of reading and maths ability. The study followed 430 children from pre-school age to adulthood. Contrary to researchers' expectations, they found that maths and reading ability did not have a significant effect on whether or not students gained a university degree. But those who could concentrate and persist at the age of four were almost 50 per cent more likely to have completed a degree course by the age of 25.

The big message from all this research and indeed from every chapter of this book, is that what practitioners do in the Early Years matters for life. As individuals we cannot stop children being born into poverty and disadvantage, but our practice can improve their long-term outcomes and support the aspirations of recent UK government policy to intervene early and prevent poor children becoming poor adults (Field and Allen Reports). The formal behaviourist view that all learning is shaped by the teacher (as in the direct instruction pre-schools of the High Scope evaluation) does not have long-term impact on aspects of life which help us sustain our learning, loving and earning power. Concentrating in the Early Years on how children learn by supporting their well-being and learning strategies enables them to be more self-reliant active learners who can exercise control over their own lives. If we concentrate on *what* rather than *how* children learn, any short-term gain soon wears off and these children are then left with insufficient emotional and cognitive self-regulation resources to manage their lives successfully. It was the concentration on *how* we learn that ensured the High Scope children were more likely to go to college, rather than filling them up with knowledge that is soon forgotten.

The third theme of this book, professionalism, links working with families and with other professionals to learning and identity. It brings the need for open and non-judgemental approaches to the fore and invites the reader to think about what professionalism means to them personally. This is a huge issue when we have such a diverse sector with a range of types of setting and practitioner qualifications. Professional identity in this context is necessarily contested but hugely important. Reading this book will help practitioners to become clearer about what the issues are and where they stand, as well as where they need to do some more reading and thinking – and/or gain some more experience of working with children or other adults. I hope that it will be read by leaders and managers as well as those seeking early childhood studies qualifications. Leadership and management at any level are about learning and development. Settings, and the adults working in them, grow and develop in response to positive relationships and enabling environments – just like the children. It is the responsibility of leaders and managers to provide an ethos where this growth, development and continuous improvement can take place. This book can help them do that.

References

Allen, G. (2011) *Early Intervention: the next steps, An Independent Report to Her Majesty's Government*. London: Cabinet Office, Crown Copyright

Banerjee, P.N. and Tamis-LeMonda, C.S. (2007) Infants' persistence and mothers' teaching as predictors of toddlers' cognitive development. *Infant Behavior and Development*, 30 (2007): 479–91

Bruce, T. (1999) In Praise of Inspired and Inspiring Teachers, in L. Abbott and H. Moylett (eds) *Early Education Transformed*. London: Falmer, pp33–40

Claxton, G. (2004) *Learning to Learn: A Key Goal in a 21st Century Curriculum*, A discussion paper for the Qualifications and Curriculum Authority, November 2004

Dweck, C. (2006) *Mindset, The New Psychology of Success*. New York: Ballantine Books

Field, F. (2010) *The Foundation Years: Preventing poor children becoming poor adults. The report of the Independent Review on Poverty and Life Chances.* London: Cabinet Office, Crown Copyright

Gussin Paley, V. (2004) *A Child's Work.* Chicago: University of Chicago Press

Holt, J. (1964) *How Children Fail.* London: Penguin

Katz (1995) *Talks with Teachers of young Children.* New Jersey. Ablex Publishing Company

McClelland, M., Acock, C.,Piccinin, A., Rhea, S.A. and Stallings, M. (2012) Relations between preschool attention span-persistence and age 25 educational outcomes. *Early Childhood Research Quarterly* 28

Robinson, M. (2003) *From Birth to One: The year of opportunity.* Buckingham: Open University Press

Schweinhart, L.J. and Weikart, D.P. (1997). *Lasting Differences: The HighScope Preschool Curriculum Comparison study through age 23* (Monographs of the HighScope Educational Research Foundation, 12). Ypsilanti, MI: HighScope Press

Sylva, K., Melhuish, E., Sammons, P., Siraj-Blatchford, I. and Taggart, B. (2012) *Effective Pre-school, Primary and Secondary Education 3-14 Project (EPPSE 3-14) – Final Report from the Key Stage 3 Phase: Influences on Students' Development from age 11–14.* Department for Education

Helen Moylett is an independent early years consultant and writer. She has been a junior, infant, nursery and home school liaison teacher, a local authority senior advisory teacher and a senior lecturer in primary and early years education at Manchester Metropolitan University. During this time she was the course leader of the B.A. in Early Childhood Studies and the M.Ed in Early Years Education. In 2000 she left academia to become head of an early years centre. In 2004 she joined the National Strategies. She was on the national steering group for Birth to Three Matters and was centrally involved in developing the Early Years Foundation Stage, as well as many of the National Strategies materials associated with the EYFS. She was also the national lead for the Every Child a Talker programme. Recently she was an expert adviser to the Tickell EYFS review team and co-authored 'Development Matters' with Nancy Stewart. Also with Nancy she wrote 'Understanding the Revised EYFS'. Helen is currently President of the British Association of Early Childhood Education (Early Education) and a Visiting Fellow of Oxford Brookes University.

Introduction: Themes and debates

Mary Wild and Alison Street

We believe that study and successful practice are about making connections, identifying themes and asking questions of ourselves, of research and of each other, while recognising the contested nature of many of the themes in the field of early childhood. This book therefore is not designed to 'provide answers' but rather it is intended to provoke enquiry and to encourage discussion and reflection among both students and practitioners. Early childhood is a broad field of study, spanning psychology, sociology, education and health and invoking historical and philosophical perspectives. This can generate a plethora of terms and approaches which can appear both confusing and at other times can give rise to simplistic mantras. For example, what do we mean by 'play'; is it too easy to slip into a discourse that emphasises its importance without taking into account the contexts and relationships in which it is situated? Similarly, terms like 'family' and 'partnership' are often treated as if they were self-evident, whereas the reality may reflect a much more complex picture.

The premise of this book is that it is important for both students and practitioners to ask of themselves *Why do I believe what I believe?* and *Why do I do what I do?* By fostering a spirit of continual enquiry, it can enable a connection between theory and practice which aims ultimately to strengthen experiences for children and their families.

The starting points for this book have come from the questions raised by students in the course of their studies in early childhood at Oxford Brookes University, and from the tensions these signify for implementing policy in practice. The relationship between theory and practice has to work in both directions. By analysing what theory has to offer practice and vice versa, new understandings can come to the fore and be questioned in the light of day-to-day experiences of children and those who care for them.

This book builds on the previous publication (Wild and Mitchell, 2007) which adopted a similarly reflective approach and foregrounded a number of seminal theories and texts. The principle of drawing on key extracts from other sources is maintained in the present book and in every chapter two extracts are included as central to the themes and debates raised in the chapter.

The nine chapters are grouped within three broad strands:

1. Exploring identities.

2. Exploring learning and well-being.

3. Exploring professionalism.

Each strand is explored by three chapters. These interlink with one another and are therefore best understood if read in relation to each other. You will find explicit links between them to help you frame relevant connections. In addition there are a number of themes that thread through all the chapters.

- The centrality of relationships and communication.

- The different agendas and voices of those involved.

- The importance of a sense of belonging for children, families and professionals.

- The interconnections between theory and practice.

Strand 1: Exploring identities

The book opens with a chapter that aims to explore the distinction between equality and equity. This is seen first in relation to social determinants of health, drawing attention to the importance of the earliest years as a foundation for children's well-being and healthy development, and how unequal children's chances are where they are affected by overlapping socio-economic factors. It then focuses on the discourse of diversity to enquire into the inequality born of prejudice and imbalance of power, and endorses Vandenbroeck's (2009) plea to maintain a spirit of open disagreement through which debate about these issues may construct better understanding of identities. The second chapter explores the complexities of the concept of children's rights in the wider context of the human rights agenda. It reflects on how children are viewed and on their perceived status in society, considering both national and international perspectives. The question of how rights are enforced and applied in different contexts and how this varies according to the child's age and maturity is considered particularly for babies and young children. In both these chapters the meanings projected by those who have a voice over those whose voice may be less often heard are seen as significant to question. In the third chapter on working inclusively, how one attends to individual voices is once again emphasised, within the context of conflicting agendas of the imposed call to raise standards with the reality for practitioners to respond to individual children's needs. You are encouraged to debate the meanings of inclusion and exclusion with reference to your own experiences and identities as they exist in relationship to other people.

Strand 2: Exploring learning and well-being

Chapters 4, 5 and 6 focus on how children learn, the importance of play and on the significance of key relationships for effective learning and well-being. Chapter 4 discusses the rationale for extending knowledge and understanding of how children learn and develop, by examining the findings of some key theorists. It highlights two clear messages: that learning is an active process that acknowledges the impetus in young children to make sense of their world, and that learning is profoundly related to the social and cultural contexts of home and everyday life. It sounds a note of warning against unquestioning acceptance of particular theoretical perspectives, however established they might appear. The challenge to professionals is rather to translate messages from theory into practice that is meaningful to children and families. Chapter 5 examines a very well established feature of Early Years practice, focusing on play and its importance in children's learning. The role of the adult is explored in relation to how to plan for and how to provide opportunities for play that strike a balance between following the child's agenda and the adult's imperatives.

It is suggested that if practitioners reflect on their own constructions and assumptions about what play is, they are more likely to create effective learning experiences for children. In Chapter 6 the importance of key relationships for supporting learning and well-being is the central focus. Attachment theory is reviewed in relation to its implications for practice, including the role of the 'key person' in settings. The tension between providing emotional security and offering emotional challenge is examined and the underpinning importance of trusting caring relationships for healthy development is reiterated.

Strand 3: Exploring professionalism

In this strand the emphasis shifts from how practitioner and professional can support learning to the dynamics of the professional roles and partnerships involved. Chapter 7 discusses various models of working with families in the Early Years, emphasising the diversity of family structures, roles and experiences. To be most effective this requires a range of skills on the part of the professional that are derived from an open and non-judgemental attitude of mind and a conscious acknowledgement of the values of the child's home and family. In Chapter 8 the different ways in which the range of professionals' roles are valued and recognised are scrutinised with reference to key policy developments. The focus is on raising awareness of the need for policy to respect the Early Years workforce and to provide frameworks that offer genuine professional growth and status. You are invited to consider the meaning of professionalism in terms of your own identity and experiences. The final chapter returns to the notion of identities, in this case, in the context where many professionals may be working together and responsible for the delivery of a complex array of services for children and families. The theme of strong and trusting relationships resonates with the theme of interconnecting relationships elsewhere in the book, but the chapter also calls for shared visions to be realised through strong communication and competent leadership. The tenor of the chapter is to pose challenges for multi-professional working rather than offering soothing platitudes for how teams can come together and move practice forward.

Through confronting challenges and debating issues, there is the potential to deepen understanding of key themes and to allow debate to enrich the construction of knowledge in the field of early childhood. In this way your own study and practice can become an integral part of the wider debates surrounding the lives of young children, their families and those who care for them.

References

Vandenbroeck, M. (2009) Editorial: Let us disagree. *European Early Childhood Education Research Journal*, 17(2), June, 2009: 165–70. Abingdon: Routledge, Taylor and Francis Group

Wild, M. and Mitchell, H. (2007) *Early Childhood Studies: A Reflective Reader*. Exeter. Learning Matters

Strand 1
Exploring identities

1 Equality and difference in the Early Years

Alison Street

This chapter will consider why equality of opportunity is important in Early Years provision. It will explore the concept of difference, both as a resource for learning and as a way of aiming for equitable practice.

By the end of this chapter you should have:

- considered the difference between equality and equity in relation to early childhood education;
- reflected on how inequalities in health and well-being can impact on children's sense of self and educational opportunities;
- thought about ways that disagreement can be a positive force for change in relation to diversity;
- considered how young children and their parents are involved in decisions about education and care.

Introduction

Inequality is now seen as the norm, regardless of how much harm it does to our shared humanity.

(Simon Callow, 2012)

In the statement above, Callow was referring to a celebration of inherited wealth through the royal 2012 Diamond Jubilee, but thereby recalling the much older meaning of a jubilee; the ancient Hebrew tradition of rebalancing rights of property, land ownership and wealth to create a more equal distribution across society. Whether you have monarchist or republican sympathies is not the debate in this chapter. But the need for redistribution of wealth is one of the emerging themes for discussion. This chapter will focus on questions for early childhood education and care that rise from considering the inequality of the socio-economic and cultural contexts in which provision is situated. Inequality has become more evident because in the second decade of the twenty-first century, publicly available data has become increasingly accessible on the social determinants of health and lifestyle. These relate both to the UK, such as the subsequent analysis of data from the 1970 cohort of children (Feinstein, 2003), and across the social hierarchies in a global context, such as researched by Wilkinson and Pickett (2010) in their book *The Spirit Level*. The latter both exposes and explains why inequality is a significant factor that influences both the structures in which people live and work, but also in how adults bring up young children and make decisions about their learning. It will be argued that early childhood is not immune and its settings cannot be protected from prevailing political and economic conditions, as these influence such everyday preoccupations as the cost of childcare, accessibility of information and support for parents, amount of parental leave at birth and availability, or lack of, parental choice.

There is not room in this space to interrogate the range of sociological, economic and political issues that impact on early childhood, and solutions are not sought. Rather, what follows is a discussion on themes emerging from two extracts that raise questions about both why and how unequal conditions and structures can influence young children's lives. In as much as family contexts, culture, ethnicity, class and gender impact on young children's developing identities and sense of belonging, there is a strong overlap with Chapter 3 in its focus on inclusive practice. The first part of the chapter will centre on the findings and recommendations of the Marmot Review team (2010) in *Fair Society, Healthy Lives.* This emphasises the links between socio-economic background, health inequalities and developmental outcomes for children in the UK. The second extract, from Michel Vandenbroeck's editorial *Let us disagree* (2009) explores the necessary move early childhood education has made away from an 'equalising' strategy towards diversity in approach, when confronting decisions about difference in families' social, physical and cultural backgrounds and beliefs. The two extracts appear to hold the view in common, that both investment in the earliest years, and also a striving to understand what underlies inequalities, are imperative for the future balance of society and for people to live harmoniously together.

Health matters

Even though the UK is generally considered to be wealthy, with universal access to healthcare free at the point of delivery, there have been numerous changes to the National Health Service in the last twenty years, including increasingly politically target-driven goals. Through a new act in 2012, the decision making on how services for patient care are commissioned has been devolved to groups led by medical general practitioners (GPs) in a Coalition policy move to reduce overall spending on public services. Simultaneously, there has been an expansion in health awareness from a global perspective, in availability of health promotion, and preventive measures for eradicating disease. One important measurement for the health of a nation is infant mortality rates. Increased prosperity in the UK led to a reduction in infant mortality from 6 to 5 per 1,000 live births, and under-5 mortality from 7 to 6 per 1,000 live births over the ten years from 1996 to 2006 (UNICEF, 1996, 2005). The long-term trend has been downwards; however, the gaps remain, both in infant mortality and male/female life expectancy between routine and manual workers and those in joint or registered partnerships (Marmot Review, 2010, 45).

Underdown (2007, ch. 4) expands on health inequalities in early childhood, drawing attention to the differences between children growing up poor in a poor country where they may lack access to clean water, sanitation, adequate nutrition and healthcare, and be vulnerable to diseases, often water-borne, with children growing up poor in a rich country, where definitions of relative poverty are not fixed. She claims that despite improvements in living conditions, general hygiene and immunisation programmes there are new threats to child health from social living conditions. These include child obesity, a reduction in many poorer urban areas of safe places to play outside, emotional and behavioural difficulties arising from breakdown in relationships and from children witnessing domestic violence, from childhood injury and smoking. Silberfield's (2007, p58) helpful commentary that raised questions about strategies needed to nurture *a strong and healthy child*, corroborated the relationship between inequality and a rise in young children's mental health problems; that conditions such as anxiety, eating disorders and depression are linked with poverty, inequality and deprivation. Children in families who experience homelessness or temporary accommodation or who have suffered as a result of conflict, such as refugees or asylum seekers, are also likely to have higher incidences of mental health problems (BMA, 2006).

The unequal chances that young children get because of their socio-economic contexts are clearly set out in the Marmot review, which was researched by nine task groups, involved scores of researchers and gathered qualitative evidence from professionals in health, involving discussion with stakeholders, focus groups and working committees. It admits inequalities in health are not a new phenomenon; there have been examples during the last two hundred years of ways seeking to address them, and that the motives behind the review may be ideological, but the recommendations are based on evidence which cannot be ignored for the sake of future society.

> *health inequalities that could be avoided by reasonable means are unfair. Putting them right is a matter of social justice. But the evidence matters. Good intentions are not enough.*

> (Marmot et al., 2010, p3)

The increasing evidence available in the public domain since records began in 1961 inform Wilkinson and Pickett (2010, p247) in the same argument:

> *The advantage of the growing body of evidence of the harm inflicted by inequality is that it turns what were purely personal intuitions into publicly demonstrable facts.*

As you read the following extract from chapter 2 of the Marmot Review, you will find links with other chapters in this book, especially those that relate to attachment and to the influence of families for young children's development. Consider what the charts indicate and how they might be interpreted in the light of your own experience and knowledge of family structures, support networks and practices.

EXTRACT 1

The Marmot Review (2010) Fair Society, Healthy Lives. Strategic Review of Health Inequalities Section 2.6.1 Early Years and Health Status, pp60–2

2.6.1 Early years and health status

What a child experiences during the early years lays down a foundation for the whole of their life. A child's physical, social, and cognitive development during the early years strongly influences their school-readiness and educational attainment, economic participation and health. Development begins before birth when the health of a baby is crucially affected by the health and well-being of their mother. Low birth weight in particular is associated with poorer long-term health and educational outcomes.

---

continued

Lower birth weight, earlier gestation and being small for gestational age are associated with infant mortality. In a study of all infant deaths in England and Wales (excluding multiple births), deprivation, births outside marriage, non-white ethnicity of the infant, maternal age under the age of 20 and male gender of the infant were all independently associated with an increased risk of infant mortality. A trend of increasing risk of death with increasing deprivation persisted after adjustment for these other factors.

Based on this analysis, one quarter of all deaths under the age of one would potentially be avoided if all births had the same level of risk as those to women with the lowest level of deprivation – fig. 2.19.

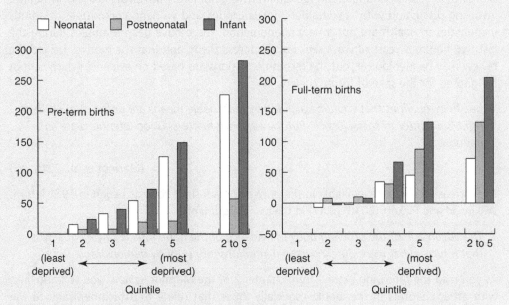

Figure 2.19 Estimated number of infant deaths that would be avoided if all quintiles had the same level of mortality as the least deprived, 2005–6
Source: Office for National Statistics Health Statistics Quarterly

The first year of life is crucial for neuro-development to provide the foundations for children's cognitive capacities. There is good evidence to show that if children fall behind in early cognitive development, they are more likely to fall further behind at subsequent educational stages. The evidence also shows that the development of early cognitive ability is strongly associated with later educational success, income and better health. The early years are also important for the development of non-cognitive skills such as application, self-regulation and empathy. These are the emotional and social capabilities that enable children to make and sustain positive relationships and succeed both at school and in later life.

There is an unequal distribution of resources across families in terms of wealth, living conditions, levels of education, supportive family and community networks, social capital and parenting skills. Abundant evidence suggests that socioeconomic status is associated

EXTRACT 1 *continued*

with a multitude of developmental outcomes for children – see fig. 2.20. Furthermore, the literature suggests strongly that socioeconomic gradients in early childhood replicate themselves throughout the life course.

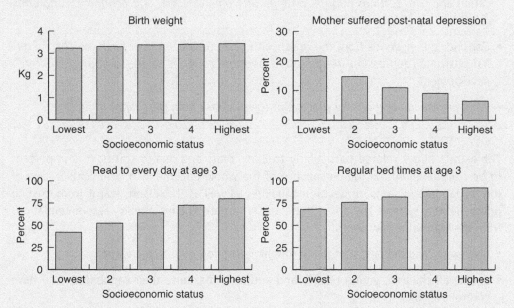

Figure 2.20 Links between socioeconomic status and factors affecting child development, 2003–4
Source: Department for Children, Schools and Families

Pre-school influences remain evident even after five years spent full time in primary school[…] A child's physical, social, emotional and cognitive development during the early years strongly influences her or his school-readiness and educational attainment, economic participation and health. Children with a high cognitive score at 22 months but with parents of low socioeconomic status do less well (in terms of subsequent cognitive development) than children with low initial scores but with parents of high socioeconomic status. Children of educated or wealthy parents can score poorly in early tests but still catch up, whereas children of worse-off parents are extremely unlikely to do so. There is no evidence that entry into schooling reverses this pattern.

In view of the differences described above, it is unsurprising that educational outcomes at school are strongly related to relative deprivation.

The acquisition of cognitive skills is strongly associated with better outcomes across the life course over a range of domains including employment, income and health. A range of empirical studies provide evidence that cognitive ability is a powerful determinant of earnings, propensity to get involved in crime and success in many aspects of social and economic life as well as health across the social gradient.

- *What do you consider to be foundational elements in the first year of life for healthy cognitive development?*

- *With reference to the charts in fig. 2.19 of the extract, how do early childhood education and care settings address a range of women's social and economic conditions relating to pregnancy and birth?*

- *Consider the evidence from the graphs in fig. 2.20. Discuss how birth weight, maternal postnatal depression, reading and bedtime routines relate to young children's development.*

- *What are the implications for practice of the evidence from the graphs in fig. 2.20?*

The extract above related particularly to Early Years and health status. It is important to be considered within the perspective of the whole document to gain a fuller view of the 'social determinants' of health inequalities as well as the lessons learnt from existing policy, delivery systems and appropriateness of targets. The main policy recommendations from the Marmot review are to:

- give every child the best start in life (the highest priority recommendation);

- enable all children, young people and adults to maximise their capabilities and have control over their lives;

- create fair employment and good work for all;

- ensure a healthy standard of living for all;

- create and develop sustainable places and communities;

- strengthen the role and impact of ill-health prevention.

For the purposes of this chapter, the implications of the first two will be explored here for their relevance to Early Years practice.

Giving every child the best start

The Review acknowledges the significant role of policy since the late 1990s focused on support for children from birth, on which it is important to build and develop. Sure Start, initiated by the Labour government in 1997, served to provide both universal and targeted local support for families and was, in its initial phases, driven by families and accountable to local community representation. This was followed by *Every Child Matters: Change for Children* (DfES, 2004) with its emphasis on fostering positive and resilient parenting. The expansion in children's centres up to 2010 as local hubs for services meeting the health, education and social needs of young children, has been contracted under the Coalition government, though services strive to continue to offer care and advice under their core programmes, balancing universal with more targeted provision. If Sure Start is thought of as the first revolution, what is recommended in the report is a *second revolution in the*

Early Years through redistribution of funding overall for the earliest years away from the later years, in line with critical and sensitive periods of a child's development, and as an economically sound preventive strategy.

It is now widely acknowledged that the earliest years are crucial in children's development; a time when attachment patterns are established through close relationships and loving and playful interactions (Stern, 2000). During their first year babies learn to manage their own emotions according to how the responses to their own signals are interpreted and extended by those around them, and to how sensitively their cues to communicate are understood. The timings and subsequent emotional engagement in interactions with close adults have been seen to be disturbed by social and emotional factors affecting adults around the child, such as mothers with post-natal depression (Robb, 1999) or in the case of newly arrived refugees (Gratier, 1999). It is therefore understood that support for mothers both pre- and post-birth is crucial, including home visiting programmes such as the Family Nurse Partnership (Rowe, 2009), and interventions that address depression and isolation. Parents' awareness and reflections on their babies' competencies, and how their own needs and assumptions influence their role have been supported by programmes such as the Solihull approach (Douglas and Rheeston, 2009). Sure Start centres have fostered interventions to strengthen positive parenting, to recognise parents as their children's first educators and to use a range of activities, including massage, songs and rhymes, play and movement, to nurture the emotional well-being of mothers with their infants.

However, where these interventions are offered to all, they have tended to be taken up by parents who recognise opportunities and already understand and value stimulating activities to support their children's learning. The evaluation for the first phase of Sure Start (Belsky et al. 2006) found that while the majority of families benefited from the initiative, the most socially deprived did not. Since then it has become increasingly evident that services need to provide both universal and targeted approaches: universal, because all families need help and advice from pre-birth and through the early years of parenting, including recognition of the father's role and paid parental leave; targeted, because there are families who avoid services, and maybe ignorant or isolated because of health, cultural, language or housing needs or chaotic lifestyles. It is arguable, however, that services that are targeted on smoking cessation, help on breastfeeding, nutrition, resolving debt problems and providing adult language programmes, while valuable, may be too focused on getting the individual to opt in and change behaviour, while the inherent problems of their lives are more complex and beyond their immediate control.

The Marmot Review also recommends the need for highly trained practitioners to continue programmes of outreach and home visiting, and to work in a non-judgemental, sensitive and flexible way to support families with complex material, social, and health needs (Marmot et al., 2010, p98). The implications for those entering the professions that offer both pre- and post-natal support, and onwards through a child's first year, require thoughtful consideration. The workforce supporting Early Years is traditionally undervalued and underpaid, and yet in terms of the partnerships and collaborative roles necessary, the associated daily decisions involving sophisticated understanding of families' conditions and young children's rights deserve to be properly recognised in time and pay. Aspects of the professional's role will be explored in more detail by Mitchell in Chapter 9.

Enable all children, young people and adults to maximise their capabilities and have control over their lives

This second recommendation relates to educational achievement, and the resulting potential benefits for employment, which has been seen in turn to be positive for mental and physical health. Evidence indicates that it is families rather than schools that have the most influence on educational attainment:

> *'Inequalities in educational outcomes are as persistent as those for health and are subject to a similar social gradient. Despite many decades of policies aimed at equalising educational opportunities, the attainment gap remains. As with health inequalities, reducing educational inequalities involves understanding the interaction between the social determinants of educational outcomes, including family background, neighbourhood and relationships with peers, as well as what goes on in schools ... Closer links between schools, the family, and the local community are needed.*

(Marmot et al., 2010, p104)

In February 2011 the figures obtained from teacher assessments of children in their Early Years Foundation Stage Profiles (EYFSP) across all local authorities in England in the term they turned five years indicated that 44 per cent did not have a good level of development, based on criteria of behaviour and understanding. This figure was an average score, meaning that some boroughs or regions showed higher or lower figures. They were not based on teachers' tests but on observations. Data from private schools were not included as they do not come under LA maintenance, but this still served to illustrate the need for ongoing or increasing support for the Early Years and for the networks in communities that can contribute to that support. The statutory framework for the 2012 Foundation Stage (DFE, 2012) obliges settings to engage parents in sharing information on child development with a view to creating positive partnerships, in an effort to narrow the gap. The expectation is that parents' increased involvement can help children's development at school. Partnership has been seen to be most effective where it has reached out to include the whole family, where it recognises existing parental expertise, and where it offers both universal and more intensive support especially in the first three years, to more vulnerable families (Siraj-Blatchford and Siraj-Blatchford, 2009). You will find partnership models for working with parents and families discussed in more detail in Chapter 7.

It is not unusual to hear the terms 'problem families' and 'problem children', and, indeed, the first extract indicates the persistence of pre-school influences of inequality in distribution of wealth, and conditions of support and parenting lasting into primary years and beyond. This suggests that in order to make chances more fair – or equitable – for young children, in the long term it is important to understand the deeper question of the costs of social reproduction. Wells (2009) outlines the role children and young people play in the global capitalist economy, and how their lives are affected in contradictory ways. She asserts social reproduction is the concept of what is needed to reproduce and continue life. This applies both to how people meet their fundamental needs – such as for food, water, shelter, medicines, maternity care, and also to how social networks and cultural practices and identities are sustained (Wells, 2009, p168). Within this concept, patterns of work and wages, terms and conditions, e.g. parental leave, are central to the function of production, and families have to earn enough to meet the costs of raising children, and their care. In advanced societies the state steps in to support where the costs of food and housing are beyond the means of those earning, though in the UK there is an increasing gap between the costs of benefits and the funding from central government that local authorities have at their disposal.

It is important to consider, however, that in the majority of the world, workers and their families more often have to sustain the costs of social reproduction, and migration is the growing strategy used by many in search of work. Families crossing borders are now the norm, not only where people are fleeing conflict and war zones but also in search of employment and quality of life. Where children live on the streets, in shanty towns and slums, or have been victims of political unrest and homelessness, the UN Convention on the Rights of the Child (UNCRC) can be invoked, and charities work to rescue young lives. But the questions remain. Is it always helpful to rescue children from conditions with which they are familiar and on which they base existing relationships and their sense of self? What criteria are employed by agencies who encourage them to reshape their lives? How does the parent of the 'problem' child perceive the expectation that she can or should adapt her style of parenting to the dominant norms of the education system? Why might she find services offered by a children's centre in an urban district in the UK very uncomfortable? In order for children and their families to *maximise their capabilities and have control over their lives*, the inequality of opportunity in diverse families' situations needs understanding by the services that set out to support them towards that goal.

Supportive networks and social capital

Wilkinson and Pickett (2010, p161) suggest that in more unequal societies, there is less social mobility. Although most of their data applies to the USA, they assert that this applies to the UK as well, based on three observations. Firstly, that inter-generational social mobility has been falling between the 1980s and 1990s, while simultaneously income differences have widened. Secondly, that public expenditure on education is strongly linked to the degree of income equality. Education is generally thought of as the 'main engine' of social mobility, leading to higher qualifications, income and social status. They refer to the US where only 68.2 per cent of money spent on schools is from public funds, with the result that there is less equal access for all social groups to higher education. By comparison, Norway, a much more equal country in income distribution, spends 97.8 per cent. Thirdly, they claim that researchers on both sides of the Atlantic have found that greater social gaps have created increasing geographical segregation of the rich from the poor, with consequent difficulties in everyday commuting, poorer health and stressful lives contributing to less social mobility.

Yet decisions about where and how people live may not depend on money alone. The French sociologist Pierre Bourdieu (1986) put forward the theory that in terms of social class, people put out and gain from cultural messages that link them. These impact on the social relationships by which they feel supported – their social capital, and the kinds of possessions and pastimes, interests and sports they partake in – their cultural capital. Understanding why people make the choices they do in relation to the kinds of people they respect or want to be like can inform the whole question about whether the concept of choice is a fair one. For example, in a study of middle and working-class parents' choices of school and childcare, by Vincent, Braun and Ball (2009), working-class parents were seen to base their decisions more on local connections and friendships, compared with middle-class parents who were more likely to have researched publications and school league tables. The study was not so much advancing one argument over another, but rather, pointing out the significant social, cultural and economic variations that govern choice and the meanings of equity in choice.

Thinking about how both people and services make choices, consider these questions.

- Why do some families avoid children's centre services?

- How can schools develop partnership with parents who they consider 'hard to reach'?

- What kinds of practice models and activities are accessible to families which build on parents' social and cultural capital?

'Let us disagree'

The chapter now turns to the second extract by Vandenbroeck (2009) in the *European Early Childhood Education Research Journal*. It focuses on attitudes to diversity in early childhood education, tracking the progress made in the last twenty years in this respect. His argument is that the growing consensus that diversity is now a significant issue for early childhood educators is in itself problematic and potentially exclusive, as it sets up structures and processes that perpetuate a discourse that remains academic and distanced from real life; that it belongs to those who educate, instead of to those who are partners in learning from and contributing to, diversity.

> *The diversity curricula, paradoxically, risk becoming a new form of expert discourse on 'the good life' for children, silencing precisely those they wished to include.*

(Vandenbroeck, 2010, p166)

POINTS TO CONSIDER

- *As you read the following extract, consider current approaches in early childhood settings that illustrate how diversity is represented in the environment; in the respect for:*

  - *children's home languages;*

  - *their particular (special) needs;*

  - *their cultural background.*

- *How do educational processes reflect children's different developing identities?*

EXTRACT 2

Vandenbroeck, M. (2009) in *European Early Childhood Education Research Journal*, 17(2), June: pp165–7

While two decades ago, publications on how to address diversity issues in early childhood education were hard to find, one can now fill several bookshelves with manuals, books, training materials and DVDs on these issues. Although in some places, diversity is still denied, in general, the early years community today cannot reasonably claim to focus on the 'average' child anymore. There is general consensus that learning processes differ depending on the contexts and that these contexts mirror the societal diversity in ethnicity, culture, religion, gender, family composition, ability etc. This evolution can be (shallowly) summarized as an evolution from an equalizing approach to a diversity approach. In short, the liberal, individualizing and equalizing approach of (roughly speaking) the 1950s up to the 1980s was based on explicit policies in which growth in wealth, welfare and well-being were considered as almost synonymous. The general modernist belief was that the growing wealth and the construction of the 'modern' welfare state would eradicate all differences and make everybody happy.

Today, the early years community is much more aware that equality and equity are not synonymous. Pursuing social justice and change goes inherently hand in hand with dealing with a multiplicity of differences in a productive way, rather than with minimizing diversity. We also begin to move beyond essentialist approaches of multiculturalism, which in the past have all too often ignored socio-economic power relations, i.e. the pitfall of culturalizing issues of blatant economic inequalities.

This is not to say that overt or covert, implicit or explicit discriminations have been eradicated. Quite on the contrary: children living in poverty and children from ethnic minorities are still often squeezed out from mainstream provisions and in many countries the children of the poorest families are overrepresented in early childhood provisions of poor quality (Vanderbroeck et al. 2008). Children with what is labelled as 'special needs' still struggle to find their place in early childhood. Homosexual parents may still daily be confronted with messages that they – and their children – do not 'belong' on a daily basis. Nevertheless, the awareness that this *is* an issue, as well as the insights in *how* to tackle these issues have substantially evolved over the last two decades.

As progressive academics or practitioners, how can we not take into account the perspective of parents who wish to 'conform' to standards of academic achievement (or to achieve this cultural capital as Bourdieu could have said), rather than to discuss holistic education? But on the other hand, how can we, if we have consecrated a major part of our lives to child centredness? As a critical pedagogue I may argue that this parental question of conformity with the dominant norms and values is to be considered as 'internalized oppression' (Freire 1970). But then again, wasn't it also Freire who said 'Dialogue cannot exist without humility. [...] How can I dialogue if I always project ignorance onto others and never perceive my own?' (1970, 78).

For 'progressive educationalists', it is hard to argue that we educate the whole child, when children leave their language and culture at the doorstep (Cummins et al. 2005). But, unfortunately, it is also hard to argue that we educate the whole child, when leaving his or her parents' opinions in the corridor.

Some key themes emerging from the text will be explored here for their relevance to early childhood practice. The first concerns how diversity has been represented. Vandenbroeck points out that essentially the current diversity agenda attempts to deal with the *multiplicity of differences in a productive way, rather than with minimizing diversity* (p165). It is useful here therefore to inquire how approaches to difference have changed over time. These have been mapped in relation to racial inequalities since the 1960s by Mirza (2005, p1), who concludes that *the more things change, the more they stay the same*.

Assimilation: 1960–70

In the 1960s children of migrant families were thought of as cognitively, socially and culturally deficient, because they had arrived from less civilised societies. It was a time when people felt that black children were expected to assimilate to British culture at the denial of their own. There was moreover a growing association of negative self-respect with underachievement – the doll experimental studies by Milner (1975) had suggested that children's lower self-esteem, as seen by their choice of colour of doll, was associated with low aspirations, that in turn became a self-fulfilling prophecy as teachers' expectations were also influenced. This lack of pride as a reason for black underachievement was countered by Coard (1971), who explained it in terms of young people feeling alienated in a white-dominated and controlled education system. In addition, English as a second language was perceived as a problem. Mirza claims that the system is still segregated according to criteria based on anti-social behaviour and discipline (2005), meaning that even though racist treatment of children might not be as blatant as it was in the 1970s, there are still problems of racial differentiation in classrooms.

Multiculturalism: 1980–90

Multiculturalism represents a liberal-reformist view of cultural democracy; a society in which all groups might live freely while maintaining their cultural and religious diversities. In education, multiculturalism often calls for an expansion (to curricula for example), to include resources, celebrations, artefacts and festivals. It emerged from a political will to promote tolerance and understanding in the wake of the Brixton riots in the mid-1980s, and from a growing awareness of the interrelated factors of underachievement with socio-economic concerns of race and class. Scholars emphasised the potential that schools could make a difference, together with home–school relations and teachers who challenged racist behaviours and assumptions. However, many of these liberal strategies for encouraging cultural inclusion have been criticised by the right as 'politically correct' and, indeed, such practices as celebrating Iraqi or Somali New Year may serve to reify and isolate 'differences' in cultures rather than promoting interaction and exchange. Approaches in Early Years settings that depend on pre-conceived perceptions of what constitutes 'Asian' or 'Indian' customs, or festivals, for example, can become tokenistic if they do not take into account the lives and interests and histories of the children and families who 'enliven' them.

Critical Race Theory

Since 1999, when eighteen-year-old Stephen Lawrence was stabbed by a group of white youths in London as he waited for a bus, and the resultant Race Relations (Amendment) Act (2000) that emanated from the Lawrence Inquiry advocated much stricter surveillance of racism within all public bodies, it became imperative on schools to maintain written race-equality policies as well as monitoring ethnic minority levels of attainment. In criticism Gillborn (2006) states:

> *But simply asserting our anti-racist intentions means nothing if we leave unchanged the dominant systems of testing, the curriculum, teacher education, and punitive inspection regimes that penalize schools serving working-class and minoritized communities.*

(Gillborn, 2006, p15)

He points out that much research on race and education in Britain is concerned with mapping the scales of inequality (*we are being seduced by a school-level focus that loses sight of the 'bigger picture*) of institutional racism. His research into the US largely law-based Critical Race Theory (CRT) has led him to promote it as a means of facilitating anti-racism to become more radical and critical, instead of it being merely reformist. Like Mirza (2005), who points out the contradictions in the rhetoric of policy extolling the importance of equality, diversity, human rights and citizenship in the face of persistent racial discrimination, both blatant and subtle, Gillborn, too, suggests that although the language may have changed, the reality of day-to-day, unwitting 'business as usual' racism has not. He cites Tate (1997) in his plea for change, through approaches which adopt CRT, as being *an iterative project of scholarship and social justice*. This is a perspective rather than a set of rules or procedures, and he considers it a coherent map for anti-racism appropriate for British education. There are within CRT defining elements. One of these is to admit that racism is endemic, and that formal equal opportunity rhetoric that treats black and white alike cannot influence the harmful racism that people experience day to day. The argument is that if racism is admitted as being all around, then its outcomes of behaviour can be addressed as a matter of day-to-day debate, as opposed to following up for proof of intent. One of the conceptual tools – or *lines of analysis* (Gillborn, 2006, p24) – used within a CRT approach, to help greater understanding of the issues is story-telling and counter-stories.

The practice of inviting personal stories from marginalised groups is not new; it has been used in ethnographical research for years. But its potential to serve the purpose of actively challenging assumptions of a dominant way of thinking, or discourse, is a concept which can be applied in trying to understand the views of others. Here there is a link with Vandenbroeck's plea in the extract above: *Let us disagree*. As an example of the need to engage meaningfully with parental expectations and knowledge he recounts how some ethnic minority parents in Belgium protested against what they perceived to be a non-academic multicultural curriculum, asking instead for a 'traditional' approach to learning and discipline for their children. This caused raised eyebrows, but it also allowed the opportunity for dialogue and challenged practitioners' assumptions of ethnic minority parents' educational expectations. In another study (Vandenbroeck et al., 2009) of newly arrived immigrant mothers' views of childcare, an emerging theme was the asymmetry of power between Neamat, a young mother of an eight-month old girl, and the prevailing ethos of care in a setting. She wanted the staff to respect her wishes to put her daughter on a potty regularly after her nap during the day. The fact that the staff after many discussions tried to carry out her wishes raised questions about the dominant discourse of Western developmental psychology and the meanings for 'different' expertise of mother and setting. This example also raises the question about hierarchies of knowledge. In early childhood education, parents, particularly of ethnic minorities and in newly arrived families, can often feel de-skilled and defer to those in authority for what are deemed suitable or acceptable procedures. This asymmetry of power in relationships sensed by new immigrant communities has been further researched by Verschueren (2008) through exploring the nature of intercultural communication, emphasising how the norms of communication, such as negotiation, are themselves taken up by authorities who dominate over the processes of how people access services and benefits. The implied challenges for the practitioner's role from an ethical point of view are explored more fully in Chapter 7.

Identity and reciprocity

'Suitable' and 'acceptable' are terms which will depend very much on who unpicks the meanings of these words, and they surround the different contexts of a young child as they move from home into early childhood settings. Answers to questions like *Am I OK?* and *Do I fit here?* depend very much on the identities children develop and adopt. Schaffer (2006) referred to the self as having multiple constructs which are complex and interrelated. This idea portrays identity not as fixed and emerging along a set series of stages, but rather as flexible and responsive to relationships. Fogel (1993) similarly emphasised the interdependence of children with significant adults and peers, arguing that children develop through their relationships. Rogoff (2003) has shown how these relationships are culturally dependent and defining, and that young children grow up through participating in the cultural events and routines of daily life, and that these contribute to a child's sense of belonging and of who they are. The fostering of a positive sense of identity is a common goal for early childhood educators and programme managers, as expressed in the second extract in this chapter. But there is no set recipe for how this can be achieved. Brooker (2008) suggests there is a danger of romanticising childhood and of sheltering it from harsh realities of 'difference'. She points out that from a young age children know already whether they are accepted or different in relation to sex/gender, race/ethnicity, dis/ability from their early relationships with their peers. They compare with the way they dress, move, interact and compete with each other. It becomes more difficult for children where groups are overtly or covertly excluded because they seem to deviate from the norm, for example in size of family, in language or attitudes to activities like music or sports. The challenge for practice is to harness this awareness of difference to make it a means for learning.

Diversity challenges practitioners to discuss with each other and with partners in learning, such as parents of young children. Vandenbroeck emphasises the need for dialogue which also involves risk taking, turning assumptions upside down and examining how different kinds of knowledge interface, for example that of the parent with that of the teacher. He suggests it is important to *challenge what is taken for granted and to acknowledge that our expertise is provisional and tentative* Vandenbroeck (2009, p169). In this way there can be a reciprocal response based on seeing the 'other's' point of view. These points imply the need for space and time for relating, for services to be meeting points and common spaces in which agreement and disagreement can be acknowledged and valued in its potential for learning and understanding. Translating this to your own experience, how can practice engage with children and their parents in issues relating to diversity within settings? What different sorts of knowledge are needed to support healthy development and learning in young children? Finally, you might reflect on how stereotypical representations influence children's identities; considering class, gender, race, ethnicity, culture.

CHAPTER SUMMARY

In this chapter you have been able to read two passages from research that illustrate the importance of issues influencing equality of opportunity for families and young children. The first, the Marmot Review, covered social determinants of health, drawing attention to the importance of the earliest years as a foundation for children's well-being and healthy development, and how unequal children's chances are where they are affected by overlapping socio-economic factors, including poverty, lifestyles, unemployment and working hours and conditions. Some global perspectives on health inequality have been explored (Underdown, 2007) as well as the costs to individual workers across the world where local economic conditions force migrations in search of work. It has been argued that early childhood education is not immune from these inequalities and their effects (Wells, 2009). Your attention has been drawn to the concepts of social and cultural capital as being significant forces in the decisions and choices parents make for their children, for example in choice of school or childcare, and how 'familiar' and 'different' may hold contrasting meanings for them. In the second part Vandenbroeck has encouraged those involved in early childhood as professionals to embrace disagreement as a healthy device in debating difference. Approaches to difference in the UK, particularly in relation to racial equality, have been traced briefly from the 1960s, with reference to assimilation, multiculturalism and their limitations. Some emphasis has been made to critical race theory as a means of trying to understand and to challenge the outcomes of racism and the harm it does in day-to-day living. Finally, the chapter returns to the importance of considering the relationships around the child in their earliest years; to the powerful influences of families and cultural background in how children form their own identities. It has been argued that if the fostering of positive identities in early childhood is a common goal in health and education, then diversity has to be a central focus for debate in which to engage both children and their parents.

References

BMA (British Medical Association) (2006) *Child and Adolescent Mental Health: A Guide for Healthcare Professionals*. London: BMA

Belsky, J., Melhuish, T. Barnes, J. Leyland, A. and Romaniuk, H. (2006) Effects of Sure Start local programmes on children and families: Early findings from a quasi-experimental cross sectional study. *British Medical Journal*. doi:10.1136/bmj.38853.451748.2F

Bourdieu, P. (1986) The forms of capital, in J. Richardson (ed.) *Handbook of Theory and Research for the Sociology of Education*. New York: Greenwood, pp241–58

Brooker, L. (2008) Defining Positive Identity, in L. Brooker and M. Woodhead (eds) *Developing Positive Identities: Early Childhood in Focus, 3. Diversity and Young Children*. Milton Keynes: The Open University Press

Callow, S. (2012) Let's reclaim the jubilee. *Guardian*, 4 June

Coard, B. (1971) *How the West Indian Child is Made Educationally Subnormal in the British School System*. London: New Beacon Books. Cited in Mirza H.S. (2005) Inaugural Professorial Lecture, 'Race, Gender and Educational Desire', delivered on 17 May 2005 at Middlesex University **http://eprints.ioe. ac.uk/2424/1/Mirza2006race137.pdf** accessed 13 November 2012

DfE (2012) *Statutory Framework for Foundation Stage*. London: DFE Publications

DfES (2004) *Every Child Matters: Change for Children*. London: The Stationery Office

Douglas, H. and Rheeston, M. (2009) The Solihull approach; an integrative model across agencies, in J. Barlow and P.O. Svanberg (eds) *Keeping the Baby in Mind: Infant mental health in practice*. London and New York: Routledge,Taylor & Francis Group

Feinstein, L. (2003) Inequality in the early cognitive development of British Children in the 1970 cohort. *Economica*, 70: 3–97

Fogel, A. (1993) *Developing Through Relationships. Origins of communication, self and culture*. Hertfordshire: Harvester Wheatsheaf

Gillborn, D. (2006) Critical Race Theory and Education: Racism and anti-racism in educational theory and praxis. *Discourse: Studies in the cultural politics of education*, 27(1): 11–32. London: Routledge

Gratier, M. (1999) Expressions of belonging: the effect of acculturation on the rhythm and harmony of mother-infant vocal interaction. *Musicae Scientiae Special Issue* 1999–2000, pp93–122

Marmot, M. et al. (2010) *Fair Society: Healthy Lives. Strategic Review of Health Inequalities in England*, post 2010. **www.ucl.ac.uk/marmotreview** accessed 6 July 2012

Milner, D. (1975) *Children and Race*. Harmondsworth: Penguin

Mirza, H.S. (2005) Inaugural Professorial Lecture, 'Race, Gender and Educational Desire', delivered on 17 May 2005 at Middlesex University **http://eprints.ioe.ac.uk/2424/1/Mirza2006race137.pdf** accessed 13 November 2012

Robb, L. (1999) Emotional musicality in mother–infant vocal affect, and an acoustic study of postnatal depression. *Musicae Scientiae Special Issue* 1999–2000, pp123–54

Rogoff, B. (2003) *The Cultural Nature of Human Development*. Oxford, New York: Oxford University Press

Rowe, A. (2009) Perinatal home visiting: Implementing the nurse–family partnership in England, in J. Barlow and P.O. Svanberg (eds) *Keeping the Baby in Mind: infant mental health in practice*. London and New York: Routledge, Taylor and Francis Group

Schaffer, H.R. (2006) *Key Concepts in Developmental Psychology*. London: Sage

Silberfield, C. (2007) Developing as a strong and healthy child? in M. Wild and H. Mitchell (eds). *Early Childhood Studies: A reflective reader*, pp48–66. Exeter: Learning Matters

Siraj-Blatchford J. and Siraj-Blatchford, I. (2009) Improving children's attainment through a better quality of family-based support for early learning. *Early Years Research Review 2*. London: Centre for Excellence and Outcomes in Children and Young People's Services (C4EO)

Stern, D.N. (2000) *The Interpersonal World of the Infant: A View from Psychoanalysis and Developmental Psychology*. Introduction to 2nd edn. New York: Basic Books

Tate, W.F. (1997) Critical race theory and education: History, theory, and implications, in M.W. Apple (ed.) *Review of Research in Education*, 22: 195–247. Washington, DC: American Educational Research Association

Underdown, A. (2007) Young Children's Health and Well-being. Maidenhead, New York: Open University Press

UNICEF (1996) *The State of the World's Children 1996. 50th anniversary issue*. Oxford: Oxford University Press

UNICEF (2005) *The State of the World's Children 2006. Excluded and invisible*. New York: UNICEF

Vandenbroeck, M. (2009) Editorial: Let us disagree. *European Early Childhood Education Research Journal*, 17(2), June: 165–70. Abingdon: Routledge, Taylor and Francis Group

Vandenbroeck, M., Roets, G. and Snoeck, A. (2009) Immigrant mothers crossing borders: nomadic identities and multiple belongings in early childhood education. *European Early Childhood Education Research Journal*, 17(2), June: 203–16. Abingdon: Routledge, Taylor and Francis Group

Verschueren, J. (2008) Intercultural Communication and the Challenges of Migration, in *Language and Intercultural Communication*, 8(1), 21–35

Vincent, C., Braun, A. and Ball S. (2009) *Local Links, Local Knowledge: Choosing care settings and schools*. London: Institute of Education, University of London

Wells, K. (2009) *Childhood in a Global Perspective*. Cambridge: Polity Press

Wilkinson, R. and Pickett, K. (2010) *The Spirit Level: Why Equality is Better for Everyone*. London: Penguin Books

FURTHER READING

European Early Childhood Education Research Journal (2009) Special Issue: Children's and parents' perspectives on diversity in Early Childhood Education ed. M. Vandenbroeck. Vol 17, No. 2, June 2009. Routledge, Taylor and Francis Group

Marmot, M. et al. (2010) *Fair Society: Healthy Lives. Strategic Review of Health Inequalities in England, post 2010*. **www.ucl.ac.uk/marmotreview** accessed 6 July 2012. The whole review to expand the extract

Rogoff, B. (2003) *The Cultural Nature of Human Development*. Oxford, New York: Oxford University Press

Wilkinson, R. and Pickett, K. (2010) *The Spirit Level: Why Equality is Better for Everyone*. London: Penguin Books

WEBSITES

www.eecera.org

www.equalitytrust.org.uk

www.c4eo.org.uk/about/default.aspx

2 Children's rights and children's voice

Catharine Gilson

In this chapter, the concepts of children's rights and children's voice are explored, examining some of the theoretical perspectives and considering how these may translate into practice. The debates are set in an international context though the examples given contextualise the discussion in the national context.

By the end of this chapter you should have:

- considered the complexities inherent in the concept of children's rights and become aware of alternative theoretical perspectives;
- explored the concept of children's voice and looked critically at the implications for implementing the right in practice;
- reflected on your own responses to the questions raised in the chapter, and on how these might affect your approach to the issues raised.

Introduction

The notion of children's rights is a relatively recent concept in the UK. Before the nineteenth century children were regarded as possessions, rather than as autonomous beings with any kinds of rights. Furthermore, the home was seen as a private space for the family, and as long as the children behaved themselves, the state took little interest in what went on. Corporal punishment was the norm at home and at school, and the emphasis was on inculcating respect and discipline in the child towards the parents and other adults. Even in the Industrial Revolution when children were working in the factories, the workplace was patrolled by the authorities but not the home (Powell and Uppall, 2012). In the late nineteenth century, orphanages and separate legal systems for children were set up and schooling was developed. The National Society for the Prevention of Cruelty to Children was founded, followed by the Prevention of Cruelty to Children Act 1889, ironically later than acts prohibiting cruelty to animals. However, the rights-based discourse that we are familiar with now was not codified until the Universal Declaration of Human Rights, which was formulated in 1948 in the aftermath of the Second World War. The Allies' determination to bring peace to Europe led to the European Convention of Human Rights (ECHR), which was drafted in November 1950 and entered into force in 1953. It is interesting to note that though there is a common misconception that the

ECHR was imposed on a reluctant UK as part of a wider Europeanisation of the country, in fact the UK was one of the leading protagonists in the human rights agenda that grew up after the Second World War. The United Nations Convention on the Rights of the Child (UNCRC) came out of the ECHR but was not introduced until much later in 1989. It has been ratified by all members of the United Nations with the exception of the USA and Somalia. By ratifying an international treaty, governments commit to implement the treaty (here the UNCRC) in law, policy and practice and report back on their progress to the United Nations Committee on the Rights of the Child. In the UK The Children Act 1989 is based on the principles of the UNCRC and lays the foundation for both private and public proceedings in child welfare law in England, Wales and Northern Ireland but not Scotland. There is an emphasis on agencies working with children and families, and parents are given responsibility for their children but not rights over them, signalling a major change in approach from the notion that children are the possessions of their parents. It was followed by the Children Act 2004, which emphasised the need for integrated working within children's services with a particular focus on safeguarding children. In the next section, we will look more closely at the terms of reference of the UNCRC.

Children's rights

The first issue is to decide what is meant by 'a right'. In the preamble to the Convention to the Rights of the Child, we read that *recognition of the inherent dignity and of the equal and inalienable rights of all members of the human family is the foundation of freedom, justice and peace in the world* (UNCRC, 1989). There is a significant amount of discussion in sociology and law about the concept of a right, but for the purposes of this chapter we will consider it to signify an entitlement that in this case all humans should be accorded. To talk of children's rights, we must also know what is a child. For example, when does life begin? Do we have rights in the womb? Furthermore, when does childhood end and adulthood start? Is it at the age of 16 or 18 in the UK? For the UNCRC, a child is considered to be every human being younger than 18, unless the age of majority in the law which applies to the child is different (article 1). The preamble states that children need special protection and care because of their immaturity, both physical and mental, and these safeguards apply before as well as after birth. So, an unborn child can be placed on the child-protection register in England, for example. Extra protection is to be given to the most vulnerable groups of children, such as children with disabilities and children in care. There are many ways of categorising the rights: they can be divided into moral rights and legal rights, for example. One useful way of considering them is to see them as falling into three overlapping areas: rights of protection (from abuse or discrimination, for example); rights of participation (as active citizens rather than passive dependents); and rights of provision to necessities (such as food, shelter, education) (Alderson, 2008). With regard to early childhood, which is our focus here, though cultural variation is acknowledged, it is defined as being from birth to eight years old (United Nations, 2005).

In the UNCRC, as we shall see, the child is presented as both needing protection and as entitled to participate and have his or her views heard. The balance shifts from one end of the continuum to the other as the children mature and get older, so babies and young children will need more protection and older children will gradually be seen to acquire legal capacities and more capabilities to participate as active citizens. For some people, however, the notion of rights comes with responsibilities or duties, and so young children are seen as incapable of having rights, given that they are not able to take on duties or responsibilities. However, one of the accepted principles of human rights, inherent in the very phrase, is that everybody has them. So, a baby can have a right but someone else is under a duty to enforce it. If the concept of human rights is accepted, then they apply to all children, not just some, in the same way as they apply to all persons rather than a selection. The children's rights discourse is not accepted by everyone, however. Guggenheim (2005), writing for an English audience from the USA, which does not ratify any United Nations treaties on rights, argues that children's rights do not necessarily work in children's best interests. He sees the children's rights movement as focusing on the exercise of power of the state over children and the exercise of parental authority. He focuses on the parent–child relationship and suggests that a child-centred approach is unhelpful, as children form only part of a society which is constructed and run by adults from their perspective. He also claims that the children's rights agenda is frequently used by adults to serve their own interests, rather than those of the child: in matrimonial disputes, for example (Guggenheim, 2005). While Guggenheim is writing in the context of a country which has not ratified the UNCRC, his views demonstrate the significance of cultural and societal influences which are acknowledged in the Convention and which contribute to the complexities of interpretation. The conceptualisation of childhood will vary between cultures, as well as historically within a given culture, and underpins our responses to the children's rights agenda.

The voice of the child

The notion of children's voice comes out of the concept of children having rights, and so power to be active citizens, not just passive dependents. While this right is enshrined in article 12 of the UNCRC, it is still a nebulous concept, with no supporting legislation, and so could be described as an aspirational right. In this chapter, we will explore what we mean by voice, as well as the role of the adult in hearing or listening to the child. If you can have the child's voice, what about the adult's voice? What do you do if there are conflicting voices, from adults working with the child, for example, or between the child and the adult? It is important to acknowledge the complexity inherent in both these closely related notions of rights and voice which involve the relationship of adult and child, power and the use and abuse of it and perceptions of childhood.

As you read the chapter, take the time to reflect on your own attitudes and beliefs regarding the questions raised, as a high level of self-awareness is necessary to be able effectively to examine critically and challenge what can be at times uncomfortable ideas and dilemmas. Do you think your view of childhood is the same as that of your parents or grandparents? Think about areas of similarity and difference between the generations, and how your generation may have been influenced by the children's rights agenda.

In the following extract and the discussion that follows, you may find it useful to have a copy of the UNCRC (1989) to hand so that you can see the scope that the rights cover.

EXTRACT 1

Alderson, P. (2008) (2nd edition). *Young Children's Rights: Exploring beliefs, principles and practice*. London: Jessica Kingsley Publishers

Limitations on rights

All rights are *limited*. As legal concepts they concern freedoms, entitlements and obligations, which can be deliberately honoured – or withheld. Parents cannot be taken to court, for example, for not loving their child. It would be useless and cruel to prosecute a mother who is too depressed to love her baby. Love and happiness cannot be willed or enforced so they cannot be rights. Yet adults can be prosecuted for obvious neglect or abuse, and children do have the right to be protected from these. The UNCRC sets possible standards, which can be enforced to help adults to give loving care, and the UNCRC's preamble states the importance of every child living 'in an atmosphere of happiness, love and understanding'. The UNCRC enshrines minimum standards, which may rise in future as the world's children come to be more respected.

Some rights are *aspirational*, not yet fully realisable, but only 'to the maximum extent of [each nation's] available resources' (4). Richer nations are expected to help poorer ones to respect children's economic rights (24.4).

Rights are not *absolute* but *conditional*, affected by the 'evolving capacities of the child', the 'responsibilities, rights and duties of parents' (5), 'the primary responsibility of the parents' (18), and the national law. 'The best interests of the child shall be a primary consideration' (3). Children's rights cannot be exercised in ways that would harm the child or other people. In exercising their rights, people must 'respect the rights and reputations of others', as well as 'national security and public order, health and morals' (13).

Rights are *shared*, being about solidarity, equality in social justice and fair distribution, 'our' rights not 'my' rights. The UNCRC is not about selfish individualism. To claim a right acknowledges that everyone has an equal claim to it and so reaffirms the worth and dignity of every person. Children's rights are part of promoting 'social progress and better standards of life in larger freedom'. The preamble states that the child 'needs special safeguards and care, including appropriate legal protection', and the UNCRC begins 'in recognition of the inherent dignity and of the equal and inalienable rights of all members of the human family [as] the foundation of freedom, justice and peace in the world'.

Rights are about *necessities* not luxuries – clean safe water, freedom to play.

One argument against children's rights is that rights cannot be bestowed. They can only apply to groups, which understand and claim and exercise rights for themselves, as some, though far from all, women, black and disabled people have struggled to do. Yet the provision and protection rights involve duties, which adults owe to children, who did not ask to be born and who are inevitably dependent at first. With the participation rights although young children may not use rights language, they repeatedly say they want adults to listen to them and take heed of their views (Lansdown and Newell, 1994; Save the Children 1999).

continued

EXTRACT 1 *continued*

It is also said that rights go with *obligations and responsibilities*, and that children are irresponsible or pre-responsible. Adults are responsible for ensuring that many children's rights are respected. Yet children often want some participation rights so that they can share more responsibility with adults, as later examples will show.

The UNCRC is about broad *principles*, which can be interpreted and applied in different ways according to local values and traditions. There is therefore at times confusion and *disagreement* about how best to honour children's rights. One example is the debates about child poverty, what it means and how it can be relieved. The UNCRC's 54 articles *combine* all children's rights, which are not seen as separate items but as complementary, and this coherent overall view can inform ways to apply the UNCRC. The UNCRC goes beyond earlier children's rights documents on provision and protection to add participation rights, which can help young children and adults to enjoy more equal and mutually rewarding lives and relationships. Central to participation is the right to form and express views.

POINTS TO CONSIDER

- *Reflect on what you understand by children's voice: you may find it helpful to think back to a time when you remember being either listened to or ignored, and consider how you felt.*

- *Discuss with a friend or colleague how you have noticed the impact of the UNCRC in the society in which you live. You might consider: (a) any experience you have of working with children, and (b) representations of children's rights issues in the media.*

- *Reflect on Alderson's view that all rights are limited. Do you agree, or do you think that some are absolute? Try to find someone else to discuss this with, and consider which areas you agree on and which you view differently.*

Equal rights?

In this extract, Alderson argues that all rights are limited and it is useful to consider in more detail how that statement might be interpreted. The European Convention on Human Rights (ECHR, 1953) distinguishes between rights that are absolute and rights that are subject to caveats. For example, article 3 of the ECHR deals with torture and inhuman treatment. This right cannot be suspended, even in a time of war. In other words, there is never an excuse for an infringement of this kind of right. This can be contrasted with article 8, which protects the right to respect for a person's privacy, family life, home and correspondence. This right is subject to certain exceptions within the legal system of the country that are considered to be necessary in a democratic society. The UNCRC similarly has some articles where the content indicates an absolute right, as for example with article 37a, which stipulates that no child shall be subjected to torture, and others which are qualified, such as article 9, which states that a child should not be separated from their parents against their will. The article then goes on to give the exceptions to this right, such as if the child is being abused or neglected, or if the parents have separated and a decision has to be made about where the child will live. So in terms of content, it does seem as if some rights are unconditional, and others conditional. However, a distinction can be made between the content of a right, the applicability and the enforceability, and then the picture becomes more complicated.

In terms of enforceability, though it may be possible for a government to legislate to ensure some articles of the convention are adhered to, such as the right to have a legally registered name and nationality (article 7), other articles are impossible to enforce, as Alderson points out, such as the right to leisure, play and culture (article 31) or the right to certain freedoms, such as the freedom of thought, conscience and religion (article 14). To complicate matters further, upholding some rights may result in an infringement of other ones. Dowty (2008) argues, for example, that the increasing scrutiny of children and monitoring using technology in the interests of child protection infringes on the entitlement to privacy (article 16). She suggests that some rights are considered more important than others and is critical of the way the concept of privacy is being undermined in the UK. She also questions the uncritical acceptance of technology. It is ironic that the increasing dependence on technology as an information and social medium is itself compromising children's safety to an extent that perhaps was not envisaged when it was introduced. Indeed the importance of the mass-media is endorsed in article 17, and we may ask how successfully children are being safeguarded against harmful mass media material and information in our society, which is an aspiration of the article. If we then consider the applicability of article 17, it then raises the question of how the importance of mass media relates to children of different ages. Would the article be interpreted and applied in the same way to a baby as to a child of eight or a teenager, for example? What is the role of the adult in ensuring the appropriate use of technology in the three different age groups? It becomes clear that this article could be interpreted and implemented in a different way depending on the age of the child. Thus Alderson's claim that all rights are limited becomes clearer, as the subtlety and complexity of the rights argument is unpicked.

Cultural and societal influences

In the extract, Alderson comments that some rights are aspirational as they may not yet be able to be fully realised but represent an ideal to strive towards. The UNCRC places responsibility for the implementation of the rights with 'state parties', and each country will have different cultural and societal factors which will influence how the rights are interpreted and applied. This is acknowledged in the UNCRC, in article 4, which states:

> With regard to economic, social and cultural rights, State Parties shall undertake such measures to the maximum extent of their available resources and, where needed, within the framework of international co-operation.

(Article 4)

Healthcare is a prime example of where the rights of the child *to enjoyment of the highest attainable standard of health* (article 24) will depend on the economic resources of the country and where provision is likely to vary widely between developed and developing countries. However, it is worth considering that even in developed countries, there may not be equal access to healthcare for all children, as access may be limited by the ability of the parent/carer to pay, as well as the geographical location which may restrict access to services (Marmot et al., 2010; see also Chapter 1). The expectation that there will be international co-operation so that poorer countries are supported by richer ones is explicitly reiterated in the articles relating to health (article 24) and to education (article 28). In particular, literacy is highlighted as a key area along with *facilitating access to scientific and technical knowledge and modern teaching methods* (article 28). You may like to consider in what ways international co-operation to support these areas is undertaken by the UK, considering for example the role of charities as well as government aid.

The UNCRC calls for respect for different cultures, cultural identities and civilisations, though this is set in the context of respect for the concept of human rights and fundamental freedoms (article 29). This acknowledges the potential tension that exists between the two ideals of valuing individual cultures at the same time as maintaining a commitment to the ideal of universal human rights. This tension arises if or when a cultural practice is embedded in a nation's identity that does not conform to the principles enshrined in the UNCRC. The preamble talks of *taking due account of the importance of traditions and cultural values of each people for the protection and harmonious development of the child* but this can be very tricky if the practices could be seen as harmful to the child. One such area in which the accommodation of traditional customs is heavily criticised is the practice of female genital mutilation in many African countries, which is both painful and of no medical benefit. The matter is further complicated when the practice takes place in countries that do not sanction the practice, such as the UK. Taking a less contentious topic, what do you do if children's work is an essential part of the family economy? Should work in a sweatshop factory be distinguished from helping out on the family smallholding? Is it just paid work or unpaid work as well? It is easy to think that this is just an issue in the developing world, but you may like to consider the situation of unpaid young carers who help look after disabled parents or siblings from a young age in this country. It is also worth noting that the responsibilities that some children take on at an early age may encroach on their right to an education as well. This issue also raises the question of the importance of how play is viewed in a culture, and also of whether children's play is a peculiarly Western concept that is being imposed on other cultures where childhood is constructed very differently. There is a difficult path to negotiate between the domination of a Western ethnocentric view of the world on the one hand and a position of extreme cultural relativism on the other (Archard, 2004).

Rights and responsibilities

One argument advanced against children being accorded rights is that rights go with responsibilities and that as children are the responsibility of their parents until they attain the age of majority, they cannot hold rights of their own (Alderson, 2008). However, the preamble of the UNCRC argues for the inherent rights of all human beings, with extra protection given to children *recalling that, in the Universal Declaration of Human Rights, the United Nations has proclaimed that childhood is entitled to special care and assistance* (UNCRC,1989). Parents (or legal guardians) are recognised as having the responsibility of bringing up the child, acting in their best interests (article 18), and taking into account the maturity of the child (article 14). However, in a rights-based discourse, everyone has rights, parents as well as children, and as Alderson points out, rights have to be exercised in a way that does not infringe the rights of other people. While children do not carry full legal responsibilities, there is much debate about whether they have duties or obligations towards their parents, as Freeman (1993) indicates. There is considerable cultural variation about this notion, and it proved to be one of the major hindrances to reaching a consensus when the UNCRC was drawn up (Freeman, 1993). You may want to consider whether in your own culture, the concept of duty towards parents varies between you and your friends, and whether there is, in your opinion, a difference of views between older and younger generations.

While the word 'duty' is not applied to children in the UNCRC, they are expected to be educated in a way that fosters *the development of respect for the child's parents* (article 29). It is interesting to bear this point in mind when we consider the debate about acceptable forms of discipline adults may use in the upbringing of children. Corporal punishment in all British schools was legally abolished in 1998, but the debate about smacking in a domestic context rumbles on with no UK government to date making the move to prohibit smacking as a form of discipline for parents or carers, despite criticisms from the United Nations Committee on the Rights of the Child in their reports in both 1995 and 2002 (Alderson, 2008). Hitting children for any reason is a contravention of the UNCRC, which seeks *to protect the child from all forms of physical or mental violence, injury or abuse, ... while in the care of the parent(s), legal guardian (s) or any other person who has the care of the child* (Article 19). However, others argue that abuse may be seen as a continuum, and that smacking is below the level they would define as harmful (Archard, 2004). This approach is directly contrary to the zero-tolerance approach to physical violence and raises the question of how to define abuse, and indeed, how to define a smack. Indeed we may want to ask why we have a special word for hitting a child? What is the difference between smacking and hitting? Is a gentle smack acceptable but a hard smack less so? What happens if a child hits the parent back? Archard acknowledges that if an adult was treated in this way, it would be viewed in law as assault, but puts forward the argument that if we are saying that children require different treatment from adults, then smacking could be seen as part of that difference (Archard, 2004). Using this argument, it would be unacceptable for a child to hit the parent back, especially an older child, as it is based on an unequal relationship where the child respects the adult's rights but the adult does not respect the child in the same way. This would seem to conflict with the fundamental principle of the UNCRC which is based on the notion of universal human rights, with vulnerable members of society such as children requiring extra protection. It also provides an example of the dissonance between policy and practice: though the UK has ratified the UNCRC, it continues to fail to implement it fully in law and in practice. The unresolved conflict also exemplifies the strong influence of cultural and societal factors, and how slow attitudes may be to change. This conflict is further exacerbated by the existence of other rights for both children and adults, such as the right to a private life, which may be justified as a reason for parents to be able to discipline children as they see best. In the second extract below, another area of conflicting rights is discussed in detail.

- *Consider what your response might be if you saw a four-year-old child being smacked in the street. You may like to think about whether you would intervene and what your thoughts might be, and then reflect on where you currently would position yourself in the debate and how this would align with the UNCRC.*

- *Are there any cultural practices in your culture which might potentially conflict with the UNCRC? Consider how you might justify these to a person from a different culture in the context of the UNCRC.*

EXTRACT 2

Freeman, M. (1993) 'Laws, conventions and rights', *Children and Society* **7(1): pp37–48 and articles 3 and 12 of the UNCRC (wording of original version)**

Articles 12 and 3 encapsulate a tension in the whole debate which has been examined here. Article 12 emphasises the centrality of a child's views. Article 3 the priority to be given to concerns of welfare. The first principle is no overriding (a Polish attempt to make welfare paramount failed), but its imperative and the philosophy of Article 12 can conflict. How, then, will conflicts be resolved? It is a real concern. Those who constructed the Convention themselves paid scant regard to children's views: do we not know that the rights enumerated in the Convention are those that children themselves would have constructed? But Article 12 cannot be underestimated. Children who are capable of forming views must be 'assured' the right to express them on 'all matters affecting' them, and these views must be given 'due weight'. Again this goes beyond the new English Children Act where a child's views and the representation of them is largely confined to the public law arena. A child has a greater 'say' in care than in school or for that matter at home.

Conclusion

The Convention is an achievement. But it is a beginning, no more. We must not get 'beyond conventions, towards empowerment' (Freeman, 1992d). We must re-examine structures, institutions and practices to make children's rights more meaningful. We have ratified the Convention; we have passed a Children Act. But children are still passed around 'like packages or pieces of property' (Lord Justice Butler-Sloss in *Re W*, 1992b), sexually abused by those 'caring' for them, whisked from their home in 'dawn raids' and held incommunicado. More live in poverty, more are homeless and fewer are entitled to social-security than was the case even a decade ago. The Children Act recognises both sides of the children's rights equation: welfare and self-determination. But is there a serious commitment to either? We have as far to go in the next quarter of a century as we have come in the last if we are truly to take children's rights seriously.

Article 3 (Best interests of the child)

The best interests of children must be the primary concern in making decisions that may affect them. All adults should do what is best for children. When adults make decisions, they should think about how their decisions will affect children. This particularly applies to budget, policy and law makers.

Article 12 (Respect for the views of the child)

When adults are making decisions that affect children, children have the right to say what they think should happen and have their opinions taken into account.

Article 3

1. In all actions concerning children, whether undertaken by public or private social welfare institutions, courts of law, administrative authorities or legislative bodies, the best interests of the child shall be a primary consideration.

2. States Parties undertake to ensure the child such protection and care as is necessary for his or her well-being, taking into account the rights and duties of his or her parents, legal guardians, or other individuals legally responsible for him or her, and, to this end, shall take all appropriate legislative and administrative measures.

3. States Parties shall ensure that the institutions, services and facilities responsible for the care or protection of children shall conform with the standards established by competent authorities, particularly in the areas of safety, health, in the number and suitability of their staff, as well as competent supervision.

Article 12

1. States Parties shall assure to the child who is capable of forming his or her own views the right to express those views freely in all matters affecting the child, the views of the child being given due weight in accordance with the age and maturity of the child.

2. For this purpose, the child shall in particular be provided the opportunity to be heard in any judicial and administrative proceedings affecting the child, either directly, or through a representative or an appropriate body, in a manner consistent with the procedural rules of national law.

The child's view versus the welfare of the child debate

Under the welfare principle, expressed in article 3, the interests of the child are paramount. A 'best interests' assessment is carried out and that outcome is followed. On the other hand, there is the concept of a rights-based discourse or assessment. Under this process, the rights of every party involved are weighed up. For example, the child's rights to a family life with both of his or her parents are considered versus the mother's rights to freedom of expression, including living where she wishes, even if that means in Australia, taking her four-year-old child to the other side of the world from the child's father. Where two rights conflict, a proportionality test is undertaken to determine the correct course in legal parlance. On the face of it, the welfare principle would appear to be more child-focused as it does not consider the interests of the parent unless they are aligned with the child's. It can be argued that a rights-based analysis gives equal weight to the parents' rights and so is likely to be less child-centred. However, in practice, the human rights discourse does not simply pitch two rights against each other in an inhumane fashion. A more helpful image is to think of weighing up the rights of all parties in this case, both parents and the child. Then the courts, on behalf of society, decide how much weight should be given to each party in each individual case. For example, it could be decided that in the example mentioned above, the child's right to freedom of expression encapsulated in article 12 is exceptionally important such that it is considered proportionate to infringe the mother's right to a very large degree in protection of the child's rights. However, as Freeman points out in the second extract (pp32–33), the requirement to take into consideration the views of the child is problematic, conflicting as it does with the paramount importance given to the welfare of the child in article 3. Firstly, the views of the child will be proportionate to their age and stage of development: in the example cited above, for example, if the child was one rather than four, it is very unlikely that the views of the child would be sought or taken into account. Equally, the views of a 14-year-old would be more likely to carry weight than those of a four-year-old on where they would like to live. Secondly, a child could express views that conflict with what are considered to be the best interests of the child – in refusing medical treatment, for example. It can be difficult to ascertain what the views of a young child are, but despite all these difficulties, Freeman emphasises the importance of honouring article 12 in taking children's views into consideration when seeking to protect their rights. Ironically, as Freeman points out, little account was taken of children's views when drawing up the UNCRC so we do not know how representative it is of their views, or what is often called 'their voice'.

The voice of the child

The notion of the child as a citizen with an entitlement to express their views and have them listened to is linked with the notion of the child as an active participant in their lives. Both these concepts are embodied in articles 12 and 13 of the UNCRC, though the degree to which these rights are exercised may vary, depending on the child's age and capabilities (article 12). It should be noted that this shift to considering all humans as having a right to a voice includes all vulnerable groups who may be partially competent so require extra protection, such as adults with disabilities, for example, and not just children. However, within the discourse of rights and participation, young children are seen as under-represented, with much of the research focusing on older children (Clarke et al., 2005). One possible reason for this is that young children are looked after and represented by parents, carers and practitioners from various agencies, who may be less active in the rights debate. Clarke et al. (2005) argue that this may be because they take a perspective informed by developmental needs rather than a rights-based approach, though Woodhead (2005) sees the right to development as being fundamental to children's rights. However, whichever paradigm dominates, fundamental to this debate is the view that is held of the child: in order to accord children a voice, adults need to commit to the notion that children have agency or power to act, and the right to do so. This is not to say that the adult does not shape the world that the child is free to speak in: James, Jenks and Prout (1998) when theorising childhood, see the debate about children's competencies and rights as existing in the space between the structures invented by the adults and the self-determinational capacities of the child. Furthermore, the question arises of what children need a voice for. There appear to be a range of reasons given, from the view that it enhances children's learning through giving them opportunities for decision-making to the wider view that it is a moral imperative within a rights-based discourse. However, a prevalent view is that it is above all a political decision, integral to a democratic approach to society (Clarke et al., 2005).

Listening to young children

Any concept of voice carries with it the concept of listening. With very young children, this may be a tricky process and involve attending to more than verbal and written language, which dominate as modes of communication. The theoretical development in Reggio Emilia, northern Italy, of the *hundred languages of childhood* is well known in this country, valuing as it does the widest possible range of communicative means, particularly visual media (Malaguzzi, 1998). Similarly the Mosaic approach, developed by Clarke and Moss (2001), uses a range of ways to listen to children, building up a multifaceted picture of the child that acknowledges that a person's voice, like their identity, will shift and be fluid, dependent on the context and the culture. There has been much research considering the importance of listening to the child and taking their views into account in two main areas: legal matters (including safeguarding) and research with young children. When writing of participatory research, Pascal and Bertram define listening thus:

> For us, listening to young children is an active process of receiving, interpreting and responding to their communications. 'Listening' includes using all the senses and emotions and accessing children's range of communication is clearly not limited to the spoken word.

(Pascal and Bertram, 2009, p255)

Listening here is seen to involve the active participation of the adult in a dialogue with the child, and importantly recognises the interpretive role of the adult in the listening process. This is problematic because as a listener, what we hear and see is mediated through our own beliefs and attitudes, which we may or may not be aware of. For example here, the interpretation will be influenced by the adult's beliefs about childhood generally, and this child and family in particular. In an article on participatory geographical research with young children, some of whom did not choose to co-operate with the researcher, Gallagher critiques early childhood studies for holding on to unchallenged notions of children's agency as entirely benign and innocent. He suggests that power constantly shifts between adult and child, and is not held exclusively by the adult (Gallagher, 2008).

Listening to anyone intently is hard work and time-consuming, and can be particularly so with young children and babies and when the meaning may be hard to construe. We may not like what we see or hear and it may present us with difficult decisions as to what to do next. While Pascal and Bertram talk about listening with our emotions, it can be necessary to overcome our feelings in order to establish a professional detachment and respond in a way helpful to the child, as a study of Early Years teacher trainees' attitudes towards child protection found (Bishop and Lunn, 2002).

It is also necessary to acknowledge that it is easier to listen to some voices than others, such as missing or marginalised voices. This may be especially the case with a group of children, either in a family or in a setting, where certain children can dominate while others become effectively invisible. How does a practitioner respond to a silent child, for example? Is the child choosing not to use their voice, which it is in their power to do, or is the child being silenced by fear of what will happen to them if they do communicate? It is important to recognise that ethically a child needs to be given the opportunity for silence, which is in itself a very powerful statement. However, it is also important to be aware that there are voices that are not heard, either because they are missing or marginalised, or because the adult does not hear them. Expressing a view involves taking a risk, and the notion of listening to the child's voice is predicated on the assumption that children are comfortable communicating with adults, which may not always be the case. There are many ways of avoiding communicating: take the child who always runs away to play outside with his group of friends when an adult approaches, for example, or the child who draws the same picture of themselves every time they do a drawing for the whole two years they are in nursery. How do we interpret their behaviour or their voices? It also behoves us to reflect back on our role as adults: as Freeman points out in this extract, young children in the UK continue to have a very restricted voice in their everyday lives.

While Freeman celebrates the creation of the Convention, he questions the level of 'serious commitment' to children's rights in practice. In the context of children's voice and participation, one of the main reasons for the gap between policy and practice is considered to be the attitudes of the practitioners both nationally and internationally, which undermine the attempts that have been to embed children's right to express their views and participate in all aspects of their lives. In the UK, Pascal and Bertram (2009) signal the need for greater changes in practitioners' underlying values and attitudes in order to make the commitment to children's participatory rights a reality in settings. This concern is reflected in other European countries. In Norway, for example, where the curricular documentation is much more explicitly democratic than that of the UK, empirical research has found that children still receive a varied experience from setting to setting, depending on the ethos of the relationship with the adult. These range from respectful and responsive interactions, in line with establishing democratic relations with the children as required, to distant and controlling interactions, which are not compatible with the curricular aims (Bae, 2009). In this interesting study, the researcher highlights the need to regard children as both dependent and competent subjects, rather than one or the other, and warns against using purely formulaic structures to satisfy the requirement for a democratic ethos – for example, asking children to press a button on the computer to indicate which computer program they would like. She also cautions against following an individualistic approach at the expense of fostering a collaborative ethos, where children use their agency to support each other as well as interact with the adult. A truly democratic ethos comes from a belief in children as fellow beings worthy of the rights and respect accorded to all people,

t on their humanity rather than any notion of competence or responsibility. If
on the advantages and possible disadvantages of taking account of children's
family or in a setting, can you think of reasons why adults may not always pro-
ght?

As practitioners (and researchers), it is incumbent upon us to question our attitudes and beliefs more critically in order to move towards making the child's voice a reality. Consider how a baby can communicate and make their voice heard. What about a three-year-old? What qualities and attitudes do you think the adult needs to have to be able to listen responsively to what the child is communicating? How might you try to hear a 'missing' voice? What means of communication could you look for? How might you respond to the child?

CHAPTER SUMMARY

In this chapter you have had the opportunity to explore the complexities of the concept of children's rights in the wider context of the human rights agenda. You have been encouraged to reflect on the wider issues of how children are viewed and of their status in society, considering both national and international perspectives. Key areas of the debate have been highlighted, such as the question of how rights are enforced and applied in different contexts, and how this varies according to the child's age and maturity. In particular, we have considered babies and young children, but situated them in the wider context of childhood as defined by the UNCRC. The issues of whether all rights are equal, and conflicting rights, have been considered, and you will have noted the multifaceted nature of children's rights, encompassing as it does the notion of a dependent child requiring protection simultaneously with a child whose views need to be given serious consideration. You have also seen the intricacies and difficulties of reaching a decision within a rights-based discourse, balancing the rights of the child and the adult while seeking to act in the best interests of the child. The notion of child's voice and agency has been explored and the significance of how the adult's own voice informs the meaning given to the voice of children signalled. Throughout, you will have seen that cultural and societal influences are pivotal in the interpretation and implementation of children's rights. Many call for more commitment to making the children's rights agenda a reality in practice: in the second extract Freeman calls the UNCRC a beginning, no more. Ultimately fulfilling this commitment comes back to examining our own perceptions of the relationship of the whole human family to each other, and our willingness to change for, as Woodhead points out, implementing the Convention does not just alter the status of young children. It also alters the status of adults. Respecting the rights of young children changes the way we think about ourselves *(Woodhead, 2005, p98).*

References

Alderson, P. (2008) (2nd edition) *Young Children's Rights: Exploring beliefs, principles and practices.* London: Jessica Kingsley Publishers

Archard, D. (2004) (2nd edition) *Children, Rights and Childhood.* London: Routledge

Bae, B. (2009) Children's right to participate – challenges in everyday interactions. *European Early Childhood Education Research Journal*, 17(3): 391–406

Bishop, A. and Lunn, P. (2002) 'I would just like to run away and hide, but I won't!' Exploring attitudes and perceptions on child protection issues with early years teacher trainees on the threshold of their careers. *Westminster Studies in Education*, 25(2): 187–99

Children Act (1989) London: HMSO

Children Act (2004) London: HMSO

Clarke, A. and Moss, P. (2001) *Listening to Young Children: The Mosaic Approach*. London: National Children's Bureau

Clarke, A., Kjorholt, A.T. and Moss, P. (eds) (2005) *Beyond Listening*. Bristol: Policy Press

Dowty, T. (2008) Pixie-Dust and Privacy: What's Happening to Children's Rights in England?' *Children and Society*, 22: 393–99

European Convention on Human Rights (1953) **www.echr.coe.int/ECHR/EN/Header/Basic+Texts/The+Convention+and+additional+protocols/The+European+Convention+on+Human+Rights/** accessed 24 September 2012

Freeman, M. (1993) Laws, Conventions and Rights. *Children and Society*, 7(1): 37–48

Gallagher, M. (2008) 'Power is not an evil': rethinking power in participatory methods. *Children's Geographies*, 6(2): 137–50

Guggenheim, M. (2005) *What's Wrong with Children's Rights*. Cambridge, MA and London: Harvard University Press

Holt, J. (1975) *Escape From Childhood*. Harmondsworth: Penguin

James, A., Jenks, C. and Prout, A. (1998) *Theorizing Childhood*. Cambridge: Polity Press

Malaguzzi, L. (1998) *The Hundred Languages of Childen*. Stanford, CT: Ablex Publishing

Marmot, M. et al. (2010) Fair Society: Healthy Lives. Strategic Review of Health Inequalities in England, post 2010 **www.ucl.ac.uk/marmotreview** accessed 6 July 2012

Pascal, C. and Bertram, T. (2009) Listening to young citizens: the struggle to make real a participatory paradigm in research with young children. *European Early Childhood Education Research Journal*. 17 (2) 249–262

Powell, J. and Uppall, E.L. (2012) *Safeguarding Babies and Young Children*. Maidenhead: Open University Press

Rinaldi, C. (2006) *In Dialogue with Reggio Emilia: Listening, researching and learning*. Abingdon: Routledge

United Nations (1989) *Convention for the Rights of the Child* **www.unicef.org/crc** accessed 24 September 2012

United Nations (2005) *Convention on the rights of the child: General Comment No. 7. Implementing child rights in early childhood*. Geneva: United Nations

Universal Declaration of Human Rights (1948) **www.ohchr.org/en/udhr/pages/introduction.aspx** accessed on 24 September 2012

Woodhead, M. (2005) Early childhood development: A question of rights. *International Journal of Early Childhood* 37(3), 79–98

Alderson, P. (2008) (2nd edition) *Young Children's Rights: Exploring beliefs, principles and practices.* London: Jessica Kingsley Publishers

Anning, A. and Ring, K. (2004) *Making Sense of Children's Drawing*. Maidenhead: McGraw-Hill Education

Freeman, M. (1993) Laws, conventions and rights. *Children and Society*, 7(1) 37–48 and articles 3 and 12 of the UNCRC (wording of original version)

James, A. and Prout, A. (eds) (1997) (2nd edition). *Constructing and Reconstructing Childhood*. London: Routledge Falmer

Rinaldi, C. (2006) *In Dialogue with Reggio Emilia: Listening, researching and learning*. Abingdon: Routledge

Samuelson, I.P (2004) How do children tell us about their childhoods? *Early Childhood Research and Practice*, Spring: 6(1)

www.unicef.org

http://ncb.org.uk

www.education.gov.uk

www.legislation.gov.uk

www.un.org

www.nspcc.org.uk

3 Working inclusively in the Early Years

Catharine Gilson and Alison Street

This chapter will explore aspects of inclusion in Early Years practice and will consider both day-to-day and broader questions that challenge the role of the practitioner in settings and impact on young children's lives.

By the end of this chapter you should have:

- inquired why the debate about inclusion vs. exclusion is important for young lives.
- considered what attitudes, structures and events might constitute barriers to inclusion in work with families and young children;
- reflected on your own identities, abilities and needs; how these develop in relationships with others;
- considered the implications of theories to inclusive practice.

Introduction

'Inclusion' is such a frequently used word in policy documents and political speeches that it has become a term often accepted without question, like a slogan, carrying assumptions that we all know what it means or stands for. The term encompasses all aspects of society but in this chapter the focus will centre on the nature of inclusive education. Thomas and Vaughan define inclusive education as *the child's right to participate and the school's duty to accept* (Thomas and Vaughan, 2004, p134). This moves practice beyond notions of integration, as it seeks not only to reject exclusion on any grounds, but also to enable all children to participate; to maximise learning opportunities for all, even if this means rethinking and reorganising existing provision. Previous notions of integration involved helping a child, for example with a special educational need (SEN), to adapt to the mainstream system, rather than taking into account the current right of entitlement. This sense of entitlement stems from the anti-discriminatory legislation and subsequent policy that has developed nationally and internationally in recent years, most notably from the UN Convention on the Rights of the Child (1989) (UNCRC), which has been discussed in Chapter 2. In the UK, the continuing climate of policy change in favour of inclusion and inclusive education is reflected in the 2001 SEN and Disability Act (SENDA), that establishes legal rights for pre- and post-16-year-olds in educational settings. This act amended the 1996 Education Act by reinforcing the government's commitment to including children with SEN in mainstream schools, unless their parent expressly wishes otherwise.

Historically, the emphasis on inclusion in the UK has focused predominantly on children with special educational needs, but the term is now viewed from a broader perspective. Inclusive education is now concerned with establishing equity of provision for all children, and rejecting the exclusion or segregation of learners for any reason whatsoever, including disability, ability, language, gender, poverty, sexuality, religion or ethnicity. The notion of equity as opposed to equality is discussed in detail in Chapter 1. It is important also to note, however, that despite the strong commitment globally to support the move towards inclusion, the implementation of ideals expressed in policy rhetoric into the reality of practice involves challenging decisions that make the issue more controversial, especially for those whose responsibility it is to support young children and families. For example, in the UK there is a tension between the drive to raise academic achievement, as detailed in the 1998 School Standards and Framework Act, and the requirements laid out in SENDA 2001 to include all students in mainstream education wherever possible, including those students with complex needs. These challenges reflect the competing discourses inherent in the education system in the UK, and are explored in more detail later in this chapter.

Inclusion and exclusion

If you include people it follows that your selection can also exclude people, and this is where the debate between inclusion and exclusion arises. Exclusion is concerned with non-participation in society, where families experience a range of conditions that make them isolated, for example because of debt, poor health, special need, housing, language, level of literacy and many other interrelated factors. Some people have more choices than others, and choice can both include and exclude others. But is this not too simplistic a view, and should it not be interrogated and challenged?

In an Early Years educational context one operational definition of inclusion has been asserted by Nutbrown and Clough (2006, p3) as:

> *The drive towards maximum participation in and minimal exclusion from Early Years settings, from school and from society.*

It follows, given the diversity of communities and multicultural nature of society in the UK that there are *as many versions of inclusion as there are Early Years settings – or indeed, the individuals who make up those cultures of living and learning* (ibid. 3). If this view is adopted, then it moves us away from a dualism in thinking in terms of inclusion and exclusion being fixed conditions – though it has to be acknowledged that some families experience life like this – towards a model where different kinds of approaches are important to consider. Practice that reflects a range of approaches founded on positive regard for difference has been seen to need dedicated time, energy, roles, decisions on an individual basis, as well as negotiation in terms of structural and policy decisions.

For inclusion to work effectively for any learning community, it involves a degree of self-awareness, of inquiring into how our own identities have been formed and go on changing. It is useful to consider how powerful adults are who work with children, and how in their everyday interactions, comments, gestures, touch, attitudes, questions, choice of story, song, etc., they can influence children's view of themselves, also their *future actions and behaviour, as well as their intentions, learning outcomes and beliefs.* (Siraj-Blatchford, 2010, p152). A more complex picture begins to emerge, in which degrees of freedom of choice to act as we wish, access to certain places, services, people and activities are determined by culture, social class, gender, accommodation, money, health, age, religion and so on. For example, consider how you have been influenced by the words or actions of a teacher in your own past, and identify how they affected you. In what ways have other factors or relationships since that time altered these influences?

As you read the two extracts selected for this chapter, try to consider what questions arise for inclusive practice: what are the challenges in the day-to-day role of the practitioner and for the development of the Early Years setting as a dynamic learning community? Equally, try to identify what constitutes exclusive practice and what or who creates barriers for families and children – and practitioners – in settings.

EXTRACT 1

Clough, P. and Nutbrown, C. (2005) Inclusion and development in the Early Years: Making inclusion conventional? *Child Care in Practice*, 11(2): pp99–102

Young children can only be truly included if their educators understand their needs, and how to meet such needs through practices which aspire to excellence. For inclusion is about much more than location – it is more than simply 'being' in a setting – it is about making sure that young children and their families are offered opportunity fully to participate in events and developments. And this is, alas, easier said than done. Despite the increasingly shared political agenda for social inclusion, there remain barriers to inclusion which have yet to be overcome. Four key themes – which cross geographical and cultural borders – seem to us to dominate the literature:

- There is an evident climate of policy change towards inclusion across Europe (*and*)

- A multinational commitment towards (and inclusive response to) education of children with learning difficulties has been established (*but*)

- A commonality of concern exists about the education of children with emotional and behavioural difficulties (*and*)

- Inclusive ideologies continue to be discussed and promoted whilst, at the same time, exclusive practices continue. (Nutbrown & Clough, 2004, p306)

Participants from a range of settings and policy contexts generally supported inclusion but with important reservations; the '*Yes – but* ...' factor that we identified highlights the mismatch between policy and practical realities – between the willingness to include all children, in principle, and the ability to cater appropriately for the diverse and sometimes demanding needs of young children. For example, two of the early years practitioners we interviewed commented:

[It] ... depends on the degree of the condition the children have. A child who has mobility problems could not pose any insurmountable problems, but a child with severe autism would be too disruptive and would affect the learning process for the rest of the children.

Children should be included, provided that there is adequate teaching support available to enable all class members to receive equal attention during lessons. It [inclusion] should promote tolerance in children without disability and enhance learning in those with a disability.

POINTS TO CONSIDER

- *In what ways do the responses of the Early Years practitioners fit with or challenge your own beliefs about inclusive practice and/or your experience of helping children to learn?*

- *Consider the possible reasons for the 'yes – but' approach of some practitioners. What might be some of the barriers to implementing a policy of inclusive practice?*

- *Reflect on what you think the benefits of inclusion are for all children, both those with a disability and those without.*

The first extract in this chapter begins by emphasising that inclusive practice for educators of young children involves not just integrating children with particular needs into their setting, but offering the chance *fully to participate* to all children and their families and/or carers. The authors acknowledge at the same time that this is not an easy aim to achieve and involves complex issues. Inclusion, therefore, is a far more radical approach than previously held notions of integration, where the emphasis was on enabling the child to fit into the established mainstream provision. Inclusive practice involves rethinking the way that learning environments are structured and organised in order to meet the full range of learning needs (Thomas and Vaughan, 2004). It is interesting to consider how Clough and Nutbrown find that despite common aspirations to share the political agenda for inclusion, there are also common concerns across different countries, over the mismatch between inclusive ideologies and exclusive practice. With reference to questions raised in the extract, three key themes will be explored in the first half of this chapter.

- The gap between policy and practice.

- Different responses to different needs.

- Different perspectives on inclusion.

The gap between policy and practice

The extract focuses particularly on the gap or mismatch between policy and practice, highlighting the 'yes – but' approach of Early Years practitioners who, while supporting the notion of inclusion in principle, are qualified in their willingness to accept and implement inclusive practices. It is useful here to reflect on what the possible reasons for the practitioners' resistance to inclusion might be. If we consider the case of a child with mobility problems, like the one mentioned in the quotation from an Early Years practitioner in the extract, there may be a range of reasons for reservations. The practitioner might be concerned about adequate resources for the child to be safely and successfully included in the setting. For example, they may want to know whether equipment will be provided for the child, such as ramps for wheelchairs or specially adapted furniture. In addition, they may want to know if there will be an allowance made for extra adult time, both in terms of providing appropriate support to meet the child's needs, as well as time to talk to the parents, liaise with external agencies and to keep the paperwork up to date.

Evidence suggests that practitioners often lack confidence in the adequacy of their own training and skills to manage the complex needs of the children for whom they are responsible in their setting (Florian and Black-Hawkins, 2011). There may equally be tensions arising between their duty of care to a child with additional needs; in keeping them safe and in helping them realise their learning potential, while also meeting the needs of the rest of the class. There are also aspects of accountability integral to the practitioner's role; in relation to a child's parents, to the articulated aims and expectations of the school through its governance and to national inspection regulations. In their study of practitioners' craft knowledge of their practice of inclusion, Florian and Black-Hawkins (2011) focused on the range of meanings of 'inclusion' as a concept for 11 Scottish primary school teachers, engaged in working with children from 3 to 11 years old. They identified practical examples of inclusive pedagogy through the adoption and observation of a Framework of Participation involving the interlinked concepts of what teachers 'do', 'know' and 'believe' about children's participation in day-to-day activities. These focused on access, collaboration, achievement and diversity. An important finding from their research in relation to the present discussion is that across schools and within education systems there are evident constraints that *counter teachers' efforts to be inclusive in their practices* (ibid. 820). They also make an important distinction between inclusive education, practice and pedagogy, suggesting that:

> *Inclusive pedagogy is defined not in the choice of strategy but in its use. While the additional needs approach to inclusion focuses only on the student who has been identified as in need of additional support, the inclusive pedagogy approach focuses on everybody in the community of the classroom.*

> (Florian and Black-Hawkins, 2011, p820)

Here, then, is a recommendation to adopt an approach that avoids the stigma of judging and labelling some students as less able, and instead, to attempt to provide a sufficiently rich environment for all. This idea is especially challenging to those practitioners who, although committed to inclusion, are also subject to contexts where they are expected to categorise children according to their ability in order to comply with the political drive to raise educational achievement.

Different responses to different needs

One of the key findings in the extract is the shared concern about educational provision for children with emotional and behavioural difficulties, indicating that practitioners may have different responses to different needs. This is exemplified in the quotation from Early Years practitioners in the extract (pp42–43), where the level of inclusion is seen to *depend on the degree of the condition* and severe autism is seen as too disruptive to manage in the classroom. While it can be argued that by including a potentially disruptive child, you may risk excluding some other children from learning opportunities, it is also acknowledged in the literature that there is particular resistance to including children seen to have 'poor behaviour.' However, there is a lack of consensus about what is seen as 'good behaviour' and 'poor behaviour' (Visser, 2003). The context is all important, so for example, being good at school may involve sitting up with a straight back on a carpet next to other children with your legs crossed, and putting your hand up to talk, none of which are likely to constitute good behaviour at home. In addition, behaviours that are considered problematic vary considerably from setting to setting, suggesting that behavioural expectations within educational establishments vary significantly.

In an interesting article examining how children come to be perceived as a problem in Early Years classrooms, Maclure et al. (2012) argue that there is a public element of being good, and how from a very young age, children develop a reputation, which then influences how they are perceived. The authors also highlight the public nature of discipline in the Early Years, and comment on the way that learning and behaviour appear inextricably linked in Early Years pedagogy. For example, listening to a story becomes as much about not interrupting, taking turns to talk, the teacher being explicit about what good listening is, and the children demonstrating that they are visibly attending, as it is about the content of the children's comments on the story. How do children demonstrate that they are conforming to behavioural expectations and make sure that they are perceived as 'good'? If a Vygotskian approach to pedagogy applies, that learning takes place through social interaction, and that modelling and scaffolding learning are essential activities, then the role of the educator naturally involves initiating the child into the social and cultural behaviours around learning (Wood, 1998). However, it is worth considering whether in practice the emphasis on good learning being linked with compliant behaviour may result at times in intolerance and discrimination against the child who does not conform to these social conventions.

Different perspectives on inclusion

In a sense, to focus on the practitioner as the source of resistance to inclusive practice is to overly simplify the complexity of the matter. There are many perspectives in the inclusion debate, and conflicting views and agendas may emerge, making a decision hard to reach in any one child's best interests. Apart from the practitioner's perspective, there is the perspective of the parents, and the views of the child to consider. In addition, there are the views of the expert agencies to take into account, such as healthcare professionals or educational psychologists. Clough and Nutbrown (2004) in an earlier European study identified reservations expressed by Early Years practitioners about working in partnership with parents to achieve inclusive education for their child. Although parents are acknowledged to know their child better than anyone else, what do you do if the parental views and practitioner or other professional views are different? How is a decision reached?

As an example, consider the case of a hearing-impaired child where the mother does not wish the child to go to the neighbourhood school (who are keen to take him), as she considers it too big and bustling for her son to settle comfortably. Having a severe hearing impairment herself, she is very aware of the need for a calm, quiet environment. So despite the inclusive and reputedly excellent practice of the setting, she decides to send her son to a much smaller and more formal school on the other side of the city, so that he can receive provision that is more akin to the specialist provision that she received as a child. What questions does this scenario raise for the practitioner who might be wondering how much s/he should try to influence the parent's choice? Whose knowledge is more appropriate in this decision-making process – the mother may well know more about what it's like to live and learn with a hearing impairment, but may her judgement be based solely on her personal experiences? There are important points for reflection here that relate to the educational environment for such a child – should it be different – more 'special'? How might the school reassess the needs of such a child? Are we listening here to the voice of the child or of the parent, whose voice is more easily heard?

If the practitioner considers the child's hearing impairment from a medical point of view, where the child can be perceived as the problem, it might be that the constraints on his learning can be judged too severe for him to remain in the busy environment of the mainstream school. If, however, a social model of his condition is explored, where the problem is seen to be the barriers that form for him, it might allow the practitioner to engage in dialogue about the boy's needs in the context of his family, friends and relations. This can then allow the practitioner to discuss more knowledgeably with the parent the social factors involved in his impairment and counteract perceptions of the child only in terms of his disability. The differences between the medical and social models of disability or illness are articulated clearly by Wade and Halligan (2004) in relation to healthcare and by the DEE (2002).

When considering the layers of influence that are contributing factors in the inclusion debate, the ecological model advocated by Bronfenbrenner (1979) is useful. You may wish to look ahead to Chapter 4 which considers how children learn from the interconnection of the social and cultural networks that surround them. So while the Early Years practitioner may be at the front line, coping with the day-to-day issues arising from trying to implement inclusive practice, the decision of whether to include the child is usually made by the manager of a setting or head teacher of a school. Similarly the practitioner will rarely be the fund holder, as funds are usually administered by the local authority, so access to resources is via gatekeepers. Thus, barriers to inclusion can be multi-layered rather than located in one or two individuals. In addition practitioners are subject to the tensions arising from competing discourses on the education of younger as well as older children, in particular the drive for improvement in academic standards which can seem at odds with the requirement to implement a more inclusive approach to education (Thomas and Vaughan, 2004). How can you know or demonstrate that all children benefit from inclusion, and is it possible to include all children so that they all achieve their potential within the current structure of the education system?

Including culturally diverse identities

The second half of this chapter aims to extend some points raised earlier, especially in relation to including parents' views. It also returns to some of the ideas explored in Chapter 1, on equality and difference, as the reality of day-to-day inclusive practice involves decisions that are influenced by attitudes to difference. The extract under discussion is from Iram Siraj-Blatchford's chapter on diversity and inclusion. Four main themes will be explored from starting points that appear to emerge within the extract. As you read it through, you may consider alternative strands that are implied, and they may equally trigger thoughts about your own experiences in Early Years practice. The main themes to be explored here are:

- including parents and extended family relationships;

- finding resources and a shared language;

- exploring citizenship;

- addressing structures and policies.

Kirsty McMonagle
2019 Nov
Call : 07853088221

EXTRACT 2

Siraj-Blatchford, I. (2010) Diversity, inclusion and learning in the Early Years, chapter 11 in G. Pugh, and B. Duffy (eds) *Contemporary Issues in the Early Years*, (5th edition), pp153–4. London: Sage

For instance, in Britain, an Indian woman who is a first-generation immigrant, and working class, will have a different identity to her daughter who is second generation British Indian, and has become a teacher. Their experience will vary because of how others perceive the combination of ethnic background in relation to their gender, socio economic status, dress, language, even age and so forth. Mother and daughter will certainly not be treated by others in the same way but they might have some shared experiences.

Staff also need to find resources and a shared language with which to work with dual-heritage children and their parents to support a strong identity. But it would be even better if staff worked with all children to make them aware that they all have an ethnic/racial identity and that they all have a linguistic, gendered, cultural and diverse identity. Surely this is the way forward? In being sure of one's own identity as multifaceted, it must be easier for children to accept that others are exactly the same – even when the combinations are different!

In their early childhood, children inevitably identify closely with a range of individuals and groups; from an early age they develop multiple commitments and solidarities. In addition to the 'sense of cultural belonging' that they develop in terms of their language and faith group, their gender and social class, educationalists support children in progressively accepting the social and moral responsibilities, and the community involvement associated with national and international (global) citizenship.

The UK has never been a monocultural society, and calls for the development of any single 'national' identity have therefore always been misplaced. Citizenship, just like identity, must be recognized as a multifaceted phenomenon. Contradictions and controversies are an inevitable consequence of diversity They are also grist to the mill of progress and creativity. In any event, democracy requires something more than simply an orientation towards common values. From the earliest years we should be preparing children to participate, critically engage and constructively contribute to local, national and global society.

continued

The sexism, racism and other inequalities in our society explain why at a structural level certain groups of people have less power while others have more. But at the level of inter-action and agency we should be critically aware of the danger of stereotyping and should focus on individuals. This is not to suggest that we should ignore structure; far from it. We need to engage in developing the awareness of children and staff through policies and practices, which explain and counter group inequalities. I will turn to the point of practice later. What I am suggesting is that educators need to work from a number of standpoints to empower fully the children in their care. Children need to be educated to deal confidently and fairly with each other and with others in an unjust society; in this way our values will be reflected in our children (Siraj–Blatchford and Clarke, 2003).

POINTS TO CONSIDER

- *In what ways do you like to define your identity or identities?*

- *How does your identity change depending on who you are with or where you are?*

- *Are you aware of situations where you tend to defer to others or conversely where you expect others to defer to you?*

Including parents and extended family relationships

Siraj-Blatchford's example of the Indian daughter and her mother illustrates the impor-tance of regard for individual differences in any one identity-forming category. In the same chapter she cites Hall's (1992) metaphor of a kaleidoscope in understanding how identities are formed from the way we can both align and differentiate ourselves indi-vidually from others according not only to race and ethnicity, but also gender, sexuality and dis/ability. She draws attention to the practices of representation of identities often considered as belonging to certain groups, such as Muslims, which can ignore individual variation and local histories of families.

Working with – and therefore understanding and valuing the educational partnership with parents and extended families in Early Years settings – has become accepted as good practice and expected via policy documents since 2000 (QCA, 2000). With the empha-sis on education and care extending from birth, which became operational through the framework of Birth to Three Matters (DfES, 2002; DfES, 2008; DFE, 2012), and the rapid expansion in children's centres in the first decade of the twenty-first century, recognition of the valuable contribution made by the home learning environment led to various com-munity models of supporting children with their families. Nutbrown and Clough (2006) traced this development since the 1960s and 1970s, from a model that was 'compen-satory' to one of increasing participation. Successful models have been seen to build on the recognition of what parents already know and do, for example in family literacy programmes (such as the REAL project, Hannon and Nutbrown, 1997), or in fostering self-esteem and early learning, working with families from birth, as in the PEEP project (Evangelou et al., 2007). It is also a fundamental principle for engaging with families in the Early Learning Partnership framework (NQIN, 2010). In the Pen Green Centre in central UK, Margy Whalley has researched and worked consistently on ways of engaging inclusively with parents, recognising the potential of 'the nurturing and supportive experiences that happen day to day within the home and with family members and friends outside the setting or group contact experienced by the practitioner' (Pen Green, 2007).

Consider the following provisions parents can give their children, in optimum circumstances, based on Langston (2006, p9), and discuss the following questions.

- *Emotional nurture*
  How does practice acknowledge the strengths and the challenging emotional behaviours in existing caring routines in families?

- *Social companionship*
  How do practitioners acknowledge children's home languages and ways of communicating including movements and gestures?

- *Cognitive and language stimulation*
  How can practice recognise and learn from the stories, games or playful songs and rhymes, names or 'pet names' families share in day-to-day routines, rituals and celebrations?

- *Care to promote physical and mental health and well-being*
  How do you think families feel about accessing medical and preventative programmes, such as in health clinics? What might make some feel excluded?

Finding resources and a shared language

The second paragraph of the Siraj-Blatchford extract emphasises the importance of helping all children strengthen their sense of their identities, and of acknowledging that identity is multifaceted. A shared language is a challenge to find, and it can be helpful to consider the many forms that communication may take, including gesture, facial expressions and body language, that both complement and add meaning to words. Baldock (2010) has explored some theoretical perspectives underlying diversity in Early Years education, and concludes that practice needs to move on from multiculturalism towards models of developing intercultural competencies. These take into account the uncertain and unpredictable situations that arise in interactions with strangers.

As societies become increasingly mobile, with adults crossing borders seeking employment, or fleeing conflict or natural disasters, so children are also caught up in the movement. In urban contexts in the UK, in places where families access services, such as offered by children's centres, it is not uncommon to find hyper-diversity within 'stay and play' groups. Here, ideally, families meet and communicate, seeking common ground in their interests of their children, or in order to develop new contacts and friendships. But the reality can often be that women huddle in small groups round the edge of a large room, preferring to chat in their own language or shared dialect. Practitioners whose remit is to support families in these contexts have to develop strategies that make room and allow for activities that are accessible and flexible to local need. Finding a language in common may involve non-verbal means of communication. The communicative elements of body language have been mentioned above, but expressive arts such as music and dance may also have their place. For example, in hyper-diverse contexts, projects that explore mothers' stories and memories of song and family members who might have sung them have been seen to have a profound effect on how women access services and articulate their own aspirations for their children's learning. Here music can act as a cohesive medium for generating meaning and cultural relevance (Young and Street, 2010).

Coping with difference in child-rearing practices and ways of expressing needs and expectations can be challenging for both parent and practitioner. The psychologist Margalit Cohen-Emerique working through the 1990s developed a framework for understanding intercultural communication and developing intercultural competence; recognising and focusing on the 'cultural shocks' that arise in everyday situations. Writing from the university in Liége, where she witnessed how practitioners in social work and education cope with migrant populations, she explained the concept of cultural shock being about:

- acknowledging attitudes we all have to our bodies;

- understanding of space and time;

- family structure;

- rules of social interaction;

- ways we ask for assistance;

- religion or beliefs;

- cultural change.

(Cohen-Emerique, 1999)

She points to the professional values that can feel threatened and may be reaffirmed in a defensive way when confronted by difference in others:

> *ces réactions défensives bloquent les attitudes nécessaires à la compréhension des situations, à la reconnaissance de l'autre et donc à la résolution des problèmes.*

> (…these defensive reactions block the necessary attitudes towards understanding situations, towards recognition of the other and therefore the resolution to these problems.)

(Cohen-Emerique, 2004)

Her emphasis lies in accepting to transform and to be transformed by those with whom we interact. This calls for an openness of mind and willingness to change, to learn more about ourselves through how we cope with 'difference'.

Exploring citizenship

A careful read of Siraj-Blatchford's third and fourth paragraphs in the extract encourages attention away from everyday interactions towards the bigger questions of how educationalists can support young children's 'sense of belonging'. What does it mean to be a citizen in the UK? Her recommendation is to accept that like identity, citizenship is also multifaceted, and therefore fraught with inevitable controversies. Debates about multiculturalism are reignited when fears are fuelled by extreme acts of terrorism, such as the gunning down of young people in Norway, in the summer of 2011; an act motivated by one man's protest at liberal acceptance of the increasing cultural diversity in a country historically more monocultural than the UK.

It might be useful here to consider how young children's identities are socially and cultur-ally constructed; to learn about the nature of citizenship from how they negotiate and navigate their relationships with others. Children, like adults, learn to decode and adapt to messages they receive from others about their own reactions to home and in wider soci-ety, including early childhood environments.

> *Identity is also the result of how other people define the young child, how he or she is understood (or not) and shown respect (or not). In these ways, children's social experiences serve as a 'mirror' for their identities.*

(Vandenbroeck, 2008, p26)

The challenge for inclusive practice is to recognise the potential creativity afforded by adopting approaches that encourage young children as co-constructors of their social and cultural identities. Vandenbroeck suggests it is important first to understand how complex it can be for young children making their transition from home to first education setting (especially where they experience contrasting views about what is expected, for example in language, dress, how to sit, or defer to authority). This can become confounded when they are confronted with a forced 'either/or' choice about how they belong (a dualist/exclusive view), instead of an 'and/and' (inclusive view) that accepts their – and our own – multiple identities (Vandenbroeck, 2008).

Addressing policies and structures

The final paragraph of Siraj-Blatchford's extract starts by acknowledging the inequal-ity within societies, the danger of stereotyping, and the respect deserved in considering children and adults as individuals. This is further reinforced by Early Years policy in empha-sising the importance of focusing on the *unique child* (DFES, 2007). But she goes further, to challenge educators and carers to confront the structures and policies that govern set-tings. Day-to-day procedures, for example, for admission to settings, for provision for children with SEN and how to afford equal opportunities, contribute to the ethos and interactions that include and exclude children and their families. To facilitate this, she has proposed that all those working in the field make regular audits of equity-based practice, that include SEN, gender, racial equality, etc., according to six stages.

> Stage 1: where diversity according to gender, class, culture and race is a 'problem' (= discriminatory);
>
> Stage 2: where a deficit model exists – a culture of blame and causal effects inappropri-ately attributed (= inadequate);
>
> Stage 3: where staff are keen to meet children's needs but lack knowledge; tokenism (= poorly informed);
>
> Stage 4: where diversity is generally valued;
>
> Stage 5: where 'equal opportunities' is firmly on the agenda, challenging discrimination;
>
> Stage 6: where staff actively try to change structures and power relations which inhibit equal opportunities, (= challenging inequality and promoting equity).

(Siraj-Blatchford and Clarke, 2003, pp15–17)

These provide a focused framework for discussion on almost any aspect of provision, for example, from the resources in home corners to the types of interactions around mealtimes and nappy changing. Where these have been explored by both students and practitioners, they expose discrepancies and feelings about communication, how information is shared, and may have a direct impact on how practitioners themselves feel included (or not) at different levels. It may be useful at this stage to take some time to consider an aspect of care or provision with which you are familiar in your practice and to think through these six stages, discussing their relevance. Alternatively there may have been a 'critical incident' where you felt uncomfortable which has caused you to reflect on your own stance or position in relation to others. It can be seen that these relate as much to management as to who does what, both with and for children on a daily basis.

This brings the chapter back to the meanings of inclusion; to the diverse views that practitioners hold. Clough and Nutbrown (2002) adopted the Index for Inclusion (Booth and Ainscow, 2004) to ask practitioners to elaborate on their personal reflections as professionals; what they saw as their own roles and needs for support. This Index was the result of a collaborative action research project whose conclusions centred on the language and terms used to mean inclusion, the identification of barriers to play and participation, the resources needed to support play, including human resources, and support for diversity across settings as a whole, rather than focusing on specific individuals.

What is clear from reading accounts of practitioners faced with difficult decisions on whether to include this or that child, or understand and meet the requests of this or that parent, is that this work can be emotionally and physically demanding. Their own strengths, vulnerabilities and ways of offering and taking support are also an inclusive part of practice in any learning community.

CHAPTER SUMMARY

In this chapter you have been able to debate the meanings of inclusion and exclusion with reference to your own experiences and identities as they exist in relationship to other people. You have explored emerging themes from two extracts that cover broad areas of inclusive practice. In the first extract some potential gaps between the rhetoric of policy and the realities of practice were explored. The discussion continued to consider how ensuring equity for early childhood education implies difference in approaches according to individuals' needs. This included recognising how children learn in social contexts (Vygotsky) and this relates not only to formal curricula but also to informal behaviours and values, special needs and genders, impacting on their developing identities. Inclusion has been considered to be fundamental to facilitating children's holistic development, taking into account family social and cultural contexts, histories and experiences (Bronfenbrenner). In the second extract you could explore four main themes; the importance of recognising existing competencies in families; the challenges of intercultural questioning through day to day interactions; the way children's multiple identities can be recognised to support their sense of belonging in early childhood contexts. Finally you have been encouraged to review and reflect on existing policies and structures in your professional life. By revisiting your own meaning of inclusion you have been able to explore what this may feel like for you in relation to both your colleagues and to the children and families you support.

References

Baldock, P. (2010) *Understanding Cultural Diversity in the Early Years*. London: Sage Publications

Booth, A. and Ainscow, M. (2006) *Index for Inclusion: Developing Play Learning Participation in Early Years and Childcare*. Bristol Centre for Studies in Inclusive Education

Bronfenbrenner, U. (1979) *The Ecology of Human Development*. Cambridge, MA: Harvard University Press

Clough, P. and Nutbrown, C. (2002) The Index for Inclusion: Personal perspectives from Early Years educators. *Early Education*, 36, Spring

Clough, P. and Nutbrown, C. (2005) Inclusion and development in the Early Years: Making inclusion conventional? *Child Care in Practice*, 11(2): 99–102

Cohen-Emerique, M.H.J. (1999) La négociation/médiation interculturelle, phase essentielle dans l'intégration des migrants et dans la modification des attitudes des acteurs sociaux chargés de leur integration. (Intercultural negotiation/mediation as an essential phase in migrants' integration and in the attitude change of social actors in charge of their integration). *Vie Sociale*. 1999, no2 (68 p) (1 p1/4), [Notes: notes dissem.], pp3–19. Paris: Centre d'études, de documentation, d'information et d'action sociales

Cohen-Emerique, M.H.J. (2004) Les réactions défensives à la menace identitaire chez les professionnels en situations interculturelles. (Defence mechanisms against the threat to self-identity amongst professionals in intercultural situations). *Les Cahiers Internationaux de Psychologie Sociale*. No. 61, p2–3

Disability Equality in Education (DEE) (2002) Inclusion in Early Years: Disability in Education Coursebook. A Human Rights Issue

DfES (2002) *Birth to Three Matters: A Framework to Support Children in their Earliest Years*. London: DfES Publications

DfES (2007) *Early Years Foundation Stage. Statutory Framework and Guidance*. Nottingham: DfES Publications

DfE (2012) *Statutory Framework for the Early Years Foundation Stage*.London: DfE Publications

Evangelon, M., Brookes, G. and Smith, S. (2007) *The Birth to School Study: Evidence on the effectiveness of PEEP, an early intervention for children at risk of educational underachievement*. Oxford Review of Education, 33(5): 581–609

Florian, L. and Black-Hawkins, K. (2011) Exploring inclusive pedagogy. *British Educational Research Journal*, 37(5), p813–828

Hannon, P. and Nutbrown, C. (1997) Teachers' use of a conceptual framework for early literacy education involving parents. *Teacher Development*, 1(3): 405–20

Langston, A. (2006) Why parents matter, in L. Abbott and A. Langston (eds) *Parents Matter*. London: Open University Press

MacClure, M., Jones, L., Holmes, R. and MacRae, C. (2012) Becoming a problem: behaviour and reputation in the Early Years classroom. *British Educational Research Journal*, 38(3): 447–71

NQIN (2010) *Principles for Engaging with Families*. London: Early Childhood Unit

Nutbrown, C, and Clough, P. (2004) Inclusion and exclusion in the Early Years: Conversations with European educators, *European Journal of Special Needs Education*, 19(3): 301–15

Nutbrown, C. and Clough, P. (2006) *Inclusion in the Early Years*. London: Sage

Pen Green Research, Development and Training Base (2007) *Parents involved in their children's learning (PICL) materials*. Corby: Pen Green. In National Quality Improvement Network (NQIN) (2010). *Principles for Engaging with families: A framework for local authorities and national organisations to evaluate and improve engagement with families*. London: National Children's Bureau

QCA/DfEE (2000) *Curriculum Guidance for the Foundation Stage*. London: QCA

Siraj-Blatchford, I. (2010) Diversity, inclusion and learning in the Early Years, chapter 11 in G. Pugh, and B. Duffy (eds) *Contemporary Issues in the Early Years* (5th edition). London: Sage

Siraj-Blatchford, I. and Clarke, P. (2003) *Supporting Identity, Diversity and Language in the Early Years*. Maidenhead: OUP

Thomas, G. and Vaughan, M. (2004) *Inclusive Education: Readings and reflections*. Maidenhead: Open University Press

United Nations (1989) *Conventions on the Rights of the Child*. New York: United Nations

Vandenbroeck, M. (2008) The challenge for early childhood education and care. In L. Brooker and M. Woodhead (eds) Developing positive identities. *Early Childhood in Focus, 3: Diversity in young children*. Milton Keynes: Open University Press

Visser, J. (2003) *A Study of Young People with Challenging Behaviour*. London: OFSTED

Wade, D.T and Halligan, P.W. (2004) Do biomedical models of illness make for good healthcare systems? *British Medical Journal*, 329, Dec 2004: 1398–401

Wood, D. (1998) (2nd edition) *How Children Think and Learn: The Social Contexts of Cognitive Development*. Oxford: Blackwell

Young, S. and Street, A. (2010) Evaluation report: Time to play: The development of interculturally sensitive approaches to creative play in children's centres serving predominantly Muslim communities. Accessible via **www.peep.org.uk**

FURTHER READING

Baldock, P. (2010) *Understanding cultural diversity in the Early Years*. London: Sage

Brooker, L. (2005) *Learning to be a child: Cultural diversity and Early Years ideology*, in N. Yelland (ed.) *Critical Issues in Early Childhood Education*. London: Oxford University Press

Nutbrown, C. and Clough, P. (2006) *Inclusion in the Early Years*. London: Sage. Chapters 1 (for an overview), 7 (about working with parents), 8 (about practitioners' experiences and accounts) and 9 (focusing on professional development)

Thomas, G. and Vaughan, M. (2004) *Inclusive Education: Readings and reflections*. Maidenhead: Open University Press

Bertram, T and Pascal, C. (2008) *Children Crossing Borders* **www.childrencrossingborders.org/ index.html**

www.diseed.org.uk

https://www.pre-school.org.uk/practitioners/387/equality-diversity-and-inclusion

www.kids.org.uk.

www.decet.org

Strand 2

Exploring learning and well-being

4 Exploring how children learn in the Early Years

Mary Wild

This chapter will consider different ways in which theorists and researchers have sought to explain how young children learn. As you read through this chapter think about your own experiences of learning, both as a child and as an adult. How do these experiences relate to the ideas that you are reading about? If you have a role that involves working with young children, think about what sorts of learning experiences you provide for them. Again, how do these relate to the ideas that are covered here? Consider also whether there are other factors that your experience tells you may be important for effective learning.

By the end of this chapter you should have:

- considered the contribution to our understanding of learning from developmental research and major theorists including Piaget and Vygotsky;
- explored the extent to which learning is an active process for children and the role of play in driving learning;
- considered the importance of social experience and interaction for children's learning;
- appreciated that a child's development is enmeshed within communities and broader cultures;
- considered the implications of different theories for professional practice within the Early Years.

Introduction

If we are to be able to provide effective learning experiences for young children then we need to have an understanding of how children learn and develop. Without that theoretical understanding the danger is that at best we do things in particular ways out of professional habit and thereby run the risk of not providing as worthwhile a learning experience as we could, and at worst we may continue with practices that could impact negatively upon the children's learning and well-being.

We all have experiences of learning something new. Think about yourself as a learner as an adult and back to your own experiences of learning as a child. When did you learn best? Was it when you were active, motivated, interested in what you were learning? Do you learn best when left to your own devices to experiment and try things out? Do you learn better when you have others around you? How much guidance do you need to help you learn? If you have experience of working with or caring for young children, what do you think helps them to learn? Do you think it comes naturally and actually you don't need to do very much or have you a more direct role to play in helping children to learn?

The active nature of learning

Learning has not always been seen as an active process in which the learner actively makes sense of the environment around him/her. For much of the twentieth century psychological accounts of learning were dominated by the behaviourist school of thinking, which sought to describe a process of learning whereby the learner reacted to external stimuli and in the course of doing so over repeated occasions learnt to act in particular ways (Skinner, 1974). The external stimuli were conceived of as mechanisms for reinforcing particular actions on the part of the child and could act to positively reinforce the behaviour, i.e. ensure that it would be repeated, or to negatively reinforce the behaviour, i.e. ensure that such behaviour would not be repeated. It is a model of learning that is akin to that used in training an animal, with the trainer, or parent or teacher, shaping the behaviours of the child over time. The role of the child is essentially as a passive respondent to extrinsic reward or punishment. Examples of this approach to learning are still evident in professional practices today. Consider for example the practice of rewarding what is seen as positive behaviour with stickers/praise in the expectation that children will repeat such behaviour. What was missing from this account of learning was any sense of what was happening within the child during the learning and any account of the intrinsic motivation to explore and learn from the environment around him/her. The idea of a child being an active explorer and mental constructor of his/her understanding was a key insight provided by Piaget.

Piaget's theory

Piaget introduced three key concepts (Piaget and Inhelder, 1966).

1. *Schemas*

   • Which are seen as the existing mental representation that the child has of a particular situation or experience.

2. *Assimilation*

   • Which is seen as the way in which the child assimilates or processes new information that is available, effectively 'how does the new situation/experiences fit, or not, with what I already know?'

3. *Accommodation*

   • This is seen as the way in which the child has to accommodate, or alter, their existing schemas to take into account the new situation/experiences effectively 'how do I now need to change what I know?'

Piaget (1983) further argued that children actively seek out patterns in their world; they are fundamentally driven to construct working models of the world around them and this has been linked to the achievement of mastery as a key driver of development (Bruner, 1966).

A second important aspect to the work of Piaget was the notion that children progress through a series of linear stages in their development. Piaget (1962) proposed that the intellectual development of the child proceeds through a series of four stages.

1. The sensori-motor stage: covering the infancy period to age 2.

2. Pre-operational: covering the age period 2–7 years.

3. Concrete operational: covering the age period 7–12 years.

4. Formal operations from age 12 upwards.

This stage aspect of Piaget's theoretical framework has been substantially re-appraised by theorists such as Donaldson (1978), who demonstrated that with subtle alteration to the methodologies used by Piaget it is evident that children are able to attain some of the decentring and logical thinking much earlier than was recognised by Piaget. This is particularly so if the types of task they are asked to undertake make what Donaldson dubbed *human sense* and are presented in contexts that are humanly meaningful to the child. Donaldson's work presaged a focus on the significance of the social context for children's learning, a theme that will be returned to later in the chapter.

Nevertheless, the notion that development may occur in a series of stages, as Piaget suggested, has popular credence and although the precise depiction of what develops and when may well be open to challenge, it possesses some intrinsic credibility when we consider children that we know or have worked with, or indeed our own experience of growing up. We can discern a pattern of becoming capable of doing things that we were unable to do when younger and we can sometimes see how an earlier ability, awareness or skill acts as a building block for later abilities. This is reflected in some approaches to curriculum development such as the Developmentally Appropriate Practices approach (Bredekamp. and Copple, 1997) or the thinking behind the Early Years Foundation Stage (EYFS) in England (DfES, 2007, DfE, 2012). However, these latter day developmentally appropriate models are much less hidebound by arbitrary age phases, offering in the case of the EYFS looser and widely overlapping age phases. Rather than detailing what children cannot do at particular ages, both versions of the EYFS stress the competences, and the active engagement of children in learning has a particular emphasis in the revised EYFS (2012). The focus is on the types of experiences that practitioners might offer to children at different ages in order to build on these characteristics of young children.

Providing opportunities for active learning

What sorts of learning opportunities are developmentally appropriate in this broader sense of the term? In this section continuing research-based evidence of the active nature of a child's engagement with their world is reviewed. As you read through these findings, reflect on what this might mean for the types of learning opportunities that are provided to children.

Children's active engagement in making sense of their physical world is evident from very early on in infancy. From as early as 2½ months of age Baillargeon (2004) has identified that babies have already begun to form expectations about how objects 'behave'. Using the methodological paradigm of violation of expectations, in which infants are noted to look for longer at events that violate rather than confirm their existing expectations, Baillargeon establishes that babies appear to be forming rules about physical properties of the world such as the fact that two small blocks resting on one other should not fall.

However, her team have also demonstrated that as babies begin to gain more physical independence they need opportunities to physically engage with their world in order to confirm or extend their understandings. To continue with the block example, they need opportunities once they are capable of sitting up and of manipulating the blocks to experiment with their understandings through independent play with such objects. Interestingly Baillargeon suggests that independent play is vital here as adults would be likely to place blocks such that they do not fall and that therefore if the infant relied solely on watching what adults do this might not trigger repeated trial and error which allows the infant to form underlying inferences about the physical world. Experiencing unpredicted outcomes is important to extend the child's mental representations. Echoes of the Piagetian view of the child's development are evident here; an adult could facilitate learning by providing the resources but the child's own experimentation is key. In further development of this work Baillargeon showed that where an adult specifically 'taught' or modelled the activity then infants achieved competence earlier. These studies raise interesting questions for practice. If early competence is the aim then maybe specific teaching or modelling should be employed, but if a deeper awareness is sought than maybe less direction and more experimentation is more effective, even (or maybe particularly) if we are working with very young children.

Another theme to emerge from developmental research is the speed or precocity with which young children pick up and apply some core principles of the physical world such as continuity (that objects exist and move continuously in time and space) and solidity (two objects cannot occupy the same space at the same time (Spelke, 2000). It is suggested that this implies that the infant brain may be primed to pay attention to such facets. Gelman (2004) writes of *psychological essentialism*, arguing that young children have an inherent tendency to search for patterns and relationships that enable them to form working categorisations of their world. It is further suggested that young children tend to see both biological properties and behavioural properties as fixed (Taylor, Rhodes and Gelman, 2009) including for example in relation to gender. Schultz et al. (2008) have noted that young children seem disposed to form theories of the world relatively quickly and once formed these working theories can be remarkably robust even when presented with evidence that contradicts their existing hypotheses about the world. It is argued that there is a trade-off between the rapidity with which children amass information about their world and mentally construe their representation of that world and the potential inflexibility of such working models. The challenge for practitioners is to simultaneously respond to the impetus from children to make active sense of their world and to be aware of how fixed a child's working models may become.

There is a theoretical challenge here also. If young children are indeed processing information from their world and formulating hypotheses with such precocity and if the indications are that some of these predispositions are fundamental characteristics of a young brain, then to what extent is learning less explicitly active and more inherently passive than has so far been the proposition of this chapter? The work of Mandler may be instructive here. Mandler (2004) makes a distinction between two forms of knowledge: procedural knowledge and declarative knowledge. Procedural knowledge is envisaged as knowledge borne of exposure to repeated opportunities that enable the brain to pick up thematic patterns and actions. An infant may or may not have a conscious aware-ness of this process and does not explicitly direct his/her actions towards accruing such knowledge. It is a knowledge base borne of engagement with the world but formed incrementally and without directed attention. In contrast, declarative knowledge is more effortful, borne of selective and focused attention that is subsequently processed inter-nally. This form of learning means that new knowledge can be derived from a single exposure or trial and is accessible to conscious awareness. Mandler cites face recognition as an example of procedural knowledge – it is said to happen automatically but not con-sciously. The child may not overtly lodge the details of a face but has logged it mentally so that if change occurs, for example a new hairstyle or glasses, this change is recognised. Learning a new fact though is declarative knowledge. It requires the child to have extrapo-lated from his/her experiences and re-shaped their expectations and understandings as a direct result. These declarative representations may be stored as images even before the child has acquired verbal language. This distinction of two forms of knowledge implies differing levels of directed activity on the part of the young children and reminds us as practitioners that we need to be aware that sometimes children may simply be picking up information, often from those of us around them, as well as requiring more discrete opportunities to explore their world.

There may be considerable variability in the extent to which children acquire new skills and concepts even for the same individual, Siegler (2005) has explored the phenomena by which children gradually increase their repertoires of skills and knowledge and found that far from being a linear trajectory, children will often seem to regress to earlier strategies and stores of knowledge when confronting a new situation. He characterises develop-ment and learning as occurring in *overlapping waves* in which children may use old and new strategies alongside one another or revert to old, tried and tested strategies even in new situations that require different learning strategies. Children need the space to revisit old strategies and patterns as well as the opportunities to encounter new activities. Siegler's work recognises the notion of the child as an active constructor of knowledge but also highlights that children's learning also involves more passive mechanisms such as recognising patterns and making associations that are evident in their environment. It is suggested that attaining fluency and automatic behaviours in this way effectively frees up the child's working memory to focus on more explicit learning and reflection.

The significance of play

Drawing on the work of both Mandler and Siegler, Glenny (2009, in Evangelou et al.) argues that there is a complex interplay between the procedural and declarative forms of knowledge and that it is the *laboratory of play* (ibid. 52) that provides the child with the ideal environment in which to both consolidate more procedural understandings and to experiment with new forms of knowledge.

Play is a crucial theme in early childhood and it therefore forms the main focus of a sub-sequent chapter in this book but meanwhile in the following extract from Vygotsky (like Piaget a seminal influence on modern psychological thinking) the significance of play as a fulcrum for both the consolidation and generation of thinking is explored.

EXTRACT 1

Vygotsky, L.S. (2004) Imagination and creativity in childhood. *Journal of Russian and East European Psychology*, 42(1): pp11–12

If we understand creativity in this way it is easy to see that the creative processes are already fully manifest in earliest childhood. One of the most important areas of child and educational psychology is the issue of creativity in children, the development of this creativity and its significance to the child's general development and maturation. We can identify creative processes in children at the very earliest ages, especially in their play. A child who sits astride a stick and pretends to be riding a horse; a little girl who plays with a doll and imagines she is its mother; a boy who in his games becomes a pirate, a soldier, or a sailor, all these children at play represent examples of the most authentic, truest creativity.

Everyone knows what an enormous role imitation plays in children's play. A child's play very often is just an echo of what he saw and heard adults do; nevertheless, these elements of his previous experience are never merely reproduced in play in exactly the way they occurred in reality. A child's play is not simply a reproduction of what he has experienced, but a creative reworking of the impressions he has acquired. He combines them and uses them to construct a new reality, one that conforms to his own needs and desires. Children's desire to draw and make up stories are other examples of exactly this same type of imagination and play. Ribot tells of a little boy of three and a half who saw a lame man walking on the street and cried, 'Mama, look at that poor man's leg.' Then he began to make up a story: the man had been riding a big horse, he fell on a large rock, he hurt his leg badly, and some kind of medicine had to be found to make him better.

In this case, the combinatorial operation of the imagination is extremely clear. What we have here is a situation the child has created. All the elements of this situation, of course, are known to the child from his previous experience, otherwise he could not have come up with them; however, the combination of these elements is something new, creative, something that belongs to the child himself, and does not simply reproduce what the child happened to observe or see. It is this ability to combine elements to produce a structure, to combine the old in new ways that is the basis of creativity.

Many authors, with complete justification, suggest that the roots of such creative combination may be noted in the play of animals. Animal play very often represents the product of motor imagination. However, these rudiments of creative imagination in animals cannot lead to any stable or major developments in the conditions under which they live; only man has developed this form of activity to its true height.

POINTS TO CONSIDER

- *The extract frames creativity as a developmental force rather than a set of particular attributes. How would you define creativity?*

- *Can you think of examples from your own childhood, or your own observations of young children, in which a play experience served to create new thinking for you or for them?*

POINTS TO CONSIDER *continued*

- *In what ways does the extract suggest children may be forming their understandings? What is the balance between consolidation of understanding and independence of thought? Do you think particular types of play might promote different patterns of thinking?*

- *In what ways does the extract suggest that part of that understanding might also be underpinned by social experiences? To what extent do you think a child needs to have specific models to imitate and emulate within his/her world as a basis for the development of new ideas? How might play with others facilitate thinking?*

Learning as a social experience

In the extract above there is reference to the child's imitation of others, in part a reproduction of his/her social experiences but also as a powerful catalyst for new thinking. The notion that imitation and modelling may be important to a child's learning is echoed elsewhere in theories such as Bandura's (1977) social learning theory.

Following on from this chapter's theme of children being active in their own learning there is also mounting empirical evidence that children are actively social and relational in their learning. Indeed, Gopnick, Meltzoff and Kuhl (1999, p194) have proposed that the brain can be thought of as a 'social brain' and in a series of studies the work of Meltzoff has continued to highlight the many social predilections of very young infants (Meltzoff, 2004). This social attunement of the baby is shown also in accounts of social referencing (Campos, Frankel and Camras, 2004) in which infants will look explicitly towards primary carers for clues as to how to respond to situations socially and emotionally. In accounts derived from our growing knowledge of the development of the brain, Meltzoff and Decety (2003) have argued that infants possess an ability to recognise equivalence between what they see others do and what they do themselves and that this is related to so-called mirror neurones in the brain. These neurones appear to be activated in the infant brain when a connection is made between the acts of another and the infant's own actions, for example in mimicking reaching actions or particular vocalisations.

Congruence between learning and a child's need to make sense of the world in social terms was noted earlier in relation to the work of Donaldson (ibid.) who critiqued Piaget's theory partly on the basis that he tended to overlook the need for human (or social) meaningfulness. The coming together of the concept of the child as an active constructor of knowledge and the profound importance of social experiences for learning (social constructivism) is the hallmark of Vygotsky's work, a small element of which you have encountered in the earlier extract.

Vygotsky and the Zone of Proximal Development

Vygotsky's work, though undertaken in the first half of the twentieth century in the USSR, only came to prominence within the West in the 1960s and 1970s (Vygotsky, 1978). His principal idea was that a child actively constructs his own knowledge from his experiences of the world around him and that there is a crucial role in this for the social experiences and interactions of the child. There is a similarity to Piaget's ideas in the notion of the child actively constructing his/her knowledge but the key element that distinguishes the theory is the prominence given to social interactions in this process. Within this account of learning Vygotsky introduced a concept called the Zone of Proximal Development (ZPD) that helped to explicate the role of others in supporting and extending the learning of children.

The ZPD is explained as the difference between a child's current or actual developmental level and a level of potential development that would be possible for the child to attain with the support of a more able other. It is interesting to note that the level of potential development is not a completely open-ended potential – the child has the potential at any given point to extend beyond his/her current level of thinking but the intellectual challenge can only be pitched a little beyond that current level of understanding. In this sense it is still a developmentally appropriate theory but 'developmentally appropriate' is calibrated to the individual and the particular social context. That is not to say that the support of learning is inevitably conscious on the part of the more able other. In theoretically allied work, Bruner and colleagues (Wood, Bruner and Ross, 1976) explored the notion of 'scaffolding' by which adults are frequently seen to provide an appropriate framework, to scaffold a child's next steps in learning and in many ways to do this quite instinctively. In the course of everyday life it can be as if young children are undertaking an *apprenticeship* in thinking (Rogoff, 1990).

In Vygotsky's core theory the more able other who supports the child's learning is usually construed to be an adult but it could also be a more able peer. For young children the more able peers could be their siblings and the positive effect of siblings on development is notable in the work of Judy Dunn (Dunn, 1984). More recently Dunn (2006) has continued to foreground the key role that siblings play in the development of social understandings in particular and as children get closer to school age the extent to which friends too can contribute to learning (Dunn, 2006; Cutting and Dunn, 2007). The benefits are seen to be mutual to both partners in the context of peer-peer learning and the importance of providing children with social contexts for learning such as co-operative conversation and co-operative play are highlighted.

As our understanding of the significance of the social nature of learning has been developed the notion of a co-construction of learning has become increasingly recognised. It is a theme picked up in the influential empirical study into the Effective Provision of Pre-school Education research project (Sylva et al. 2004) and the associated Researching Effective Pedagogy in the Early Years (REPEY) project (Siraj-Blatchford et al.; Sylva, et al. 2002). This project identified sustained shared thinking as a crucial determinant of effective practice, within Early Years settings. Sustained shared thinking is defined within the REPEY report as: *An episode in which two or more individuals 'work together' in an intellectual way to solve a problem, clarify a concept, evaluate activities, extend a narrative, etc. Both parties must contribute to the thinking and it must develop and extend* (pp8–9).

The sense of learning as a co-construction has resonance with more general theories of development that emphasise the bidirectional or transactional nature of development. Looking at children's development in the family context, Sameroff (1975) shifted the focus from seeing how what the parent does (or doesn't do) shapes the child's learning and development to a transactional model which recognises the ways in child and parents each affect the other's responses in a mutual and progressive manner. In social relationships as in cognitive endeavours the child is seen as an active player rather then a passive responder to parental actions. Building on this understanding of development, some theorists now conceptualise child development within a *dynamic systems* paradigm (Lewis and Granic, 2000; Sameroff, 2010). Dynamic systems theories draw attention to the multiconnected nature of development, a theme which is explored further in Chapter 7.

Forms of interaction to support children's learning

What are the implications of co-construction of learning for the role of the adult in an Early Years setting? How might a practitioner facilitate productive interactions? In this section some ways in which you might support a child's thinking as a practitioner are suggested in the light of a review of developmental research that was undertaken to inform the revising of the EYFS in England (Evangelou et al., 2009). Underpinning many of the specific developmental findings the review highlighted: the importance of adult responses being contingent to the child's actions and needs. Responses need to flow logically and clearly from the child's lead. This might take the form of *social biofeedback* (Campos et al., 2004).

Here an adult mirrors and exaggerates a child's expression, serving to affirm and validate the child's actions. It might be contingent on the child's expressed thoughts in conversation rather than his/her actions (Bartsch and Wellman, 1995) but the form the conversation takes may be crucial if the child's thinking is to be extended. As Laible and Thompson (2007) have suggested, adopting an *elaborative narrative style*, involving open questions for example, is likely to be most effective. As adults working with children we need to provide children with specific opportunities to explore, explain and reflect upon the feelings and intents of others (Wellman and Lagattuta (2004, p494). This can be relatively straightforward building on existing Early Years practice such as the sharing of picture books. In a study carried out by La Bounty et al. (2008), positive associations were found between adult's references to emotions and emotional causality in conversations observed during the sharing of picture books with children at age 3 and their concurrent and subsequent emotional understanding at age 5.

Helping children to form 'narratives' of their own experiences can be a key 'tool for thinking' enabling them to make sense of both their social and physical worlds. This is most effective when children are encouraged to form their own accounts, rather than passively accepting those of adults (Evangelou et al. 2009). Once again this can be relatively straightforward to incorporate within everyday Early Years practice, for example using prompts such as pictures and photographs of what is personally significant to a child and talking together about them (Atance and O'Neil, 2001). However, to extend thinking these narratives require more than mere recounting (Fivush, 2001) and will be more effective if adults engage the children in evaluation of past events and predictions of future events (Hudson, 2001).

Helping children to construct a narrative can also be effective in developing their problem-solving and reasoning skills. Following a series of studies looking at children's scientific thinking, Kuhn (2004) stresses that it is not sufficient to always leave children to discover new ideas and concepts. Her evidence is that children younger than five years need support to elaborate their thinking and that adults can facilitate the development of logical and evidence-based thinking by involving children in conversation about the processes of finding things out, by talking about why things happen and how we know. It has also been shown that encouraging children to begin to provide their own explanations rather than descriptions is beneficial in promoting a child's capacity for causal reasoning (Siegler, 2005). A child's imaginative capacity can also be supported by fostering dialogues that include speculation and hypothesising; encouraging children to think about *what might be*, what Chappell et al. (2008) have called *possibility thinking*.

Another interesting finding to emerge from the developmental review (Evangelou et al., 2009) was the idea that there are some things that children are unlikely to discover though first-hand experiences, e.g.microscopic processes or remote geographical or historical events (Harris and Koenig, 2006). In such instances children rely on the testimony of others to understand their world. Though it runs counter to many of the cherished mantras about discovery learning and exploration in the Early Years, there may be times when as adults we simply have to tell children certain things. This has important consequences for the adults in whose testimony the children place their trust and it also raises interesting dilemmas if the testimony of different significant adults in their lives varies. What happens for example if home and setting provide the children with different versions of truths?

It is not too difficult to envisage how the various strategies already noted in this section might be adopted in activities that are structured and led by an adult but it is perhaps more difficult to determine how they might be incorporated into more spontaneous activities such as children's thinking in more free-flowing and child-led activities. Or maybe you feel that these activities should be less adult directed? If so, we might be missing some valuable opportunities to extend children's thinking. In a study of children's free-flowing role play for example, the power of explicit adult intervention has been demonstrated (Siraj-Blatchford, 2007).

In an elucidation of the concept of sustained shared thinking, Siraj-Blatchford (2005) points out that adult intervention to support and extend children's thinking can take many forms: *tuning in; showing genuine interest; re-capping; offering own experience; clarifying ideas, suggesting, reminding, offering alternative viewpoints, speculating, reciprocating, asking open questions, modelling thinking.*

What these strategies all share is a sense of purposeful engagement with the children and they imply that extending children's thinking can sometimes be more or less directive. It is not simply about asking open questions but embraces concepts such as tuning in and showing interest. It is worth remembering too the value of the companionable silence while pondering something together and to remember sometimes to resist the urge to immediately intervene and say or do something. Such debates will be considered further in Chapter 5.

Before leaving the theme of interactions to support children's thinking you might also like to reflect more broadly, and perhaps more controversially, on the implications of being constantly aware of the significance of social interaction for learning and of how as adults we might move children on in their thinking. Does this mean that practitioners need to turn every interaction into a learning opportunity or can we sometimes give ourselves and the children a 'rest' from learning? Or maybe that isn't quite possible; children will always be learning something from us, even if it is just that it is pleasant to sometimes relax!

Learning as a cultural process

Vygotsky's socio-constructivist account of learning (Vygotsky, 1978) went beyond ascribing a key role for one-to-one social interactions in learning. He argued that the particular social interactions that take place, and the language and forms of communication that are used, are themselves shaped and driven by the broader cultural context in which they take place, not just at the level of what you know but in terms of how your thoughts and concepts are formed. Hence the learning of an individual is a fundamentally social and cultural process. These ideas are developed in the following extract from Rogoff et al.'s influential monograph on the theme of guided participation (Rogoff et al., 1993). As you read the extract think about the extent to which knowledge is being described as something that is a co-construction between individuals and how this interaction with other individuals is also seen as a co-construction within a broader culture.

EXTRACT 2

Rogoff, B., Mistry, J., Göncü, A. and Mosier, C. (1993) **Guided participation in cultural activity by toddlers and caregivers.** *Monographs of the Society for Research in Child Development* serial nos 236, 58(7): pp5–6

We regard children's development as occurring through their active participation in culturally structured activity with the guidance, support, and challenge of companions who vary in skills and status. The concept of guided participation is used in an attempt to keep individual, interpersonal, and cultural processes simultaneously in focus, representing inseparable aspects of whole events in which children and communities develop (Rogoff, in press). The concept provides a perspective on the process by which children develop through their participation in the evolving practices of their community. It stresses guidance – not only in the sense of explicit instruction but also in the sense of development in specific directions that are based on the models of human activity provided by previous generations. It stresses participation in the sense of shared endeavours – not just the focused interactions on which research on communication often centres but also the side-by-side or distal arrangements of activity without co-prescence, in which children and social partners participate while developing their own contributions to, and extensions of, cultural practices.

The concept is not a classification scheme by which one could evaluate whether guided participation is occurring or effective in any particular situation. Rather, it is a perspective through which to view individual, group, and community transformation. It is not limited to the kind of dyadic interactions that have often been the focus of research but instead

continued 69

promotes a focus on systems of relationships (including present and distant partners, groups, and institutions) that must be described in terms of local models of implicit developmental goals – not imposed definitions of the 'ideal' goals of development.

The concept of guided participation extends Vygotsky's notion of the 'zone of proximal development,' in which individual development is regarded as occurring during joint problem solving with people who are more skilled in the use of cultural tools, including interventions such as literacy, mathematics, mnemonic skills, and approaches to problem-solving and reasoning (Laboratory of Comparative Human Cognition, 1983; Vygosky, 1978; Wertsch, 1979). Cole (1985) suggested that, in the zone of proximal development, culture and cognition create each other. Cultural tools and practices are both inherited and transformed by new members of cultural communities. Culture itself is not static; it is formed from the efforts of people working together, using and adapting tools provided by predecessors and in the process creating new ones.

We assume that children advance their understanding in a creative process in which they transform their understanding and become more responsible participants in the practices of their communities as they participate. Learning to coordinate understanding and effort is inherent in observation and participation in social activity because, without some shared understanding, communication and shared activity could not proceed.

The concept of guided participation refers to the process and system of involvement of individuals with others, as they communicate and engage in shared endeavours. It emphasises children's involvement in structured and diverse relationships and activities with a variety of other people. It includes distal structuring that occurs as children choose (or choose not to) watch television, do chores, or eavesdrop on their parents, as parents extend or limit opportunities by making decisions regarding day care or saving chores until toddlers are asleep, or as communities construct institutions that include or exclude children.

POINTS TO CONSIDER

- *It is suggested that development is more than just the product of direct social interactions. Do you agree? Are there examples from your own upbringing that support this broader concept of how development is shaped by the community or culture into which you were born?*

- *In what ways were such understandings passed on to you by those closest to you? Can you think of implicit understandings that you acquired as well as more direct and explicit examples?*

- *If children are encultured into their community, how is it simultaneously possible for that culture to evolve/change as is suggested in the extract?*

- *Can an Early Years' setting have its own cultural rituals and practices? What might be the implications of these for children's learning?*

- *The extract suggests that guided participation is a mechanism that brings together individual aspects of development, interpersonal aspects and cultural values and practices. It is therefore seen as a unifying theory. Do you agree or can you think of instances where these facets might be in conflict with one another? Have you ever directly experienced such conflict? If so, how was it resolved and how might you support children to make sense of such clashes?*

Rogoff has elsewhere noted *Human functioning cannot be separated from the cultural and more immediate context in which children develop.* (Rogoff and Morelli, 1989, p19). The significance of the cultural context extends beyond being one of many influences on a child's development; it is foundational in its impact. Nor are young children mere passive recipients of a culturally transmitted corpus of knowledge and understandings. Akin to the notion explored earlier that children are born primed to respond to their immediate social context, Trevarthen (1998, pp87–9) argues that children have a profound and fundamental need to connect to a culture: an *innate need that children have to live and learn in culture, as fish swim in the sea and birds fly in the air*.

Another classic theory linking development of the child to multiple levels of influence is Bronfenbrenner's ecological model of human development (1979), which underlines the nested nature of human development in which a child is seen as nested within a series of ever wider and yet interconnected layers of social interaction comprising:

- the microsystem: face-to-face, direct interaction with an immediate social world;

- the mesosystem: interactions between the aspects of the child's immediate world such as the family and external but directly experienced environments, such as the neighbourhood and local religious or community groups;

- the exosystem: environments that impact on the child indirectly such as the policies, practices and relationships that shape the experiences of a child within the microsystem or mesosystem;

- the macrosystem: wider cultural influences;

- the chronosystem: timeframe.

The socially situated nature of learning forms a complex backdrop and stage for the development of children's thinking. The precise configuration of socio-cultural influences that a child experiences may be diverse and as practitioners it is incumbent upon us to be aware of what Hedegaard and Fleer (2008, p1) refer to as the *social situation of children's development*. What are considered to be appropriate behaviours, appropriate parenting and so forth are meaningful only in relation to particular social and cultural understandings. This may also extend to what is considered to be normative in terms of development and behaviours. There is an imperative case for our practices in Early Years to reflect and nurture the different cultural repertoires of the children and families with whom we work and the rewards and challenges this can bring are featured in a number of chapters in this book.

CHAPTER SUMMARY

There are two key messages in this chapter. Firstly, that learning is an active process that recognises the impetus that young children have to make sense of their world and to actively seek out meaning. Secondly, that learning is profoundly connected to a child's social context, and this direct social interface also mediates wider socio-cultural factors to shape and hone the active engagement of the child. However, beneath these twin messages it is hoped that you have detected an important undercurrent to the chapter that guards against the unquestioning adoption of key messages such that they become easy slogans or mantras. Though the child as an active learner is highlighted there are times when the locus of activity and direction may need to shift towards the adult. Similarly, though aspects such as the role of play and the significance of culture are emphasised, they have real meaning only if they are interrogated as concepts and the challenges for practice are acknowledged and explored.

References

Atance, C.M. and O'Neil, D.K. (2001) Planning in 3 year olds: a self-reflection of the future self?, in Moore, C. and Lemmon, K. (eds) *The self in time. Developmental perspectives*. New Jersey/London: Lawrence Erlbaum Associates

Baillargeon, R. (2004) The acquisition of physical knowledge in infancy: A summary in eight lessons, in Goswami (ed). *Blackwell Handbook of Childhood Cognitive Development*. Oxford: Blackwell

Bandura, A. (1977) *Social Learning Theory*. Englewood Cliffs, NJ: Prentice-Hall

Bartsch, K., and Wellman, H.M. (1995) *Children Talk About the Mind*. Oxford: Oxford University Press

Bredekamp, S. and Copple, C. (1997) *Developmentally Appropriate Practice*. Washington, DC: National Association for the Education of Young Children

Bronfenbrenner, U. (1979) *The Ecology of Human Development*. Cambridge, MA: Harvard University Press

Bruner, J. (1966) *Toward a Theory of Instruction*. Cambridge, MA: Belkapp Press

Campos, J.J., Frankel, C.B. and Camras, L. (2004) On the nature of emotion regulation. *Child Development*, 75(2), 377–94

Chappell, K., Craft, A., Burnard, P. and Cremin, T. (2008) Question-posing and question-responding: The heart of 'Possibility Thinking' in the Early Years. *Early Years*, 28(3): 267–86

Cutting, A.L. and Dunn, J. (2007) Conversations with siblings and with friends; link between relationship quality and social understanding. *British Journal of Developmental Psychology* 24(1): 73–87

David, T., Goouch, K., Powell, S. and Abbott, L. (2003) *Birth To Three Matters: A Review Of The Literature*. Nottingham: Queen's Printer

DfES (2007) Early Years Foundation Stage, **www.standards.dfes.gov.uk/eyfs/site/index.htm** accessed 27 March 2007

DfES (2007) *Early Years Foundation Stage: Statutory Framework and Guidance*. Nottingham: DfES Publications

DfE (2012) Statutory Framework for the Early Years Foundation Stage and Development Matters **https://www.education.gov.uk/publications/standard/publicationDetail/Page1/DFE-00023-2012** accessed 24 September 2012

Donaldson, M. (1987) *Children's Minds*. London: Fontana Press, pp19–24

Dunn, J. (1984) *Brothers and Sisters*. Cambridge, MA: Harvard University Press. London: Fontana

Dunn, J. (2006) *Children's Friendships: the beginnings of intimacy*. Maiden, MA: Blackwell Publishing, 2004

Evangelou, M., Sylva, K., Wild, M., Glenny, G. and Kyriacou, M. (2009) *Early Years Learning and Development Literature Review*. DCSF RR 176 **http://www.education.gov.uk/publications/eOrderingDownload/DCSF-RR176.pdf** accessed 13 November 2012

Fivush, R. (2001) Owning experience developing subjective perspectives in autobiographical social narrative, in Moore, C. and Lemmon, K. (eds) *The Self in Time: Developmental Perspectives*. New Jersey/London: Lawrence Erlbaum Associates

Gelman, S.A. (2004) Psychological essentialism in children. *Trends in Cognitive Sciences*, 8(9): 404–08

Gopnick, A., Meltzoff, A. and Kuhl, P. (1999) *How Babies Think*. London: Weidenfeld and Nicolson

Harris, P. and Koenig, M.A. (2006) Trust in testimony: How children learn about science and religion. *Child Development*, 77(3): 505–24

Hedegaard, M. and Fleer, M. (2008) *Studying Children: A cultural historical approach*. Maidenhead: McGraw-Hill

Hudson, J.A. (2001) The anticipated self: mother–child talk about future events, in Moore, C. and Lemmon, K. (eds) *The Self in Time. Developmental perspectives*. New Jersey/London: Lawrence Erlbaum Associates

Kuhn, D. (2004) What is scientific thinking and how does it develop, in Goswami (ed.) *Blackwell Handbook of Childhood Cognitive Development*. Oxford: Blackwell

La Bounty, J., Wellman, H.M., Olson, S., Lagutta, K. and Liu, D. (2008) Mothers and fathers use of internal state talk with their young children. *Social Development,* 17(4): 757–75

Laible, D.J. and Thompson, R.A. (2007) Early socialization. A relationship perspective, in Grusec, J.E. and Hastings, P.D. (eds) *Handbook of Socialization Theory and Research*. New York/London: The Guilford Press, pp181–207

Lewis, M.D. and Granic, I. (2000) *Emotion, Development and Self-organization*. Cambridge: Cambridge University Press

Mandler, J.M. (2004) *The Foundations of Mind: The origins of conceptual thought.* Oxford: Oxford University Press

Meltzoff, A.N. (2004) 'Imitation as a mechanism for social cognition', in Goswami (ed.) *Blackwell Handbook of Childhood Cognitive Development.* Oxford: Blackwell

Meltzoff, A.N. and Decety, J. (2003) What imitation tells us about social cognition: a rapproachment between developmental psychology and cognitive neuroscience. *Philosophical Transactions of the Royal Society: Biological Sciences,* 358: 491–500

Piaget, J. (1962) The stages of the intellectual development of the child, reprinted in Slater, A. and Muir, D. (1999) *The Blackwell Reader in Developmental Psychology.* Oxford: Blackwell Publishers

Piaget, J. (1983) Piaget's theory, in W. Kessen (ed.) *Handbook of child psychology: Vol. 1. History. Theory and methods* (pp103–26). New York: Wiley

Piaget, J. and Inhelder, B. (1966) *The Psychology of the Child.* London: Routledge and Kegan Paul, pp5–6

Rogoff, B. (1990) *Apprenticeship in Thinking.* Oxford: Oxford University Press

Rogoff, B. and Morelli, G. (1989) Perspectives on children's development from cultural psychology, reprinted in Gauvain, M. and Cole, M. (eds) (1993) *Readings on the Development of Children.* New York: Scientific American Books

Rogoff, B., Mistry, J., Göncü, A. and Mosier, C. (1993) Guided participation in cultural activity by toddlers and caregivers. *Monographs of the Society for Research in Child Development* serial nos 236, 58(7), 5–6

Sameroff, A. (1975) Transactional models in early social relationships. *Human Development,* 18: 65–79

Sameroff, A. (2010) A unified theory of development: A dialectic integration of nature and nurture. *Child Development,* 81(1): 6–22

Schultz, L.E., Goodman, N.D., Tenenbaum, J.B. and Jenkins, A.C. (2008) Going beyond the evidence: Abstract laws and pe-schoolers' responses to anomalous data. *Cognition,* 109: 211–23

Siegler, R.S. (2005) Children's learning. *American Psychologist,* 60, 769–78

Siraj-Blatchford, I. (2005) Quality interactions in the Early Years. Paper presented at TACTYC Annual Conference, November, in Cardiff, Wales

Siraj-Blatchford, I. (2007) Creativity, communication and collaboration: The identification of pedagogic progression in sustained shared thinking. *Asia-Pacific Journal of Research in Early Childhood Education,* 1(2): 1–13

Siraj-Blatchford, I., Sylva, K., Muttock, S., Gilden, R. and Bell, D. (2002) *Researching Effective Pedagogy in the Early Years.* London: DfES/Crown Copyright

Skinner, B.F. (1974) *About Behaviourism.* London: Jonathan Cape

Spelke, E.S. (2000) *Core knowledge. American Psychologist,* 55: 1233–43

Sylva, K., Melhuish, E., Sammons, P., Siraj-Blatchford, I. and Taggart, B. (2004) *The Effective Provision of Pre-school Education: Final Report.* Nottingham: DfES Publications

Taylor, M.G., Rhodes, M. and Gelman, S.A. (2009) Boys will be boys; Cows will be cows: Children's essentialist reasoning about gender categories and animal species. *Child Development*, 80(2): 461–81

Trevarthen, C. (1998) The child's need to learn a culture, in Woodhead, M., Faulkner, D. and Littleton, K. (eds) *Cultural Worlds of Early Childhood*. London: Routledge/Open University, pp87–9 (originally published in *Children and Society*, 9(1), 1995)

Vygotsky, L.S. (1978) *Mind in Society. The Development of Higher Psychological Processes*. Cambridge, MA: Harvard University Press, pp84–7

Vygotsky, L.S. (2004) Imagination and creativity in childhood. *Journal of Russian and East European Psychology*, 42(1): 11–12

Wood, D., Bruner, J. and Ross, G. (1976) The role of tutoring in problem solving. *Journal of Child Psychology and Psychiatry and Allied Disciplines,* 17(2): 89–100

Wellman, H.M. and Lagattuta, K.H. (2004) Theory of mind for learning and teaching: The nature and role of explanation. *Cognitive Development*, 19(4): 479–97

Piaget, J. and Inhelder, B. (1966) *The Psychology of the Child*. London. Routledge and Kegan Paul, pp5–6

Rogoff, B. (1990) *Apprenticeship in Thinking*. Oxford: Oxford University Press

Sameroff, A. (2010) A unified theory of development: A dialectic integration of nature and nurture. *Child Development* 81(1): 6–22

Vygotsky, L.S. (1978) *Mind in Society. The Development of Higher Psychological Processes*. Cambridge, MA: Harvard University Press, pp84–7

DfE (2012) Statutory Framework for the Early Years Foundation Stage and Development Matters https://**www.education.gov.uk/publications/standard/publicationDetail/Page1/DFE-00023-2012** accessed 24 September 2012

DfE (2012) Effective provision of pre-school education

www.education.gov.uk/childrenandyoungpeople/earlylearningandchildcare/evidence/a0068162/effective-provision-of-pre-school-education-eppe accessed 14 November 2012

Archive of Soviet Constructivist psychologist Lev Vygotsky at **www.marxists.org/archive/vygotsky/** accessed 14 November 2012

www.early-education.org.uk/

5 The place of play in the Early Years curriculum

Nick Swarbrick

This chapter looks at a classic definition of play – that of Tina Bruce – and asks about the notion of the 'use' of play by teachers and other practitioners. This links with the previous chapter on how children learn, and this chapter explores how play is seen as fundamental to what happens in the Early Years.

By the end of this chapter you should have:

- come to an understanding about how play can be seen in theory;
- begun to see some of the tensions around the debates about play in the curriculum;
- explored ways in which play may and may not be a medium for adult-directed learning in the Early Years.

Introduction

Psychologists and educators have found it difficult to come to an agreed definition of what play is – partly, perhaps, because the phenomenon is more easily recognised than it is pinned down to a rigid classification. However, understanding some of the complexities of play needs some unpicking. We can identify play when we see it, but going beyond a mere description is a more complex business. Vygotsky, for example, begins his discussion (1978: 92) of the role of play in development by describing what play is not, and Fisher is clear that *there is no single definition of play, and, therefore, playful activities in one form or another have been open to interpretation in different ways* (2007, p118). Like play, childhood itself is a concept that has been open to interpretation for centuries (Nutbrown, Clough, and Selbie, 2008, chapters 1 and 2, or the exploration of the history of play in both Wood and Attfield (2005) and Whitebread, Basilio and Mohini (2012)). Do we see children as 'little sponges', ready to soak up the experiences we offer? Do we take a more romantic view, and think that children are innocent, unworldly beings and it is the practitioner's role to protect them from the corrupting influence of society? These are some of the complexities we need to confront when we start to think about play. At the very least we need to recognise that when we discuss play, our own model of what childhood is (or somehow 'should be') may well colour our understanding of play.

It has nevertheless become usual for curricula in the Early Years in the UK to make use of the idea of play. Many Early Years books look at how educators have sought to see play as integral to the experience of young children learning: Tina Bruce's *Time to Play in Early Childhood Education* (1991), which we will explore later, is a key work here, but it is worth noting that Wood and Attfield (2005), by looking at play as something that is planned for and provided by adults, have been very influential in setting up what they call (2005, pp158–83) a *pedagogy of play*. Moyles, too, has written extensively on the place of play in early childhood, and uses a slightly different phrase when she discusses *playful pedagogies* (2005, pp13–29). These writers have been of tremendous significance, and their work will be referred to later in this chapter. The most recent Early Years curriculum documentation for England (DfE, 2012) talks explicitly about *play* and *active learning* as key to children's learning. It would seem obvious, therefore, that practitioners should have some understanding of what is meant by those terms.

Something very like human play is observable in many animals, and one of the greatest explorations of play – a collection of essays and lectures edited by Bruner, Jolly and Sylva (1976) – looks at a variety of phenomena from children's street games, to rock climbing, and at the activities of cats and chimpanzees: clear enough evidence of how wide-ranging play is seen to be, but also, perhaps, an indication of how big an issue we are dealing with. Watch a group of young otters sliding around in water, or fox cubs involved in not-very-serious jostling and rough-and-tumble. Are these animals involved in the same behaviours as young chimpanzees? Are chimps at play doing what young humans do? There are certainly common features to this exploration in young animals, and even if we restrict our observation to young humans we see certain behaviours coming through again and again.

Categorising these behaviours can be tricky, and using them to come to some sort of 'distilled' version that gives us a definition of play is even harder. Whitebread and colleagues (2012) take a fascinating, detailed look at play from an historical (including evolutionary) and psychological perspective, as well as attempting an interesting description of play behaviours – physical, object-play, symbolic play, socio-dramatic play and play with rules – but they give, from their consultation and research, a wide variety of definitions. It is as if we know it, but that it slips away from us when we try to pin it down. Is play always social, or can it be solitary? To what extent must it have a physical element to it? How is a two-month-old waving his hands different from his big sister's block play at two, or complex, imaginative constructions at five? Which of them is play – or are they all play?

Bruce's work has become a key way of looking at play. She describes play as having a number of dimensions, which receive different stress from different theorists. Play can be seen as recreation (1991, pp36, 37); in this way of looking at it, play *only takes place as a break from work,* (1991, p57) so that play time in a school reproduces the adults' desire to stop working with the children. Play can also be seen as preparation for adult life (p38), in which case play as genuinely child-centred is replaced by adult-led activities that children will find fun. In Bruce's theory, however, play is seen as an *integrating mechanism* (1991, p55); a complex phenomenon in which the child brings together feelings, ideas and technical mastery. In the extract below, Bruce describes the essentials of this high-level play she calls *free-flow play*. It is worth noting that Bruce suggests that where seven or more of these features are present, *we are likely to see effective learning.*

As you continue through this chapter you will be introduced to other perspectives. In the second extract, for example, Rogers (2010, p161) suggests that schools *are designed to control and sanitize play.* While practitioners might try and tread, in Fisher's words, a fine line (Fisher 2010: 94) *between intervening in children's play and interfering in it* the idea that play might be something adults can use to get the best learning out of children (an instrumental view of play) might be at variance with Bruce's view of play as *without a product.*

Here, then, is a significant area for enquiry in relation to play: how much value should adults place on play as an activity, and why?

EXTRACT 1

Bruce, T. (1991) Free-flow play and its features, in *Time to Play in Early Childhood Education*. London: Hodder and Stoughton, pp59–60

The 12 features of free-flow play

Rubin, Fein and Vandenburg (1983) formulated criteria of play... and these have been absorbed, where indicated, in the first four features below. However, free-flow play has other crucial features which need to be present. If all 12 features are there, we can be more confident that we are observing free-flow play than if only a few are present.

Feature 1

It is an active process without a product (Rubin *et al.*, adapted).

Feature 2

It is intrinsically motivated (Rubin *et al.*, adapted).

Feature 3

It exerts no external pressure to conform to rules, pressures, goals, tasks or definite direction (Robin *et al.*, adapted).

Feature 4

It is about possible, alternative worlds, which involve 'supposing' (Rubin *et al*, adapted), and 'as if' (Atkins, 1988), which lift players to their highest levels of functioning. This involves being imaginative, creative, original and innovative.

Feature 5

It is about participants wallowing in ideas, feelings and relationships. It involves reflecting on and becoming aware of what we know, or 'metacognition'.

Feature 6

It actively uses previous first hand experiences, including struggle, manipulation, exploration, discovery and practice (Rubin *et al.*, adapted).

Feature 7

It is sustained, and when in full flow, helps us to function in advance of what we can actually do in our real lives.

Feature 8

During free-flow play, we use the technical prowess, mastery and competence we have previously developed, and so can be in control.

Feature 9

It can be initiated by a child or an adult, but if by an adult he/she must pay particular attention to features 3, 5 and 11.

Feature 10

It can be solitary.

Feature 11

It can be in partnerships, or groups of adults and/or children who will be sensitive to each other.

Feature 12

It is an integrating mechanism, which brings together everything we learn, know, feel and understand.

If we want a shorthand way to summarise the 12 features of free-flow play, we can express their essence in an equation.

Free-flow play = wallowing in ideas,   + application of
                 feelings and   developed
                 relationships   competence,
                                          mastery and control

- *In what ways does Bruce's definition of play challenge you to rethink play?*

- *Do any of these 12 features seem more important to you than any others? If seven features might be seen as an indicator of effective learning, are some features essential components?*

- *You might want to spend some time observing a sustained session of play. How do you record play, so that the 'effective learning' can be seen by others? Is there a single method that will suit every situation?*

POINTS TO CONSIDER continued

- *Watch a child you know deeply involved in an activity of their own choosing. Can you see evidence of any of the 12 features of free-flow play? Then watch a child of a different age. What similarities and differences do you notice?*

- *In your experience, does play principally allow children to explore their real relationships and situations or does it generate imaginative worlds? Might the two overlap or are they distinct from one another?*

- *Are Bruce's ideas universal? Would all families, for example, value play like this? Could you think of situations, or cultural differences, in which play might be considered differently?*

It is worth noting that practitioners often use the term *free-flow* to represent something different from the play Bruce is describing here. You can for example hear practitioners describing the kind of Early Years set-up where children make their own choices about activities indoors and out as *free-flow*. The term accurately captures the image of a group of children moving easily through their environment. However, Bruce is not talking here about how children move or make choices about activities in their first educational surroundings, but uses a phrase from earlier theorists to suggest some play is of a higher order than simple exploration.

Planning for play

Time and again, trainee teachers going out on a first school experience placement ask anxiously *How do we plan for child-initiated play?* They are not wrong to ask. In fact, in asking this, they are at the heart of the debate about how much adults can or should 'use' children's play to further the adults' curriculum needs. Drawing on the earlier work of Wood and Attfield, Martlew, Stephen and Ellis (2011) suggest that this is *evidence that play develops children's content knowledge across the curriculum and enhances the development of social skills, competences and dispositions to learn* (Martlew, et al., 2011, p72), although their findings are not without some criticism of the adults who do not always have a clear, shared understanding of a play-based curriculum.

The Revised Early Years Foundation Stage document talks about *Planned, purposeful play* which begins with more child-initiated activity and gives way to more adult-directed tasks so that a child is ready for *more formal learning, ready for Year 1*. Whitebread et al. (2012, p3) seem opposed to this:

> *While in some European countries the emphasis continues to be upon providing young children with rich, stimulating experiences within a nurturing social context, increasingly in many countries within Europe and across the world, an 'earlier is better' approach has been adopted, with an emphasis upon introducing young children at the earliest possible stage to the formal skills of literacy and numeracy. This is inimical to the provision and support for rich play opportunities.*

It is true that in the UK external pressures and what can sometimes seem like arbitrary demands on curriculum time appear to be destructive of 'rich play opportunities.' In the past, some of these initiatives have been opposed, some dismissed, and some accepted by professionals working in the sector and by people commenting on their work. It is often worth looking at current debates or government initiatives in the news and asking: how does this initiative support children's learning today? How might it help these children be better learners in the future?

Whitebread et al. (2012) note elsewhere in their report how school work can be seen as inhibiting play opportunities, and when looking at how young children learn, it is always worth asking yourself how the initiative you are considering takes into account the time required for the project, and whether it inhibits children's opportunities for other things. They do, however, note that some theoretical explorations of play allow that not all learning is done through play, and Fisher likewise lists a number of aspects of the curriculum that play does not teach effectively such as mathematical calculation or phonological awareness, both of which need adult focus to remain *relevant and purposeful* (2010, p98). Here we are dealing with the complex issue of curriculum design: what part can play have in the learning and teaching that we desire in Early Years settings?

Programmes and curricula

The Council of the European Union (commented on by Whitebread et al., 2012) proposes that quality provision in Early Childhood might include:

> *Promoting developmentally appropriate programmes and curricula, which fosters the acquisition of both cognitive and non-cognitive skills, whilst recognising the importance of play, which is also crucial to learning in the early years.*

> (Council of the European Union 2011, p4)

This short, bullet-point document is not clear what is meant by *programmes and curricula*. A lot of good Early Years practice, for example, has a sensitive mix of both adult-led and child-initiated activity, where adult-led activity is developed sensitively from the child's interests and from what the adults have observed a child can 'nearly do' This could be described as a 'programme' or at least part of the teaching and learning that make up a large part of what may be viewed as a curriculum. Such an approach evokes the Vygotskian Zone of Proximal Development (defined in Chapter 4), and sometimes broadly described as a *child-centred approach*.

However, we have to be careful: a 'programme' might also be a set of adult-composed activities through which a child is taken systematically and with a larger element of direct instruction. One argument that could be put forward for this more formal kind of teaching (what might be called a curriculum-centred or outcome-led approach) is that children are *eager to learn what we have to teach them*. In other words, since children are by and large happy to comply with adult requirements, teachers and others working with children are in a prime position to pass on the skills, knowledge and understanding that we judge they need. It might then be argued that the best way to do this is with a clear lead from the adults and an amount of direct instruction. This may be behind a current emphasis of the Early Years Foundation Stage that children need to have acquired skills and knowledge early, so that they can make good progress later on.

This has a number of dangers. The first is that Early Childhood can become merely a place for children to gain school readiness skills for their future rather than their current needs. The second is that just because a child can be taught something doesn't necessarily mean they should be. Perhaps more invidious is the suggestion that simply because a child displays pleasure at being praised for compliance this means that the teaching activity is worthwhile and/or successful. Note that the Council document cited above qualifies its use of the word 'programme' by the phrase *developmentally appropriate*.

The key to resolving this dilemma is to enquire of any teaching programme:

• What do the people who wrote this programme seem to understand about how children learn and develop?

• How does this programme support children's learning?

These are, in effect, the questions we looked at earlier. There is nothing intrinsically wrong in teaching and learning experiences being led by the adults in a setting, except where the experiences become detached from a real understanding of how children develop and learn. When an activity is developmentally appropriate, it will, as the Early Years Foundation Stage document insists, be *planned around the needs and interests of each individual child and are assessed and reviewed regularly* (DfE, 2012, p2) rather than being generated by external pressure and pursued regardless of the children's progress or interest. Play, because of the way it allows a child to use his or her developmental maturity hand-in-hand with self-motivation and first-hand experience, allows any programme to be grounded in what a child genuinely needs, and what a child is truly interested in.

In the second extract (below) Rogers is sounding a note of caution. Exploring a pedagogy of play (a term referring back to the thinking of Wood and Attfield, 2005), she expresses a concern that play can be controlled by the adults to the exclusion of a child's original intentions. Earlier in the chapter from which Extract 2 is taken, Rogers is concerned that *a pedagogy of play is described principally from the adult's perspective* (in Brooker and Edwards 2010, p155; see also Fisher, 2010, p95). Rogers sees play as having the child as its *prime agent* in which social relationships are of major importance – not as an area that is open to interference from the adults in a setting. It is, perhaps, tempting to see play as a tool for the adults to shape the learning, to use a play experience to create a picture, a model, a learning outcome or product that accords with the desires of the adult. However, just as Bruce claims that play is *without a product* (see above), Rogers is keen for practitioners to move their vision of play so that it is seen as neither *undisciplined* nor *regulated*. This requires a big leap, intellectually, so that the adult working with a child is empowered to live with an ambiguity, namely that play is seen as more than *down time*, and something different from a fun activity directed by a grown-up.

EXTRACT 2

Rogers, S. (2010) Powerful pedagogies and playful resistance, in L. Brooker and S. Edwards (eds) *Engaging Play*. Maidenhead: Open University Press, p161

Two distinct positions are suggested by these examples: first, that play is viewed as the undisciplined activity of young children. Thus schools and other early childhood institutions are designed to control and sanitize play so that it reflects adult views of what is good play/bad play. Second, that play is viewed as less important than other activities in classrooms because of the way it is positioned at the margins of what counts as real and necessary activity such as reading with an adult and other literacy-related activity, including 'changing books'. From either perspective, play is used as a pedagogical device for delivering the demands of schooling and society, in other words, as an instrumental activity. My argument then is that play is regulated and controlled by more subtle forces of pedagogy, even when a pedagogy of play appears on the surface at least to prevail.

Set against this, opportunities for social pretend play offered children the possibility to explore identities within their relationships with others and in the process of navigating the dominant pedagogical practices of their classrooms. These identities are not fixed but rather shift with particular play events and social groupings. It is precisely because play allows for such social interactions and pretence (which enables also the exploration of pretend identities) that children are able to act and speak in ways that would not be possible in other social contexts. Within the formation of identities in play, children may also desire, and hence seek, acceptance from their peers, and membership of the play group. Part of the imperative to play witnessed in many children is tied up with this social recognition and acceptance within a social group. Play is also an occasion for children to demonstrate to their peers their autonomy from teachers, to display boundaries of inclusion and exclusion from shifting peer groups, and to experience power and control; friendships developed, in and sustained by play are tied up with power and desire.

POINTS TO CONSIDER

- *What according to Rogers happens to play when it is sanitized and controlled by adults?*

- *Do you think the view of play she explores differs from that of Bruce – and, if so, in what ways?*

- *If you have spent some time observing a child of maybe three or four involved in their own play – something they have chosen to do and have really 'made their own' – can you see ways in which a child's involvement in a fun adult-chosen activity looks different? If so, how is it different?*

- *It might be argued that the three prime areas of the Early Years Foundation Stage – communication and language, physical development; and personal, social and emotional development (DfE, 2012, pp4, 5) are exactly those areas in which play helps children in their development, but what about the more specific areas and the skills they require such as skills in reading (or, for that matter, tree climbing)?*

What becomes clear is that, while play is a key factor in a child's learning and development, it does not take place independent of other learning; the provision of good quality experiences (in the home or in another setting) takes account of play as an enriching experience, so that adult-led experiences go hand-in-hand with the learning that arises from the children themselves and their play. As the Early Years Foundation Stage expresses it:

> *Children learn by leading their own play, and by taking part in play which is guided by adults. There is an ongoing judgement to be made by practitioners about the balance between activities led by children, and activities led or guided by adults. Practitioners must respond to each child's emerging needs and interests, guiding their development through warm, positive interaction.*

(DfE, 2012, p6)

Making choices about play

So how do adults make choices about play? No child really arrives at a school, or nursery or playgroup to find an empty room that practitioners can miraculously furnish with the equipment a child desires or needs. Adults choose from what they have available in cupboards and stores, make choices from catalogues of equipment, or what they can get readily (such as recyclable/reusable materials), and either set these out as suggestions, or at least have them available for children to choose from on shelves or in drawers. This might make a nursery classroom look like an Aladdin's cave, but while imagination might allow things to be combined in a large variety of ways, the equipment list is finite.

In the following two examples, children use the equipment on offer in very different ways. Try to think about what these activities might have meant to the children, and to the adults working with them. Child A chooses from ropes and milk crates and, by using the tree in the nursery garden, makes a swing that (just about) works: she enlists her friends to help get her off the ground, and spends an afternoon organising goes on her swing. Child B takes the same equipment and by adding cups and bottles from the water tray equips a pub, writing notices as he does so: it takes him an afternoon and a morning of intense concentration. The adults have supported both these projects by questioning – with genuine interest – what is being created, by suggesting additions and improvements, by going and getting blocks from the block play, or more bottles or paper, by supervising the activity (so that the swing is fairly safe and that the pub does not exclude anyone) and by observation of what is going on, so that they can get to the heart of the learning that they can see. An attempt to sanitise either of these play incidents could have weakened the learning that was taking place: a swing might be considered too dangerous, a pub in some way encroaching on the innocent world of the nursery. But to smooth out the edges of these activities – for example to ask Child A to pretend she was on a swing, or to insist that Child B made a more genteel café, not a pub – might have missed the children's intentions. At this remove, it is difficult, of course, to discern what learning was going on; without knowing what went before, for example, it might be tempting to make judgements about these children's lives that were wholly wrong. You might, however, take them at face value and ask what value the children placed on the activity. This might lead you to reflect on the role of the practitioners in this 'edgy' play: should they stand back? At what point might they intervene, and why?

It has to be said that play is not always like this. At times it can exclude, be an occasion for inappropriate behaviour, or be simply 'stuck': failing to move beyond a dull repetition of activities. An adult might then choose to intervene to move the play along, to provide a new experience that will challenge. But this needs to be done with care; adults sometimes act hastily to ban the latest media craze – see, for example, Grieshaber and McArdle's discussion of banned play in which one child discusses why adults might ban play as 'a bit rough' (2010, p66), or Rogers' warning (above) about sanitising play. Similarly a reflective and thoughtful attitude towards play might show reference that repetition is often worthwhile for a child, of course; novelty is not always needed, especially when s/he is exploring or testing a skill or a concept. One very valuable, way of looking at play is to explore how children learn, and to reflect, from that understanding, on what the adults might need to do next. This might be to rethink some planning, so that the children's needs are met in different ways; it might be to join in the play with a timely conversation or question; it might also be that the adults look at repeated patterns in play and leave the children to work out the problem without adult interference. All three ways forward are possible.

Observation

Play therefore needs further action (or a set of actions) from the adults: choices about when and how to intervene which should be made sensitively and with an understanding of the individual child's needs and intentions, and this can only really be gained through observation. As Fisher states *if you invest time in observation you will save time planning experiences or activities or experiences that are either way beyond a child's ability or do not stretch and challenge him* (2010, p139). To follow up on the play of Child A and Child B (described above) books were chosen (by the adults, in both these cases) to reflect the children's interests, and other activities such as painting brought in to support the main play project. Adult intervention is not allowed to dominate the play by the practitioners demanding a turn on the swing (or swooping into the pub and overturning the play by asking for a drink, or how much things cost), but the adults make choices about how to intervene through conversation that seeks to deepen everyone's understanding of what is going on. Here *the pedagogy is play* is taken seriously, as children are genuinely allowed to act as the agents and prime movers in the play they undertake.

There is a wealth of guidance on how to observe children's learning and development, from suggesting quickly scribbled notes to lengthier narratives which require the observer to sit outside the action for a set amount of time. Technological solutions – cameras, voice-recording, e-portfolios of records – mean that the methods are constantly changing. From pencil and paper through to webcams in the nursery, they all have their place, and which you choose to use may depend on the purpose of your observation. Some individuals may be looking to gather information for a research project, while others might be thinking in terms of their practice as Early Years workers, in which case their information-gathering is likely to lead directly to planning for the next day or week, and then fed into a record-keeping system. In both cases, understanding of children is deepened by detailed observation of what children are doing, and by questioning what we see and hear. Observation and the reflection that crucially arises from the observation are seen as ways of investigating children's learning and development but also in supporting the adults *so that they can argue the merits of playful practice with parents and practitioners in other key stages and that learning skills in a playful way is advantageous to children*. (Howard and McInnes in Moyles, 2010, p38). To use the information gathered like this demands detail, and gathering this level of detail takes time, but this should not deter us; the kind of reflection on our own practice is an important element in improving work with children.

Interaction

To take two concrete examples: it is seen as critical to successful adult intervention that practitioners go beyond simplistic questioning that merely tests a child's understanding of adult concepts or seeks to continue a conversation the adult controls. There are examples in the wonderfully named article by Iram Siraj-Blatchford et al., 'Would you like to tidy up now?' (2008) in which nursery workers keep too rigidly to their own agenda, to the detriment of the interactions between themselves and the children. *Guess what's in my head* is a sort of rootless questioning activity practitioners play all too frequently. The effective practitioner, however, will try to look for a way to interact with children that sustains the play, motivates the wary and challenges children's thinking. In another interesting piece (with an equally fascinating title, 'The Trampoline Tree and the Swamp Monster with Eighteen Heads'), Waller (2007) shows how children at play in the outdoors carry themes through into different contexts competently and imaginatively. Using these observations in conjunction with observation of the adults and with subsequent practitioner reflection allows Waller to assert with confidence that organising for effective learning in the Early Years means practitioners need to move *from one-off listening events to a sustainable participatory culture with children, leading to the construction of knowledge through shared reflection and collaborative enquiry* (Waller, 2007, p404).

In some way, a certain closeness between adult and child both engaged in solving a problem that has arisen during play might be a mark of its naturalness; the adult isn't trying artificially to fulfil the role of the teacher, and the child may have abandoned the role of eager-to-please pupil. They are co-players, in much the same way as Anning and Edwards describe mother and child interactions (2006) – but they warn that this ease of interaction does not come effortlessly to the practitioner. Fisher's research with teachers suggests that much of the adult–child interaction that happens is of a kind that can actually stop children from exploring their thoughts satisfactorily She cites some observations where adult attempts to engage children in conversation *interrogates children rather than illuminating their thinking* (2010, p188). Have you seen this kind of questioning happen in your practice or experience? What would be the implications (of time and space) to enable genuine collaborative enquiry?

Play as a reward

Practitioners sometimes use play as simply a reward – what one teacher described as *coffee-time for children: when you've done your work you can go and play*. This can lead to 'Golden Time' or 'Choosing Time' being a corner of the school week where nothing really important happens, as Rogers suggests, a time *at the margins of what counts as real and necessary*. (Rogers, 2010, p161) This in turn can lead too readily to a teacher using this as a reward for good behaviour rather than an opportunity for the child, and a catch-up time, to hear the odd straggling reader, for example, and not to be genuinely involved in the play s/he has provided for. According to the EYFS (DfE, 2012) a practitioner needs to respond to children's needs in play, to become the mentor who guides a child through quality interactions, through being where they are needed. Wood and Attfield's work (2005) suggests that, as well as supervising for safety, a responsive teacher plans flexibly enough to allow for children's interests, finds those interests (and explores the meanings and themes of the children's play) through observation. Key to their argument is an enthusiastic and sensitive co-player; a hard task if all the class is offered is an hour on a Friday afternoon!

Observing colleagues

One way that practitioners might extend their repertoire of ways of interacting is to ask a colleague to look at these events in the course of a session. It would be possible for an adult, properly briefed, to observe their colleague with the specific intention of commenting on how the adult becomes involved in play. What kind of questions do they use, and, perhaps most important of all, are they able to show a real sensitivity to the children's ideas and needs? As Waller suggests (2007), we can begin to see the need here to reframe how we understand learning. With a new understanding arising from your own observation of children's play, you might then organise the learning experiences in the Early Years in a way that raises the status of a child's knowledge. This allows adults and children to be partners in the learning experience, rather than setting the adult up (sometimes wrongly) as the expert whose task it is to transmit the correct information to the child.

Allowing the child to flourish

Vygotsky's concept that play allows a child to step into the Zone of Proximal Development was explored in Chapter 4 – you may recall that the ZPD is conceived as *the distance between the actual developmental level ... and the level of potential development ... under adult supervision or in collaboration with more capable peers* (1978, p86). We might choose to put the emphasis within play on aspects other than those Vygotsky describes, but nonetheless the notion that *in play a child is always above his average age* is a powerful one. How do we organise experiences for children – at home, in a childcare or educational setting – which allow this flourishing, this *highest level of pre-school development*?

Practitioners need to think carefully about what they do and why they do it so that they can plan to improve practice in their setting or defend existing practice. If there is a potential danger that external pressures on the curriculum could limit effective play provision, then teachers, parents, students and theoreticians need to be able to look beyond romantic notions of innocent childhood, and beyond an uncritical mantra of play as the teacher's best tool for children's learning, to come to a deeper understanding of the place of play in children's development.

CHAPTER SUMMARY

You will have seen by now that play is a complex area of academic debate. Take some further time to observe play: in what ways can you see the play of a two-year-old as differing from that of a child at the end of the Foundation Stage? What is the role of the adult in any play you observe? If you are a co-player with children, in what ways do your interactions move the play forward? Do your actions and questions help children's thinking to develop? Can you allow yourself time to reflect and record in detail what you see and hear?

Reflect on the theories that practitioners draw on – often unconsciously – when they say that their approach is based on 'play-based learning.' Do they spend time involved in children's play, or do they organise fun learning activities for the children in their care?

Play is sometimes misunderstood, and in many ways the debate about what constitutes play is still unresolved, but if you work with young children, or are thinking of doing so, you might reflect on the issues that this chapter raises. How could we define play in such a way that the adult's role is clear? Should we involve ourselves in children's play, and in what ways? Try to list the factors that might encourage play in any situation: are play partners important? What about time? Is the physical environment a central element for you?

Play can be seen as the way in which children act creatively and imaginatively, often independent of adults, engrossed in an activity of their own choosing. The children's need to 'wallow' in the feelings and ideas they encounter is seen as vital; the adults' need to feel in control will have to take second place.

References

Anning, A. and Edwards, A. (2006) *Promoting Children's Learning from Birth to Five: Developing the New Early Years Professional.* Maidenhead: Open University Press

Bruce, T. (2004) *Developing Learning in Early Childhood.* London: Paul Chapman

Bruner, J., Jolly, A. and Sylva, K. (1976) *Play: Its role in development and evolution.* Harmondsworth: Penguin

Council of the European Union (2011) Council conclusions on early childhood education and care: providing all our children with the best start for the world of tomorrow. 3090th EDUCATION, YOUTH, CULTURE and SPORT Council meeting Brussels, 19 and 20 May 2011 **www.consilium.europa.eu/ uedocs/cms_data/docs/pressdata/en/educ/122123.pdf**, (accessed 26 September 2012)

Department for Education (2012) *Statutory Framework for the Early Years Foundation Stage* **http:// media.education.gov.uk/assets/files/pdf/e/eyfs%20statutory%20framework%20march%20 2012.pdfEYFS** (accessed 26 September 2012)

Fisher, J. (3rd edition, 2007) *Starting from the Child.* Maidenhead: Open University Press

Fisher, J. (2010) *Moving on to Key Stage 1: Improving transition from the Early Years Foundation Stage.* Maidenhead: McGraw-Hill, Open University Press 2010

Grieshaber, S. and McArdle, F. (2010) *The Trouble with Play*. Maidenhead: Open University Press

Howard, J. and McInnes, K. (2010) in Moyles, J. (2010) *Thinking About Play: Developing a reflective approach*. Maidenhead: McGraw-Hill, Open University Press

Martlew, J., Stephen, C. and Ellis, J. (2011) Play in the primary school classroom? The experience of teachers supporting children's learning through a new pedagogy. *Early Years: An International Journal of Research and Development,* 31(1), (March 2011): pp71–83

Moyles, J. (2nd edition, 2005) *The Excellence of Play*. Maidenhead: Open University Press

Moyles, J. (2010) *Thinking about Play: Developing a reflective approach*. Maidenhead: McGraw-Hill, Open University Press

Nutbrown, C., Clough, P. and Selbie, P. (2008*) Early Childhood Education: History, philosophy and experience*. London: SAGE

Rogers, S. (2010) Powerful pedagogies and playful resistance: Role play in the early childhood classroom, in Brooker, L. and Edwards, S. (2010) *Engaging Play*. Maidenhead: McGraw-Hill, Open University Press

Siraj-Blatchford, I. and Manni, L. (2008) 'Would you like to tidy up now?' An analysis of adult questioning in the English Foundation Stage. *Early Years*, 28(1): 5–22

Vygotsky, L. (1978) *Mind in Society*. Cambridge, MA: Harvard University Press

Waller, T. (2007) 'The Trampoline Tree and the Swamp Monster with 18 heads': Outdoor play in the Foundation Stage and Foundation Phase. *Education 3–13*, 35(4): (2007) 393–407

Whitebread, D. with Basilio, M. and Mohini, V. (2012) *A report on the value of children's play with a series of policy recommendations*. Written for Toy Industries of Europe (TIE)

Wood, E. and Attfield, J. (2nd edition) (2005) *Play, Learning and the Early Childhood Curriculum*. London: Paul Chapman

Brooker, L. and Edwards, S. (eds) (2010) *Engaging Play*. Maidenhead: Open University Press

Bruce, T. (1991) *Time to Play in Early Childhood Education*. London: Hodder & Stoughton Educational

Fisher, J. (3rd edition, 2007) *Starting from the Child*. Maidenhead: Open University Press (NB: a new edition is promised for the near future)

Moyles, J. (2nd edition, 2005) *The Excellence of Play*. Maidenhead: Open University Press

Wood, E. and Attfield, J. (2nd edition, 2005) *Play, Learning and the Early Childhood Curriculum* London: Paul Chapman

Council of the European Union (2011) Council conclusions on early childhood education and care: providing all our children with the best start for the world of tomorrow. 3090th EDUCATION, YOUTH, CULTURE and SPORT Council meeting Brussels, 19 and 20 May 2011 **www.consilium.europa.eu/ uedocs/cms_data/docs/pressdata/en/educ/122123.pdf**, (accessed 26 September 2012)

Department for Education (2012) Statutory Framework for the Early Years Foundation Stage **http://media.education.gov.uk/assets/files/pdf/e/eyfs%20statutory%20framework%20march%20 2012.pdfEYFS** (accessed 26 September 2012)

www.righttoplay.com/uk/Pages/Home.aspx

www.playengland.org.uk/

6 Ensuring children's emotional well-being in the Early Years

Mary Wild and Ingram Lloyd

The issue of children's well-being can be considered on a range of levels. There is persistent and appropriate concern for children experiencing extremes of hardship and adversity and the continued prevalence of neglect and abuse is shocking. It is salutary to remind ourselves of such extremes but it is not the principal focus of this chapter. This chapter will consider the ways in which children's well-being can be supported within the immediate social contexts in which they live. The focus is on the developmental foundations of positive well-being rather than on issues of safeguarding children. After outlining some of the theoretical concepts around children's emotional well-being, the chapter will present two extracts for your consideration. The first will invite you to revisit some of the longstanding debates as to whether, and if so how, emotional well-being can be effectively sustained in non-familial care contexts. The second extract will explore issues around the balance between providing security and offering challenge to children.

By the end of this chapter you should have:

- an understanding of the crucial importance of emotional security and the significance of warm and contingent relationships for children's development;
- considered attachment theory and the importance of significant adults to a child's well-being in the context of childcare settings;
- examined the concept of resilience;
- reflected on the balance between providing security and challenge to enable children to develop to their full potential.

Introduction

There is some unease about the lived experiences of children even where superficially their basic security and prospects might appear relatively assured. The pressures of living within fast-paced and socially changing environments are highlighted by authors such as Palmer (2006) who writes of modern childhood as a *toxic* experience for many children. In a report on children's well-being in the UK, Layard and Dunn (2009) drew attention to a number of sociological forces that may be contributing to a growing sense of unhappiness among children including the rise of excessive individualism, changes in family structures and pressures from peers and wider society based on changing and sometimes contra-dictory social values. They also highlight the impact of social policies and provision on children, for example changes to schooling and the significant power of economic forces to shape individual experience. Children's well-being is a theme that threads throughout many chapters in this book, drawing attention to how children are impacted by a multitude of socio-cultural influences and societal frameworks and provision. This chapter, however, adopts a more psychologically oriented consideration of well-being, focusing on the features of a child's immediate experience that might foster or diminish a child's sense of his or her own well-being. The connection between a child's sense of emotional security and the capacity to understand their world is highlighted.

What is well-being?

Well-being is one of those seemingly 'obvious' concepts, in the sense that we use the term almost without thinking; but if you begin to try to define it the concept can prove less easy to pin down. How would you define it? Take a few moments to think through what is important to your own sense of well-being.

It is likely that you had a range of factors in mind, maybe particular people or places that make you feel happy, maybe a list of things you like to do, or things you have achieved, particularly those that didn't come easy to you. Or maybe for you well-being involves a sense of being needed and valued by others. As Roberts (2010, p22) notes, well-being has been likened to a 'travel bag', containing very many different elements that are both separate and yet bound together.

Did your list include more basic needs such as things you like to eat or drink, or feeling safe and being free to do what you want? In some accounts of well-being such as the Hierarchy of Needs proposed by Maslow (1943) well-being is seen as hierarchical such that more basic needs are foundational to being able to develop higher-order aspects of well-being. At the base of Maslow's well-known pyramid of needs are physiological needs followed by safety needs. Building on these, sequentially, are social needs, self-esteem and finally at the pinnacle of the pyramid is the potential for self-actualisation.

More recently Roberts (2010) offers a model of well-being founded on three distinct layers, or constructs. Her so called ABC model, like Maslow's theory, places Agency (A) at the pinnacle. The other two are explained as Belonging-and-Boundaries (B) and Communication (C). Underpinning these three constructs stands the determinant of physical well-being, which is conceived in this model as an important prerequisite to the others, and reflects both young children's physical development including health, and the context of their physical world, including home life, family and neighbourhood relationships. It is useful to see in the scenarios Roberts introduces from her observations of young children and their companions, that these different constructs can be discerned both separately and also in the contexts of each other. She reminds us that states of well-being, agency and boundaries and belonging, may not always depend on strong physical health. For example, a child with a disability may suffer from a chronic medical condition, but even so, enjoy a strong sense of belonging and of agency (Roberts, 2010, p32), especially if those around him are emotionally supportive and communicative.

For Roberts well-being is envisioned as more than just feeling happy; it spans tradition-ally separate developmental domains such as cognition and affect. It is a positive model because it is about the presence of key constructs rather than the absence of negative fac-tors. Though this model is not explicitly invoked in the new Early Years Foundation Stage for England (DfE, 2012), it corresponds in content and emphasis to the three 'prime' areas of learning and development; physical development, personal, social and emotional devel-opment, and communication and language.

In their review of factors influencing child well-being Layard and Dunn (2009) highlight seven key areas that contribute to a child's sense of well-being: loving families; friends; positive lifestyle; social values; good schools; mental health; and enough money. They show how each of these factors may impinge on well-being but in their conclusions they note that: *love is the most important backdrop for children's well-being. That is what chil-dren say they want, more than anything else. And if well cared for, that is what they learn to give* (Layard and Dunn, p151).

In 2011 an international study comparing the well-being of children in three countries (UK, Spain and Sweden) similarly explored the interconnections between intra-personal factors and social influences on children's well-being (UNICEF and Ipsos Mori, 2011). The study included meetings with some 250 children aged 8–13 years and steering groups (children aged 14 years) in each of the three countries and provides a direct insight into the views of children and young people. The authors report that:

> *The message from them all was simple, clear and unanimous: their well-being centres on time with a happy, stable family, having good friends and plenty of things to do, especially outdoors.*

> (p1)

You may wish to reflect on the meaning of *happy, stable family* and this is a theme revis-ited in Chapter 7. Nevertheless, these reports seem to indicate that children focus on the relational aspects of their life and that these are more profoundly significant than other indicators of well-being. This is not to say that well-being is one-dimensional: both the reports cited recognise that there are many factors that contribute to well-being. For exam-ple, the sharing of activities and time is a significant factor in sustaining well-being but the relationships with the people with whom a child shares the activities and time are cen-trally important. Do you feel that love and relational stability are the foundation stones of a child's well-being? If so, what does it mean to love and be loved? What about families that from the outside seem unloving and to which children still espouse love, loyalty and a sense of belonging? What about children who have been loved but 'go off the rails'?

Emotional security as a foundation of development

The importance of warmth and responsiveness in relationships in children's development is well noted in developmental reviews (David et al., 2003; Laible and Thompson, 2007, Evangelou et al., 2009). Writing specifically of experiences in the first year of life, Robinson (2003) stresses that what *others do with our feelings actively influences how we express them and in the Early Years, their effect is powerful* (p36). Just how powerful and how influential early emotional experiences and relationships are is explored in this section in the context of the long-standing but still debated attachment theory (Bowlby, 1953, 1969, 1973 and 1980) and in the light of summaries of more recent research into early child-hood brain development (Gerhardt, 2004; Barlow and Svanberg, 2009).

Attachment theory

Attachment theory was first elaborated by John Bowlby in the 1950s and is focused on the bonds between the parents, more specifically the mother, and children that are forged during infancy and early childhood. Attachment is seen to have a biological basis, with infants exhibiting what Bowlby calls *proximity maintaining behaviours* (Bowlby, 1969) and he highlights the occurrence of *separation anxiety* that can be observed in infants aged between 6 and 18 months as further evidence for the importance of attachment between infants and their special people, especially the mother.

> *What is believed to be essential for mental health is that an infant and young child should experience a warm, intimate and continuous relationship with his mother (or permanent mother-substitute – one person who steadily mothers him) in which both find satisfaction and enjoyment. It is this complex, rich, and rewarding relationship with the mother in the early years ... that child psychiatrists and many others now believe to underlie the development of character and mental health.*

(Bowlby, 1953, p13)

How do you feel about the emphasis on the mother figure? Is this borne out in your own experiences and observations? Note the sense that this relationship is seen as more than just beneficial: it is described as *essential*. What are the implications of this? What is meant by *continuous relationship* – does this mean that mothers should never be absent from their children in infancy? Is this possible or reasonable to expect? It is further argued that this early attachment relationship provides the child with a secure emotional base that will impact on their emotional well-being long into adulthood (Ainsworth et al., 1978).

There have been many critiques of Bowlby's theory, particularly his focus on the singular-ity of the mother–child relationship. Rutter (1972) was among those who emphasised that children are in fact capable of forming multiple attachments and more recent iterations of attachment theory do allow for this. Nevertheless, there appears to be an abiding recog-nition that strong early relationships are vital for the development of a child's emotional well-being. Research into the impact of early attachment continues to link secure attach-ment to a range of socio-emotional outcomes, for example, in the realms of emotional understanding (Kochanska, 2001; De Rosnay and Harris, 2002), as well as conscience and self-regulation (Laible and Thompson, 2000; Kochanska, 2002; Kochanska et al. 2004). Nor has the emphasis on the mother figure been entirely abandoned. Writing in 2007, Richard Bowlby notes that by six months of age babies are *already showing a preference for one person. By nine months old, their primary attachment bond to this person, usually the birth mother, is well advanced* (p309). However, a primary attachment bond does not nec-essarily mean that other bonds cannot be formed and in the same article Richard Bowlby explores how daycare settings might foster development of an infant's bonds with sec-ondary figures. The ramifications of attachment theory for childcare practice are returned to later in this chapter.

The emotional health of infants

Barlow and Svanberg (2009), writing from a health perspective, invoke the concept of attachment, re-emphasising the extent to which the patterns of early attachment between mother and infants set an internal mental template for the child for his/her emotional experiences throughout life. This includes in due course the individual's capacity to provide a secure emotional base for their own children. They note how this can serve to perpetuate patterns of attachment and emotional security from one generation to the next. In doing so they make new links to the work of Meins (2004), who has demonstrated the importance of maternal *mind-mindedness*, which is the degree to which a mother is able to interpret and react contingently to her baby's emotional signals. It is suggested that the parents' implicit recognition of a child's own emotionality and their explicit contingent reactions provide the child with the mental building blocks to understand and regulate their own emotional well-being as well as to recognise the emotions of others. In these recent accounts of emotional well-being it is the relational processes, the interactions between the parents and the child, that are central to the development of a child's emotional well-being.

The centrality of relational security for children's emotional well-being has been directly linked in to research on the development of the brain by authors such as Gerhardt (2004) and Sigman (2011). Gerhardt stresses a concept of *emotional flow* and draws on a range of neuropsychological studies to make the case that the development of significant neuronal connections within the brain is impeded by early negative emotional experiences. Over- and under-production of the stress hormone cortisol are linked to poorer patterns of attachment and it is argued that long-term emotional well-being is in large measure determined by early emotional experiences; Gerhardt further suggests that for positive emotional development babies need a *caregiver who identifies with them so strongly that the baby's needs feels like hers* (p23). Gerhardt's claims are echoed and amplified by Sigman (2011), who like Gerhardt highlights the role played by the hippocampus, which is part of the limbic system in the human brain that regulates emotions and emotional response. It is claimed that many of the essential emotional connections within the brain are set by the age of three years.

Other authors are less convinced of the irreversibility of some of these early influences. Blakemore and Frith (2005) for example, draw attention to the amazing plasticity of the brain, capable of adapting and forming new connections beyond infancy, and Belsky and Fearon (2002) have found that early negative experiences can be subsequently mitigated, for example by later sensitive parenting.

The childcare debate

Although the degree of irreversibility of early negative emotional experiences may be contested, there is a growing consensus that the very first years of life are profoundly important in potentially shaping a child's current and later emotional well-being. As Belsky (2001) points out, attachment theory continues to pose some uncomfortable questions for many modern Western societies in relation to the provision of childcare for young children. In a longitudinal study of over 1000 children from 1991 onwards conducted for the National Institute of Child Health and Human Development in the USA, Belsky and colleagues identified a tendency for better cognitive/linguistic outcomes but a greater risk of anti-social and aggressive behaviours in children who had experienced higher degrees of early childcare (Belsky et al. 2007). However, they also point out that there is a complex interplay of quality, quantity and types of childcare and differential individual susceptibility. In the UK, the findings from the Effective Provision of Preschool Education (EPPE) study also noted that the socio-emotional outcomes of pre-school education were less beneficial than the positive effects noted for linguistic and cognitive outcomes (Sylva et al. 2008). However, this research study had previously noted the significance of adult/child relationships as an indicator and mediator of quality experiences within the most effective settings (Siraj-Blatchford et al. 2002).

More stridently, Sigman's analysis (2011) is that the increasingly dominant patterns of non-familial childcare, at least in Western countries, are likely to be highly detrimental to children. This is a contention that is also raised by Gerhardt (2004) in the following extract.

EXTRACT 1

Gerhardt, S. (2004) Why love matters. How affection shapes a baby's brain. London: Routledge, pp214–217

I believe that we have swung from one unworkable situation to another, where either mothers pay or children pay the price. Betty Friedan first described the oppression of young mothers in the 1960s, suffocating in the suburbs, unable to play any social role except that of 'mom' or wife. But our current situation may be equally oppressive to babies and toddlers who are increasingly being shunted to and from nurseries or child-minding groups, plonked in front of videos, fitting around the parents' busy lives which are elsewhere. How are such children learning to regulate their emotions?

The implicit message of such practices is that relationships are not a priority; work is the priority. Relationships have become a kind of 'treat', encapsulated in the concept of 'quality time'. The regulatory aspect of close relationships is all but lost in this approach. Whilst adults may be able to get by with a conversation at the end of the day, or a phone call when regulation is needed from their partner (or often end up being regulated by their colleagues at work), children need much more continuous regulation. This is usually only available in expensive childcare arrangements, where there is the possibility of good quality attention from a familiar adult. Substitute care on a more economic scale is less likely to provide this kind of attention and will be depriving the child of the essential emotional learning that characterises this period of early life.

The qualities of good parenting (and of close relationships in general) are essentially regulatory qualities: the capacity to listen, to notice, to shape behaviour and to be able to restore good feelings through some kind of physical, emotional or mental contact, through a touch, a smile, a way of putting feelings and thoughts into words. These capacities are personal ones, but they cannot be expressed fully in a culture which relegates children to the margins.

To turn the situation around, to provide more children with the optimal start for being emotionally equipped to deal with life, we need to invest in early parenting. This

EXTRACT 1 *continued*

investment will be costly. To bring about conditions where every baby has the kind of responsive care that he or she needs to develop well means that the adults who do this work must be valued and supported in their task. This in itself would involve a sea change in our cultural attitudes. Instead of hiding breastfeeding away, we would accept and value it. Instead of isolating women in their homes with a baby, parenting – whoever takes on the role – would be much more based in a local community of adults.

POINTS TO CONSIDER

- *Do you think the prevalence of daycare for young children is a positive or a negative development for society? Have we 'marginalised' relationships?*

- *Do you think there are any links to the chapter on children's rights here? How do they relate to the rights of the adults concerned?*

- *What is 'quality time' for children? How can it be provided in a setting? Is it about what the children do in terms of activities or is it more important who they share their time with?*

- *Do you think that parents will inevitably provide better quality time?*

- *How can children's individual emotional needs be made central in settings?*

Forming close bonds with babies and young children – the role of the key person

Elfer, Goldschmied and Selleck (2003, pp5–11) outlining requirements for a baby to develop and flourish within a non-familial setting, propose that one specific adult should take a lead role for each child. This is known as a key person approach. In delineating the role Goldschmied asks why it is *worth the time and trouble to introduce a key person system* and answers the question by noting that *we need to think of our own relationships as adults ... if we look back we may recall important people in our early lives who, though not there in person, give continuity and significance to how we conduct our present lives.* (Goldschmied et al., 1994, p37 cited in Elfer et al. 2005, p12). The contention is that the key person will enable the child to feel specially cherished and secure when they are away from home. Underdown (2007, p41) further suggests that it is the ongoing daily care-giving role the child receives from this key person as well as parents that enables the child to learn to rely and trust these adults. In turn, this constancy underpins the child's developing attachment and gives them independence and 'mastery' in later years.

The value of the key person role has been recognised in Early Years policy and practice and it is a requirement in the Early Years Foundation Stage (2012) for each child to be assigned a key person (EYFS, 2012). What are your views on this role? Do you remember closely identifying with an adult in your childhood; was it just one person or several? Why do you remember this? What happens if adults for some reason do not forge close ties? What are the implications for working with parents?

Geddes (2006) notes that even very young children are capable of strong independent relationships with a supportive and understanding adult, beyond the traditional mother–child dyad. These close strong bonds must be mutually established if this is to be successful and the care giver must remain a constant person for the child. This has important implications for the organisation of settings, where staffing arrangements are often complex to organise and ensuring the individual continuity and consistency required for children could be a challenge in some settings.

The key person approach can pose emotional challenges too. Elfer (2012) summarises some concerns of Dahlberg (1999) around the notion of the particular *closeness and intimacy* the child may develop with the key person, highlighting the difficulty parents can have in understanding that they are not being replaced in their child's affections even though the key person may spend longer with their child during the day than they do. Another issue is that having one key person could be restrictive for the child by possibly inhibiting them from exploring and forming a wider range and networks of close relationships with other adults and may negatively impinge on the fluidity of team working within a setting.

However, important differences are noted by Elfer (2012) between the role of the key person and parent. Nursery is not the same as home but nevertheless the baby or young child needs to feel valued and cared for with consistency and understanding. This will be enhanced if there is regular and strong communication between the home and setting. One of the understandings that can strengthen the relationships between a child and the key person is their recognition of the importance of multiple relationships in a child's life. This theme of co-operation and mutual interest in the child's welfare is developed and explored in Chapter 7.

Elsewhere, Elfer (2007) has also noted the sometimes challenging nature of the key person role for the professionals involved and suggests that to be most effective for the adults involved, and ultimately for the children, it is essential for training and support to be available for professionals. The emotional expectations and demands placed on professionals are high if we are to provide the emotionally sustaining environments that young children need and deserve, which in turn demands proper recognition and status within society. This theme will be pursued further in Chapter 8.

Resilience

David et al. (2003, p20) have described resilience as the extent to which *some children are able to overcome the effects of negative events or experiences* and in this review they note the powerful impact of at least one deeply nurturing relationship in equipping children to face challenging circumstances in their lives.

In a longitudinal study spanning thirty years Sroufe et al. (2005) tracked the life trajectories of 180 children born into poverty in the USA. They concur with the proposition that the early years are enormously important in determining these life trajectories and that early relationships based on a secure parent–child attachment can form a *positive plat-*

form (p227) for the development of resilience in the face of life's adversities. However, the authors also point out that *balancing supports* in later childhood can serve to redress some earlier negative effects.

In another seminal study, Rutter and colleagues explored the experiences of children who had spent their early years in the severely deprived emotional environments of Romanian orphanages in the 1990s and were subsequently adopted by families in England (Rutter et al. 2007). In studies of these children at ages 4, 6 and 11 years these children exhibited remarkable psychological catch-up, although there was evidence that this was greater for those children who were adopted at a younger age than others. Elsewhere, Rutter (1999) demonstrates that there is individual temperamental variability in the extent to which early psycho-social risks can be overcome but, notwithstanding, such variability exposure to new and more positive experiences can offer children *turning points* (Rutter, 1999, p129). More generally Rutter has argued that resilience can be actively fostered rather than reactively redressed by providing children with *controlled exposure to risk* (Rutter, 2006). By facilitating the development of a range of coping strategies children can be proactively primed to deal with future adversities.

In a three-year study of 152 pre-school children aged 3–4 years, Blair et al. (2004) found that children who were encouraged to explore emotional issues developed constructive emotional resilience skills; for example, children were encouraged to address their anxieties through discussions using stories and other imaginary scenarios. Another benefit of this approach was that carers and children gained deeper understanding and appreciation of the trusting and supportive relationship they had with each other. The contention is that the overt consideration of emotionally challenging themes can be beneficial even for quite young children and that specific teaching about feelings should be considered for young children. This resonates with an approach supported by Laevers (2000, p26) who developed *A Box Full of Feelings* to structure such experiences for young children. Echoing this chapter's earlier theme about the centrality of secure and trustful relationships, Denham (2007) stresses the need for young children to gain awareness of themselves and of the power of emotions and feelings within a relational context.

You might want to reflect on these propositions as you read the following extract in which New et al. relate a number of 'risky' experiences provided to young children. In particular they mention two projects that were undertaken in their setting. One project involved bringing a pet dog called Tucker into an early childhood setting on a regular basis. This was initiated by the chance meeting of a mother and her blind young son when they were visiting the boy's nursery. The mother and boy had encountered a dog in the university building; the child asked if it was a 'seeing dog'. The child's teacher decided to follow up on the boy's interest and bring the dog into the setting. However, the dilemma was that Tucker had been diagnosed as having cancer and it was known that he would die soon, which would be likely to be upsetting for the children. Nevertheless the authors of the article note the teacher's belief that *Tucker would provide a context in which the children could learn about each other's individual's needs even as Tucker also offered them an opportunity to learn about the needs of a dog* (New et al., p5).

Though less directly relevant to the theme of this chapter, the second project referred to in the extract is a project around the theme of democracy. This second project was borne out of the tensions generated by some children wanting to retain a classroom artefact they had built together and another group of the 'builders' wanting to demolish the artefact. Following on from this the children were encouraged to think about issues such as collective versus individual fairness and the right of a majority versus minority voices. The extract below is the conclusion of their research paper which explores the underlying issues raised by their project about young children's well-being, and the role of a *risk rich environment* in developing a child's sense of self.

EXTRACT 2

New, R., Mardell, B. and Robinson, D. (2005) Early childhood education as risky business: Going beyond what's 'Safe' to discovering what's possible. *Early Childhood Research and Practice*, 7(2) Fall: pp1–15

We have described teachers (ourselves and others) making choices on behalf of children and working in the guise of curriculum that reflects beliefs about what seems best, right, necessary, essential. What is not always acknowledged is that each of these decisions about what to do entails implicit if not explicit decisions about what *not* to do.

Effective teaching in this light has recently been described as akin to jazz or improvisation, such that the teacher's responses to children link with what they have proffered and, in the next moment, take them to a place not yet fully defined but ripe with possibilities (Sawyer 2004). And yet scholars have documented the general aversion to such ambiguity; more recent research of classroom dynamics attests to the anxiety that teachers often feel when they are unable to predict or control the outcome of their interactions with children. That teachers would be averse to purposefully adding risk taking to their professional repertoire is thus not surprising. And yet, when we consider the alternative possibilities consciously eliminated or unconsciously precluded as teachers go about their daily planning and interactions with children, we are left with an image of teaching that is unavoidably risk filled.

We do not propose to redefine the parameters of safety and risk as applied to early childhood education, nor do we mean to suggest that teachers disregard concern for children's well being. Rather, our aim has been twofold: (1) to suggest that the topic of risk is more complex and culturally situated than is typically understood, and (2) to highlight the potentials of an explicitly risk rich curriculum. Our stories – about, a dog and a project on democracy – have in common a willingness to embrace unknown territories, new ideas, and new relationships. In sharing stories of our own experiences with risk taking, we argue in favor of being less fearful and more open to an early childhood curriculum characterized by purposeful and collaborative risk taking. Such a 'risk rich' early childhood curriculum

1. acknowledges children as capable *and desirous* of testing their developing skills and understandings of and in the world,

2. invites parents into collaborative relations that inform decision making about what and how children can learn, and

3. encourages teachers to trust themselves and their children to learn together while exploring meaning making in the real world they inhabit.

Such an approach to the early childhood curriculum requires more than courage to 'move out and beyond' the status quo (Gitlin, 2005). It also requires curiosity and imagination as well as faith in the collective intelligence of teachers, children, and families. Such a curriculum has the potential to not only benefit children – it also reminds adults of the purposes of an early childhood education In a democratic society. This orientation to the care and education of young children is also consistent with an image of teaching as a means to expand 'the space of the possible' (Davis, 2004). Given the multiple challenges facing children, families, and teachers in an increasingly unpredictable global society, it may well be that the best way to keep children safe is to be willing, as adults, to take more risks on their behalf.

POINTS TO CONSIDER

- *What are your views on the role the teacher took? The teacher had proposed a course of action that would raise difficult emotional situations. Was this a wise decision or should other alternatives be considered?*

- *In what ways do you think his closeness to the children underpinned his appreciation of what the children might learn?*

- *What do you understand collaboratively courageous to mean? To what extent can such actions be genuinely collaborative between adults and young children? Whose decisions/agenda carry the most weight?*

- *How should the teacher or other professionals include parents in such decisions?*

The theme of decision-making is raised in this extract. Buchanan and Huczynski (2004) define decision-making as being shaped by two categories of outcome: 'certainty' and 'risk or uncertainty'. Within a setting there are often tricky decisions to be made and possible consequences of decisions being wrong. In making decisions about whether or not to introduce a particular practice or experience, overall aims and desired outcomes may be more or less explicit. Sometimes making a decision may be based on what not to do and as New et al., (2005) indicate, deciding not to do something may have its own consequences for children's learning. In the setting portrayed by New et al., taking a lead from children's interests and following them through was normal practice, but outcomes were not usually so risky, unknown and emotionally fraught. By choosing to follow this more challenging option the children's understanding of their world expanded in an area not planned for.

Providing a risk-rich environment

Is this a paradoxical phrase given the important theme of providing security and well-being? What if any are the connections between the two?

Little (2006) sees risk taking as having positive and negative sides but that risks need to be taken if we are to gain confidence and skills outside our current expertise — if we are to reach our full potential. Indeed Little (2006, p152) views one of the key indicators of a 'high quality' Early Years provision as providing a safe learning environment that is also an environment where children can experience stimulating and challenging experiences, risks and mistakes can be taken and made. Yet she feels the important role of risk taking in child development has minimal recognition. Similarly, Hostetler (2011, p1) values the importance of wider and unplanned-for opportunities, as without them education would be *flattened or narrowed*. The associated inclusion of challenging ideas can support a child's resilience and well-being. Well-being in the curriculum is greatly undervalued in his eyes.

Referring to personal construct theory, Butler and Green (1998) write of the child gaining greater self-knowledge as new situations are confronted. They further recommend that if we are to support this process we need to look at the situation through the eyes of the child, unbiased by our own ideas and prejudices. This may raise questions for you in relation to your own experiences. Are you a risk-taker and have felt constrained by others being over protective of you? Or conversely, have there been times when you felt uncomfortable being challenged? What is the balance to be struck here?

Experiences outside the home and in a setting may be of considerable significance because of the length of time a child spends in them. Geddes (2006, p64) believes that supportive environments can provide good opportunities for close bonds to be formed and in turn these bonds of trust can facilitate the provision of challenging experiences. Underdown (2007, p15), too, suggests that the foundation of supportive environments is the quality of attachment between the carers and the child. The relationship needs to be secure, warm, and affectionate, drawing on humour and good communication. From such a basis of positive attitudes risk-taking can be encouraged, and opportunities for reflection and problem solving will flow more readily.

CHAPTER SUMMARY

This chapter has focused on the notion that relationships are crucial to children's emotional well-being. This is superficially an uncontroversial proposition, but Extract 1 drew attention to the contentious nature of the implications that can flow from this premise. In the consideration of attachment theory, for example, if some relationships are more significant than others and if early emotional security is foundational to a child's development of self, then what are the implications for society regarding the organisation of childcare? This chapter has sought to show that the family is imperative but the 'core' of people that the child relates to can extend beyond the family, although as the discussion of the key person concept shows, this can pose challenges in practice.

The second extract drew attention to the debate between offering security and challenge to children. There is a quite natural instinct to want to protect children from facing difficult issues and yet some of the research concerning emotional resilience suggests that if we can find 'safe' ways to provoke emotional challenge and reflection on the part of children then this may expand their emotional understanding and foster greater internal resilience. This second debate extends the earlier emphasis in the chapter on the fundamental importance of secure relational foundations as the base from which the child feels safe to explore their world.

References

Ainsworth, M., Blehar, M., Waters, E. and Wall, S. (1978) *Patterns of Attachment.* Hillsdale, NJ: Lawrence Erlbaum Associates

Barlow, J. and Svanberg, P.O. (2009) *Keeping the baby in mind*, in Barlow, J. and Svanberg, P.O. (eds) *Keeping the Baby in Mind: Infant mental health in practice.* London: Routledge

Belsky, J. (2001) Emmanuel Miller lecture: Developmental Risks (Still) Associated with Early Childcare. *Journal of Applied Psychology and Allied Disciplines*, 42(7): 854–60

Belsky, J. (2006) Early child care and early child development: major findings of the NICHD study of early child care. *European Journal of Developmental Psychology*, 3(1): 95–110

Belsky, J. and Fearon, R.M.P. (2002) Early attachment security, subsequent maternal sensitivity, and later child development: Does continuity in development depend upon continuity of caregiving? *Attachment and Human Development*, 4(3): 361–87

Belsky, J., Burchinal, M., McCartney, K., Vandell, D.L., Clarke-Stewart, K. A. and Owen, M.T. (2007) Are there long-term effects of early child care? *Child Development*, 78(2): 681–701

Blair, K.A., Denham, S. A., Kochanoff, A. and Whipple, B. (2004) Playing it cool: Temperament, emotion regulation, and social behaviour in preschoolers. *Journal of Social Psychology*, 42: 419–43

Blakemore, S.J. and Frith, U. (2005) *The Learning Brain: Lessons for education.* Oxford: Blackwell Publishing

Bowlby, J. (1953) *Child Care and the Growth of Love.* Harmondsworth: Penguin

Bowlby, J. (1969) *Attachment and Loss Volume 1: Attachment.* New York: Basic Books

Bowlby, J. (1973) *Attachment and Loss Volume 2: Separation.* New York: Basic Books

Bowlby, J. (1980) *Attachment and Loss Volume 3: Loss.* New York: Basic Books

Bowlby, R. (2007) Babies and toddlers in non-parental daycare can avoid stress and anxiety if they develop a lasting secondary attachment bond with one carer who is consistently accessible to them. *Attachment and Human Development* 9(4): 307

Buchanan, A. and Hudson, B. (eds) (2000) *Promoting Children's Emotional Well-being.* Oxford: Oxford University Press

Buchanan, D. and Huczynski, A. (2004) *Organizational Behaviour* (5th edition). Hemel Hempstead: Prentice Hall, pp69, 648, 765–70

Butler, R. and Green, D. (1998) *The Child Within. The exploration of personal construct theory with young people.* Oxford: Butterworth-Heinemann

Dahlberg, G. Moss, P. and Pence, A. (1999) *Beyond Quality in Early Childhood Education and Care: Postmodern Perspectives.* London: Falmer Press

David, T., Goouch, K., Powell, S. and Abbott, L. (2003) *Birth to Three Matters: A review of the literature.* London: Department for Education and Skills

Denham, S. (2007) Dealing with feelings: How children negotiate the worlds of emotions and social relationships. *Cognition, Brain Behaviour*, 11: 1–48

De Rosnay, M. and Harris, P. (2002) Individual differences in children's understanding of emotion: the roles of attachment and language. *Attachment and Human Development*, 41: 39–54

DfE (2012) *Statutory Framework for the Early Years Foundation Stage and Development Matters* **https://www.education.gov.uk/publications/standard/publicationDetail/Page1/DFE-00023-2012** accessed 24 September 2012

Elfer, P. (2007) Nurseries and emotional well-being: Evaluating an emotionally containing model of professional development. *Early Years Journal of International Research and Development*, 27(3): 267–79

Elfer, P. (2012) (2nd edition) *Key Persons in Early Years: Building relationships for quality provision in Early Years settings and primary schools*. London: Routledge

Elfer, P., Goldschmeid, E. and Selleck, D. (2003) *Key Persons in the Nursery. Building relationships for quality provision*. London: David Fulton Publishers

Elfer, P., Goldschmeid, E. and Selleck, D. (2nd edition) (2005) *Key Persons in the Early Years. Building relationships for Quality Provision in Early Years settings and primary schools*. Abingdon: David Fulton Publishers

Evangelou, M., Sylva, K., Wild, M., Glenny, G. and Kyriacou, M. (2009) *Early Years Learning and Development Literature Review*. DCSF RR 176 **www.education.gov.uk/publications/eOrdering Download/DCSF-RR176.pdf** accessed 15 November 2012

Geddes, H. (2006) *Attachment in the Classroom*. London: Worth Publishing

Gerhardt, S. (2004) *Why Love Matters. How affection shapes the baby's brain*. Hove: Routledge

Hostetler, K. (2011) *Seducing Souls. Education and the experience of human well-being*. London: Continuum International publishing Group

Kochanska, G. (2001) Emotional development in children with different attachment histories: The first three years. *Child Development*, 72(2): 474–91

Kochanska, G. (2002) Mutually responsive orienting between mothers and their young children: a context for the early development of conscience. *Current Directions in Psychological Science*, 11(6): 191–95

Kochanska, G., Aksan, N., Knaack A. and Rhines, H.M. (2004) Maternal parenting and children's conscience: early security as moderator. *Child Development*, 75(4): 129–42

Laevers, F. (2000) Forward to Basics! Deep-Level-Learning and the Experiential Approach. *Early Years: An International Journal of Research and Development*, 20(2)

Laible, D.J. and Thompson, R.A. (2000) Mother-child discourse, attachment security, shared positive affect and early conscience development. *Child Development*, 71(5): 1424–40

Laible, D.J. and Thompson, R.A. (2007) Early socialization. A relationship perspective, in Grusec, J.E. and Hastings, P.D. (eds) *Handbook of Socialization Theory and Research*. New York/London: The Guilford Press, pp181–207

Layard, R. and Dunn, J. (2009) *A Good Childhood. Searching for Values in a Competitive Age*. London: Penguin Books

Little, H. (2006) Children's risk-taking behaviour: Implications for early childhood policy and practice. *International Journal of Early Years Education*, 14(2): 141–54

Maslow, A. (1943) A theory of human motivation. *Psychological Review*, 50(4) 370–96

Meins, E. (2004) cited in Barlow, J. and Svanberg, P.O. (2009, p5) Keeping the baby in mind. In Barlow, J. and Svanberg, P.O. (eds) *Keeping the Baby in Mind: Infant Mental Health in Practice*. London: Routledge

New, R., Mardell, B. and Robinson, D. (2005) Early childhood education as risky business: Going beyond what's 'safe' to discovering what's possible, *Early Childhood Research and Practice*, 7(2) Fall: 1–15

Palmer, S. (2006) *Toxic Childhood: How the Modern World is Damaging Our Children and What We Can Do About It*. London: Orion Books

Roberts, R. (2010) *Wellbeing from Birth*. London: Sage Publications

Robinson, M. (2003) *From Birth to One. The year of opportunity*. Buckingham: Open University Press

Rutter, M. (1972) *Maternal Deprivation Reassessed*. Harmondsworth, Penguin

Rutter, M. (1999) Resilience concepts and findings: implications for family therapy. *Journal of Family Therapy*, 21(2): 119–45

Rutter, M. (2006) Implications of resilience concepts for scientific understanding. *Annals of New York Academy of Science*, 1094: 1–12

Rutter, M., Beckett, C., Castle, J., Colvert, E., Kreppner, J., Mehta, M., Stevens, S. and Sonuga-Barke, E. (2007) Effects of a profound early institutional deprivation: An overview of findings from a UK longitudinal study of Romanian adoptees. *European Journal of Developmental Psychology*, 4(3): 332–50

Sigman, A. (2011) Mother superior? The biologist. *Mother Biologist,* 58(3): 28–32

Siraj-Blatchford, I., Sylva, K., Muttock, S., Gilden, R. and Bell, D. (2002) *Researching Effective Pedagogy in the Early Years*. London: Department for Education and Skills, Research Report 356

Sroufe, L.A., Egeland, B., Carlson, E.A. and Colins, W.A. (2005) *The Development of the person. The Minnesota Study of Risk and Adaptation from Birth to Adulthood*. NY & London: The Guilford Press

Sylva, K. Melhuish, E., Sammons, P. Siraj-Blatchford, I. and Taggart, B. (2008) *Effective Pre-school and Primary Education 3-11 Project (EPPE 3-11) Final report from the primary phase: Pre-school, school and family influences on children's development during Key Stage 2 (Age 7–11)*. (Research Report). Nottingham: DCSF Publications

Underdown, A. (2007) *Young Children's Health and Well-being*. Maidenhead: Open University Press

UNICEF/IPSOSMORI (2011) Nairn, A., Duffy, B., Sweet, O., Swiecicka, J. and Pope, S. Children's Well-being in UK, Sweden and Spain: The Role of Inequality and Materialism **http://www.ipsos-mori.com/DownloadPublication/1441_sri-unicef-role-of-inequality-and-materialism-june-2011.pdf** accessed 1 August 2012

Barlow, J. and Svanberg, P.O. (2009) *Keeping the baby in mind*, in Barlow, J. and Svanberg, P.O. (eds) *Keeping the Baby in Mind: Infant mental health in practice*. London: Routledge

Elfer, P. (2012) (2nd edition) *Key Persons in Early Years: Building relationships for quality provision in Early Years settings and primary schools*. London: Routledge

Gerhardt, S. (2004) *Why Love Matters. How affection shapes the baby's brain*. Hove: Routledge

Roberts, R. (2010) *Wellbeing from Birth*. London: SAGE Publications

www.ncb.org.uk/policy-evidence/research-centre

www.childrenssociety.org.uk/what-we-do/research/well-being/promoting-positive-well-being-children

www.coram.org.uk/

www.unicef.org.uk/UNICEFs-Work/What-we-do/Issues-we-work-on/Child-well-being/

Strand 3
Exploring professionalism

7 Working with families in the Early Years

Alison Street and Mary Wild

This chapter will consider different models of families and their role in young children's learning. It will encourage you to explore and debate the nature of partnership and implications for practice.

By the end of this chapter you should have:

- considered what is meant by a 'family';
- recognised the role of the family in supporting children's learning and examined the potential impacts of home learning environments;
- reflected on different models of partnership;
- explored the nature of partnership relations in practice;
- considered the ethics of agency of those who both care and are cared for.

What is meant by a 'family?'

Family is one of those evocative words that conjure up an instant mental image for most people and most probably an image that is based on your own family. It is also likely that the image you have of the family evokes strong emotional responses within you whether positive or negative. You may look back upon your own childhood experience of the family and be certain that if you have or intend to have children you would wish to offer them a similar upbringing to your own, or alternatively you may be convinced that you will definitely do things differently from your own parents. Even if you did not experience life within a family unit as a child you are likely to hold opinions about the desirability of growing up within a family and of the potential effects of family life for the development of children. As Allan and Crow (2001) note:

> *Everybody knows what 'family' means; it is a term we use routinely, normally without any need for reflection or self-awareness.*

(Allan and Crow, 2001, p1)

However, take a few moments to try to define the term 'family'. Though a superficially easy task, this can prove quite difficult, particularly if you are asked to come up with a workable definition within a group of other people. You will probably start from the model provided by your own family but after only a few minutes conversation with the others you will appreciate the very different forms that a family can take.

The UK Office for National Statistics (ONS) offers the following definition:

> *Households are defined as people who live and eat together or people who live alone. Families are defined by marriage, civil partnership or cohabitation or, where there are children in the household, child/parent relationships exist.*

(ONS, 2011, p3)

How sufficient and inclusive is this? Does it capture other manifestations of family life? For example, in some cultural traditions the understanding of 'family' would be a far less nuclear concept and would embrace an extended model of the family.

As well as acknowledging the diversity of family life it is also important to bear in mind that the family is not a static concept either for individual families or within society in general. As Draper and Duffy (2006) point out, *Families are changing, as they always have done. Parents are not a homogenous group* (p151). Smart et al. (2001) reviewed the changes within UK society that had taken place in the preceding half-century, noting the diversity and fluidity of families, borne of increasing rates of divorce, separation or repartnering. They argue that it is no longer appropriate to think of the more traditional married couple plus children as a benchmark for other groupings. Neither can it be assumed that children will experience only one form of family within their childhoods.

It is one thing to acknowledge at a rational level that families are not homogenous or easily accommodated within a single accepted definition, but it is not always so easy to personally acknowledge the internal model of the family that you almost certainly hold. So, as you read through the rest of the chapter, mentally question not only the models or definition of the family and family relationships that are explicit or implied, but constantly reflect also on how your own idea of the family is contributing to your evaluation of the material presented.

The role of the family in supporting children's learning

In Chapter 4 the different ways in which theories of learning highlight the significance of the social context on a child's development and learning were charted. It is logical to extrapolate that a child's family members might form key role models within the framework of social learning theory and modelling (Bandura, 1977) or act as key scaffolders of children's leaning within the ZPD as depicted in Vygotsky's work, (Vygotsky, 1978) or Rogoff's notion of children as apprentices in the learning process engaged with those around them (Rogoff, 1990). The extract in chapter four from the paper by Rogoff et al. (1993) on guided participation also provides a powerful example of the ways in which important adults within the family might structure their children's learning and simultaneously induct them in cultural norms and traditions.

Over the last decade two significant trends can be discerned in the literature concerning how families support children's learning: a shift towards seeing the family in more sociocultural terms and a separate trend within psychologically oriented literature to re-align their models of family as 'dynamic systems'. Both trends have implications for the ways in which non-familial settings might interact and work with families.

Socio-cultural models of the family

Rogoff (2003) has built on her earlier work looking at the culturally embedded nature of the family and contends that we can only understand the development of individuals *in the light of the cultural practices and circumstances of their experiences* (pp3–4). She rightly acknowledges that it would be erroneous to assume that everyone or every family within a certain cultural milieu will act in a uniform way, but she highlights the ways in which interactions within families may be very different according to dominant cultural traditions. This raises questions for the ways in which non-family-based childcare contexts work with families. Are professionals open to different models of the family and different sets of traditions and values?

In a similar vein, the work of Brooker (2002) highlights how family expectations of schooling and education may be very different based on differing cultural expectations. Focusing on the experiences of children and their families from different cultural backgrounds as they transfer to school, Brooker shows how settings may have dominant expectations, or practices, that do not necessarily accord with the expectations of families. One example is the arguably dominant discourse among Early Years practitioners of the importance of play for learning in the Early Years and yet for some families the expectation may be that school is supposed to be about 'work'. If not addressed by practitioners then the dissonance between family and school expectations may result in difficulties for the child's experiences of school. Brooker also draws on the work of Bourdieu around *cultural capital*, and some of these issues are covered in more detail in Chapter 1.

Families as dynamic systems

Many long-standing theories of development were fundamentally linear and often focused on one-to-one interactions between individuals as the engine of development. However, more recent conceptualisations of development acknowledge that interactions cannot be seen as free standing. Each new interaction is in part shaped by previous interactions and the partners to an interaction are both active players. Such models are now being applied as appropriate to the family as a whole. Cox and Paley (2003) for example, highlight the need to regard the family as being shaped and re-shaped on the basis of the complex web of relationships within it. These relational patterns are not static but are capable of changing, to circumstances within and beyond the family. You will probably recognise shifting alignments and patterns of engagement within your own family. You may feel more in tune with some members of the family about certain issues and at certain times and more in tune with other family members on other occasions. As a child, did you find that you could row with your brother or sister one moment only to ally yourself with them later on the day against your parents? Yet despite this adaptive and fluid nature of the family you will also recognise a sense of wholeness about your family; it may be difficult to describe exactly but there will be a sense of the family as something with its own coherence and integrity that you identify with above and beyond the individuals within it. If we accept the tenets of dynamic systems theory then we must recognise each family as having a unique and constantly evolving identity. This too will have implications for how professionals work with children and their families. To what extent are we always or indeed ever aware, of the complexities of the families with whom we work? Are we genuinely making an effort to engage with the family situation as a whole or only with certain individuals? Most likely the mother? In some family situations it may not be possible to engage more widely but, if not, are we factoring in the importance of differing dynamics within the family when we consider the child?

The impact of the home learning environment

Developmental theory clearly indicates that the family plays a key role in supporting and forming a location for children's learning. In more everyday terms Brooker (2002) points out that:

> *All of children's early experience – from being picked up and cuddled fed and changed, rocked and soothed, to being taken to the library or shown how to count – is a form of learning...*

> *Children acquire an incalculable amount of knowledge before starting school.*

> (Brooker, 2002)

Desforges with Abouchaar (2003) recognise the significance of the home as a learning environment and stress that even though social class, poverty and health issues can affect the capacity of parents to support children in their learning, what they call *at home good parenting* can still exert a powerful positive effect on children learning. Indeed, Feinstein (2003, 2004) has also demonstrated that parental involvement can be hugely important in breaking the cycle of disadvantage and children's underachievement.

Similarly, the influential EPPE project (Sammons et al., 2007) has shown that what parents do to support their children's learning is more significant than a variety of demographic factors in promoting children's intellectual and social development. What parents do is shown to be more important than who parents are. The notion of the home learning environment as a powerful enabler of children's learning is discussed in the following extract, based on the work of the EPPE team.

EXTRACT 1

Edward C. Melhuish, Phan. M.B., Sylva, K., Sammons, P., Siraj-Blatchford, I. and Taggart, B. (2008) Effects of the home learning environment and preschool center experience upon literacy and numeracy development in early primary school. Journal of Social Issues, 64(1): pp108–9

The effects of the home environment and parenting upon children's development may partly be due to the teaching and learning of specific skills (e.g., letter–sound relationships). However, the multiplicity of learning opportunities included in the HLE suggests that the effects may be related to more generalized and motivational aspects of child development (e.g. learning to learn). Also, children may internalize aspects of parental values and expectations (implicit in the activities of the HLE) as they form a self-concept of themselves as a learner. Such a perspective is congruent with Vygotsky's (1978) theory that children learn higher psychological processes through their social environment and specifically with adult guidance operating within a child's 'zone of proximal development' (stimulation within the child's comprehension) and reinforces the idea that children acquire cognitive skills such as literacy through interaction with others who aid and encourage skill development.

It is quite possible that the strong relationship between home learning environment and cognitive scores is mediated by some intervening unmeasured factor. Those parents, who answer the questions in a way leading to a high score, may have other characteristics that lead their children to have higher cognitive scores. Even if this were so, the HLE would still be an efficient proxy measure of such unmeasured factors.

Whatever the mechanisms, the influences of parenting upon child development are pervasive. Research involving 0-to-3-year-olds from the evaluation of the Early Head Start (EHS) program, which provided combinations of home visits and center child care intervention for disadvantaged families, found that the intervention increased both the quantity and quality of parents' interaction with children, as well as children's social and cognitive development (Love et al., 2005). A review of early interventions concluded that, to gain the most impact, interventions should include both parent and child together with a focus on enhancing interactions (Barnes & Freude Lagevardi, 2003). Such work indicates that parenting behaviors are learnable, and changes in parenting are associated with improved child development. Similar conclusions derive from a study by Hannon, Nutbrown, and Morgan (2005) in the United Kingdom, where children showed better literacy progress when parents received a program on ways to improve child literacy during the preschool period.

POINTS TO CONSIDER

- *To what extent does the extract suggest parental intervention is an explicit process, i.e. a deliberate and focused effort to support their children? Do you believe parents need to be aware of how they might be supporting their children in order for that support to be most effective?*

- *The extract speculates that the advantages for children's learning might derive from their acquisition of positive attitudes and dispositions to learning from their parents. Do you feel that if parents can generate a 'love of learning' this is more important than trying to teach specific skills or knowledge?*

- *Positive learning interactions between parent and child are noted as important but what is the key component of a positive interaction? Is it relational, i.e. to do with the shared spending of time between parent and child, or does the focus of that time also matter?*

- *The extract refers to the Vygotskian principle of the ZPD (see Chapter 4). It does so in relation to the support a parent might provide for a child's learning. To what extent might this principle apply to professionals working with parents to help them to build on the skills they already have even if they may not always recognise their own skills?*

Elsewhere in the article from which the extract is drawn Melhuish et al. (2008) make the point that recognising the key role of parents in supporting their children's learning does not mean that such responsibility *should be placed solely on parents*. The article emphasises that *provision of good quality preschool education is likely to produce further benefits, especially if the setting works closely with parents.*

Models of partnership between parents and settings

The idea that there will be benefits to children's learning if parents and settings work together within Early Years education is now widely accepted. It is enshrined for example in the previous and new versions of the EYFS in England (DFES, 2007; DFE, 2012). However, as Bridges (2010) notes, the acceptance of needing to work together has not always been held to be the case and the development of the concept of such partnership in education has taken differing forms over the years.

In a notable typology of partnership, albeit in relation to schools rather than Early Years settings, Epstein suggests six potential forms of involvement (1995 Epstein, cited in Sheldon and Epstein 2005):

Type 1. Parenting: Helping all families establish supportive home environments for children.

Type 2. Communicating: Establishing two-way exchanges about school programmes and children's progress.

Type 3. Volunteering: Recruiting and organising parent help at school, home, or other locations.

Type 4. Learning at home: Providing information and ideas to families about how to help students with homework and other curriculum-related materials.

Type 5. Decision-making: Having parents from all backgrounds serve as representatives and leaders on school committees.

Type 6. Collaborating with the community: Identifying and integrating resources and services from the community to strengthen school programmes.

Each of these types betokens a form of relationship between parents and the professionals in the school setting but is that the same as genuine partnership? Where does the locus of control lie in each of these levels?

Within the Early Years a number of programmes and approaches explicitly foreground engagement and involvement of parents such that this is seen as a core principle of their philosophy and practice. The following exemplars are not a definitive selection. Take time to follow up these through the websites listed under further reading at the end of the chapter, and consider the similarities and differences in how they perceive and position relationships with families. This should demonstrate how a core principle may be applied in subtly different forms.

• Pen Green Centre for Children and their Families.

• Parents, Early Years and Learning (PEAL).

• Peers Early Education Partnership (PEEP).

• Reggio Emilia.

The nature of partnership relations in practice

The models above have in their individual ways both contributed to and been guided by local and national policy guidance in how settings might build and extend relations with parents and families in their communities. A literature review by Smit et al. (2008), who surveyed international experts in the Netherlands, Germany, Sweden, Belgium, England, France and the USA, explores partnership in a more international perspective. They researched the relationship between parenting, education and childcare and found the educational roles of pedagogues and parents have become increasingly intertwined. Secondly, formal curricula draw on international treaties such as the European Declaration of Human Rights in promoting the *primacy of parents* and thirdly, these curricula emphasise citizenship and workplace readiness as goals for learning. Increased parental 'choice', contractual arrangements and parents-as-clients were also seen as current developments. Important though the identification of these trends are, they do not take into account the transitory migratory patterns of families crossing borders, nor do they inquire into parents' own aspirations, needs, expectations and skills. Some of these parental attributes will be relevant to the nature of partnership relations explored next.

The focus now turns to current UK policy and research findings that underpin how practice relates to families' home environments: how true partnership is founded on respect for what families are and create. You may note that it is not considered here how families might contribute to their children's learning; rather the emphasis is on how already they are providing and educating young children. The task therefore for practitioners in settings is how to work with that parental knowledge and understanding – which may range from being very limited to very sophisticated – in a reciprocal way, and to understand the challenges that emerge.

The role of parents in the EYFS

In the original EYFS (DfES, 2007) framework there was a strong recommendation on how practitioners and parents might work together; how the relationship might be built through respect for diversity, through clarity and effective communication and towards the mutual learning benefits from each other. The more recent statutory requirements for the Foundation Stage (DfE, 2012) by contrast, consider parent involvement under the heading of assessment under a new formal appraisal of their child during their third year – in time to inform the Healthy Child Programme health and development review at age two – and to contribute towards priorities for learning. It therefore sets a prescriptive role for parents in line with preset early learning goals, where, it is arguable, the professional practitioner's expertise and knowledge are likely to be perceived as being more important than the parent's knowledge because it both formalises and structures assessment. Practitioners who seek a collaborative partnership with parents and carers may have to develop even more sophisticated and sensitive strategies to engage with parents and carers about their child's care prior to this stage, and to establish trust early on in their relationships with families. The establishment of trust raises ethical issues within day-to-day interactions in practice. These will be explored to some extent in the extract by Brooker (2010) that follows. First, though, some theoretical perspectives that can help to situate relations between practice and family life will be discussed, with reference to research into parents' and practitioners' views.

Parents' and practitioners' views of partnership

Loreman (2009) considers three intersecting segments in these partner relationships: society, home and school. He draws on Bronfenbrenner's ecological systems theory (1979) to show the distinction between, on the one hand, the independent, autonomous child, learning to gain control over their own destiny, and, on the other, the interdependent child, interconnected, decentred and essentially related and relating to their social and cultural daily companions:

> *In practice … perhaps a narrow focus on the individual does children a disservice, and that in order to properly support and respect children one needs to support the ecosystems, the contexts, in which they live.*

> (Loreman, 2009, p35)

In terms of the home, Loreman emphasises the crucial role of media representation, digital technologies and popular psychology that all play their part in the dynamics of family life, and influence parents' values, their perceptions of their roles, and daily interactions around routines, play, children's interests and setting boundaries. In the home–school relationships, Loreman recommends that professional interactions be *warm, caring, empathetic, respectful, contextually relevant and understanding* (2009, p49). But what do these idealistic terms really mean in a day-to-day context? What has been seen to work for both parents and professionals?

In the Parents as Partners in Learning (PPEL) project (DCSF, 2007) the evaluation on parental involvement, an initial audit of 150 local authorities in England, called for greater precision and clarity in the definitions of 'parental support', parental engagement' and 'parental involvement', in terms of strategy development. Following this, the Early Learning Partnership Project (ELPP) (Evangelou et al., 2008) involved a range of projects focused on parents with children aged 1–3 considered at risk of learning delay. The findings from this evaluation identified a major shift in services for practitioners to regard parents as parents rather than clients, and as strong potential partners influencing their children's learning, through working together to reduce risks, especially among those families most at risk of exclusion. What participating parents most enjoyed was the range of activities offered in groups; the opportunities for learning together, the interaction with other parents and seeing their children mixing with others, knowing and gaining from professional support for their own learning and having a safe and structured, spacious environment which was relaxed and where they could talk freely (Evangelou et al., 2008, p106).

In a health model (Kirkpatrick et al. 2007) 20 women, considered at risk, were interviewed following an intensive programme of weekly home visiting, in the second trimester of their pregnancy and on through the first year of their baby's life. They most valued the contact with a professional who came to know them well, became someone they could 'open up to' and who had very practical advice as well as empathy. The relationships which developed also served to counteract previous negative exchanges with health professionals and suggest that this model of partnership, being non-directive, gave the participating women the self-confidence to deal with their own difficulties more effectively.

Practical support and safety appear to be important to parents engaging with Early Years centres, together with a sense that their views are valued through being listened to and being consulted (Robson, 2006). What becomes clear from Robson's research is that individual and personal factors demand responses that are tailored to individual contexts. It follows that practitioners need flexibility in approach and a range of skills and strategies available and accessible in their 'tool kit' of resources when relating to parents.

Even informal contexts like 'stay and play' drop-in sessions are not without their dilemmas for those who host them. A comparative study of supported playgroups in England and Australia (Needham and Jackson, 2012) exposed the friction felt by facilitators between allowing socialising between parents and encouraging them to focus their chat through purposeful interactions with their children perceived to support their learning. While long-term developmental outcomes for children have been found to be stronger in programmes that provide for parents and children together (Shonkoff and Phillips, 2000), what tensions might arise through this kind of provision? Are group activities and talk child-focused or parent-focused? How important is it to nurture parents and understand their needs in order to support their children's development? As you read this it may well be that you have experienced similar dilemmas especially in centres running programmes for 0–3s together with their carers.

The second extract under discussion in this chapter is taken from an article by Brooker (2010). It draws attention to the complex nature of caring and to the equally complex understandings of how 'professionalism' is constructed and perceived by both practitioners and by parents in relation to care. As you read it through, try to identify the different qualities which constitute care in early childhood education contexts, with particular regard to the meanings of both caring 'for' and caring 'about' another person.

EXTRACT 2

Brooker, L. (2010) Constructing the triangle of care: Power and professionalism in practitioner/parent relationships. *British Journal of Educational Studies*, 58(2): p183, p184

Since the care-giver is aware of caring, and the cared for person is simultaneously aware of *being* cared for, a reciprocal bond develops which is mutually satisfying and mutually reinforcing: in other words, both the care-giver and the cared-for person contribute to the relationship, and both gain from it. Noddings' model for the development of such relationships has its origins in the home, which she views as the ideal crucible in which caring feelings are first forged (2002). While this model may prove unrealistic in practice – not all homes supply children with 'adequate material resources and attentive love' (2002, p. 289) – it is perfectly possible for policymakers and providers to build their own aims and objectives around this principle of reciprocal, attentive care. In both *Birth to Three Matters* (2002) and the EYFS (2007), the idea of the key person who bonds with the child on their entry into a group setting and remains a support throughout their early years reflects an attempt to create these ideal conditions for development. The successful enactment of such conditions within a sector characterised by an extremely variable quality of environment, resourcing, staffing, leadership and so on, cannot be assumed, as this paper goes on to show.

continued

More recently, Dahlberg and Moss (2005) have applied Noddings' arguments to their project of re-thinking the nature of relationships and provision in early childhood more broadly. They advocate that the traditional care relationships which have evolved in European societies should be reconsidered in order to develop a more ethical stand-point and one which acknowledges the child's own agency as an individual who actively contributes to the care relationship. In doing so they call on a range of philosophical traditions of which two are relevant here: those of Tronto (1993) and of Levinas (1989). Tronto's far more wide-ranging approach to caring is to describe it as 'a species activity that includes everything that we do to maintain, continue and repair our 'world' so we can live in it as well as possible' (cited in Dahlberg and Moss, 2005, p.74). Applied to human relationships, this requires the qualities of 'attentiveness (to the needs of others), responsibility, competence and responsiveness' (ibid). In a further development of this argument, Dahlberg and Moss offer Levinas' notion of 'the ethics of an encounter' (2005, p.80) as an encounter with 'the Other' (child or parent) in which the professional's role is not to know, or grasp, the other but to respect and 'welcome' the other as a stranger. In offering a respectful welcome, the professional is open, attentive and caring at the same time as safeguarding the other's difference and individuality – in effect, taking care not to try to make the Other, whether child or parent, into 'someone like us'. These fundamentally ethical re-definitions of care and caring may sit awkwardly with traditional models of childcare in which a more competent and able individual (an adult) 'cares for' a weaker and less competent individual (a child).

These approaches are arguably as important in the formation of parent–practitioner relationships as in those between the key person and the child. In this case too, the differentials of power and expertise which are present, though less visible than those between adults and small children, may set the parameters for each partner's role, agency and identity within the relationship. There is a tendency, in considering the role of power in home–school relations, to assume that the differentials favour the teacher, who is the professional or 'expert' by virtue of her qualifications and knowledge of 'all children', as compared with the parent who is the expert only in her own child's development (and may even misconstrue or misunderstand that). While this may often be the case (Vincent, 1996), the reverse can be true, and that parents who view themselves as 'professionals' may exercise power over practitioners whose professional qualifications they hold to be of little value. In every case, an absence of genuine care for the other members of a relationship may impact on the well being of both adults and children.

- *If you consider the parent as being 'cared for', how can practitioners and parents both gain from their relationship? What strengths and expertise can they recognise in each other?*

POINTS TO CONSIDER *continued*

- *The key person role ideally strengthens the bond for the child and their family within a group setting. What kinds of challenges influence the effectiveness of this role in terms of practitioners' and parents' attitudes and knowledge?*

- *Brooker is advocating how children need to be understood and treated as dynamic agents in caring relationships. What does this mean in day-to-day practice?*

- *How might the caring professional maintain an 'openness' that does not conflict with their responsibilities, particularly where communication in a multi-professional team is required?*

For a better understanding of how everyday caring relations in home-setting partnership give rise to ethical questions that reach beyond the proscribed policies and advertised procedures, the article should be read in full. It also relates to Chapter 3 on inclusive practice. The four points above will now be explored.

Whose expertise? Whose knowledge? Whose gain?

Brooker (2010) takes three procedures which are widely viewed as supportive of pre-school transitions: home visiting, daily communications about the child and the role of the key person. She suggests from analysing interviews with both practitioners and parents, that care relationships in the triangle are in practice problematic and need to be informed by a *relationship of attentiveness, responsiveness and thoughtful consideration between caregiver and cared-for* (p194). The article draws on key theoretical concepts of Noddings (1984) and Levinas (whose philosophical theories she interprets for everyday teaching contexts), to explore the part of the cared-for person as a dynamic agent in the partnership. Noddings emphasises care ethics as a relational ethic (2010, p7); that being 'in relation' to someone comes before 'caring for' them and that it takes both parties to play their part. For teachers she distinguishes between virtue-caring and relational-caring. Virtue-caring teachers focus on planning what children need to learn and how they must behave, where their care is based on actions to support their progress, knowing what is in their best interests. Relation-caring is more dependent on listening to children, and working to their expressed needs. So care ethics are not so much about rights as about responding to needs, where emphasis is on attention, listening and understanding. Care ethics can be considered as moral education, and Noddings explains four components of caring in this respect.

- Modelling: what older siblings, parents and teachers do to show young children how they can learn or behave.

- Dialogue: the talking and listening and responding.

- Practice: from a caring perspective this is about how empathy develops, how one learns to see what others may be going through or feeling about the process.

- Confirmation; that acts of caring can help another 'recognise and develop his/her better self'.

Care therefore involves understanding how the other person feels. But essentially, and in the teaching context, care is not seen as warm and fuzzy, but includes the competence and critical thinking needed to carry out the caring responsibilities, as teachers respond to a host of diverse needs and evaluate their capacity to respond. Competence refers to professional knowledge and skills with which teachers meet parents' and children's needs through expanding their own intellectual repertoire.

It has been suggested previously, in relation to Loreman's (2009) work, that parents can feel deskilled and inadequate and blamed by popular psychology. Media can be quick to portray parents as the ones at fault for society's ills and Loreman advocates for their empowerment, as experts in their knowledge of their own child. Yet might this become problematic where their knowledge is perceived as less relevant, or perhaps being more specialised, or out of date, or even unhelpful to their child's development? How does the practitioner balance the interests of parent with those of the child?

The imbalance of power permeates the caring relationships, particularly in contexts driven by targets and standards where time and space become contracted and procedures and information cannot meet the relational needs of parent and practitioner. With such constraints it becomes important to set time aside for reflection and discussion, to allow exploration of issues about power or whose knowledge counts. Looking back to Neamat's story in Chapter 1 (Vandenbroeck et al., 2009) we read that the practitioners agreed after some discussion to comply with her wishes to have the child use the potty at such a young age, when possible in their day. The consequence was that Neamat became more respectful and understanding of the routines and the individualised attention given to her daughter. What is central to this account is that practitioners were prepared to go along with her needs and concerns even though they did not understand them. Vandenbroeck interpreted the mother's desires as a need perhaps to be somehow 'present' for her daughter through her instructions. The relational knowledge that Neamat demonstrated was not devalued, and neither did she feel her views were disregarded as unimportant. She came to see the practitioners' expertise as different and appropriate, through dialogue, while their compliance allowed her to become aware of her own agency in the face of the 'expert' gaze of the professionals.

In this context the practitioners took a risk and acted with imagination. Garrison (2008), in his reflections on the ethical obligations in caring for others, reinforces the role of moral imagination and the potential gain through understanding the other's point of view:

> *moral imagination ... allows us to 'see' future consequences and even respond in terms not just of the person before us, but with regard to his or her, and our, best future responsibilities. Relationship-building is a transaction wherein the participants, if they succeed, create meaning in common as a consequence of their relationship.*

(Garrison, 2008, p283)

The key person role

You will find further exploration of the role of the key person in Chapter 6. In the study which contained the second extract, Brooker draws attention to two main findings. The first one is that practitioners as key persons prioritised physical care, such as nappy-changing and feeding over relations with parents. There was generally a lack of reflection on how the parents' needs for reassurance in their own role might be met, in coping with the balance of work and leaving their child, or, for example, at the end of a day, needing *just two minutes of a trust-building face-to-face exchange* (Brooker, 2010, p190). There appeared to be a lack by both parties to see the other's point of view: how it might feel to be the other caregiver.

The second point is the question of whether the key person's role is perceived as mother-substitute or as companion/playmate to the child. Friendship can also be a key question for exploring the practitioner–parent relationship. Brooker illustrates the sensitive balance needed by professionals in maintaining some distance – as strangers – even though informal interactions are friendly and informative. This is often difficult to achieve. In the extract above it was seen how parents and practitioners can hold different understandings of the same child and different views of what may be right for their development. To apply care ethics means to both care *for* the child and to care *about* him/her. This can feel risky for both parties:

Responding with ethical responsibility to the other always involves some risk and vulnerability.

(Garrison, 2008, p283)

The child's own agency

Noddings refers to dialogue as an important component of moral education. This involves both speaking and listening. Dahlberg and Moss (2005) emphasise the *pedagogy of listening,* where the voice of the child may be heard, even when it involves silences, where listening to thought or what another person implies in their gestures and looks is important in understanding and educating. This term comes from the Reggio Emilia approach that sees the child as an intelligent meaning maker, interpreting the world from their own experiences, where the *teacher and children become partners in a process of experimentation and research* (Dahlberg and Moss, 2005, p107). How might a child's silence tell you what they are thinking? You might turn back to Chapter 2 to explore this again.

Gregory (2006) illuminates the home–school relationships through her research on the playful talk between bilingual and monolingual children in the 'interspace' linking home and school. She suggests even very young children bring home talk into classrooms and school contexts into their socio-dramatic play at home, thus making games and developing the cultures of both contexts. Extended families including siblings and grandparents are drawn into their play as they construct significant bridges for themselves and each other in the discourses of home and school. This highlights the competence of young children working across a range of languages and illustrates the sophisticated nature of their insights into the hierarchies of power and influence in the relationships with adults and peers in their everyday experiences.

The openness of the professional relationship

Brooker draws on Dahlberg and Moss's (2005) interpretation of Levinas's notion of 'encounter' when considering the triangle of care. This concerns the way one meets 'the other' and relates in a way that does not seek to consume, to grasp or persuade the other. It is about feeling that the other person is there in relation, not necessarily at a conscious level, but nevertheless constituting an ethical responsiveness and responsibility for the other person. This is where the chapter turns back to consider the asymmetry of the face-to-face relation. Both Derrida (1997), cited in Vandenbroeck et al. (2009), and Levinas have used the words *welcome* and *hospitality* in making sense of how people coming together have both the potential to build a friendship and to disagree and part. Levinas' writing on ethics has been influential over the last twenty years but has also been criticised for not being practical as it lacks an everyday context like teaching. As professional carers and educators it is all too easy to feel one is continually in a responding role where care giving can be both rewarding and exhausting. Noddings (1992) helpfully focuses on consequences in relation to ethics of care, emphasising the reciprocal nature of caring where both carer and cared for take responsibility for relating, and for preserving the relationship. She explains how the carer puts their own interests temporarily aside in order to give open attention which can be detected and experienced by the cared-for (Noddings, 2010). These roles are not fixed. They may change places as the balance of power alters from one moment to the next. When genuinely open, this balancing can make working with parents and extended families feel both rewarding and terrifying.

Time for dialogue appears to be crucial for fostering trust both at an individual and at a wider level. Glenny and Roaf (2008) clarify how when professionals have good relationships with each other they are likely to have time for recognising each other's expertise, where communication and information sharing are crucial in multi-professional teams. You will find more about this in Chapter 9. As professionals cope with change in policy and its consequent demands of accountability, regulation and measurement in Early Years settings, the focus on how relations of trust and care are built and maintained in the best interests of young children's lives becomes ever more relevant to practice.

CHAPTER SUMMARY

This chapter has offered you the opportunity to read two extracts which complement each other in their themes and arguments in relation to working with families. The first has drawn attention to the diverse nature of family structures and their influence on young children's development. Two important changing trends for conceptualising how families are viewed were identified. The socio-cultural model is where social and cultural contexts and interactions determine how families interact in their communities. The family as a dynamic systems model is where interactions and transactions are part of and contribute to the complex web of relations. Both have been seen to be constantly changing and to influence the attitudes and practices that affect young children's development before and outside educational settings. Both models have implications for how formal settings work with families. The importance of the home learning environment and of what parents 'do' at home as first educators has been emphasised. Models of home-setting partnerships have developed as schools and Early Years settings have increasingly recognised the powerful role played by parents. While children's needs have appeared to be foremost, these have been seen differently by different groups or individuals. The provision is therefore complex and varies in local management structures and professional teams. Within this network of care and education relations of trust and understanding have become imperative. These relations depend on understanding the diversity of families' parenting beliefs and knowledge, and on ethical approaches and actions that are founded in dialogue and reflection on practice.

References

Allan, G. and Crow, G. (2001) *Families, Households and Society*. Basingstoke: Palgrave Macmillan

Bandura, A. (1977) *Social Learning Theory*. Englewood Cliffs, NJ: Prentice-Hall

Bridges, D. (2010) Government's construction of the relation between parents and schools in the upbringing of children in England 1963–2009. Educational Theory, 60(3): 299–324

Bronfenbrenner, U. (1979) *The Ecology of Human Development*. Cambridge, MA: Harvard University Press

Brooker, L. (2002) *Starting School – Young children learning cultures*. Buckingham: Open University Press

Brooker, L. (2010) Constructing the triangle of care: Power and professionalism in practitioner/parent relationships. *British Journal of Educational Studies,* 58(2): 181–96

Cox, M.J. and Paley, B. (2003) Understanding families as systems. Current directions in psychological science. *American Psychological Society*, pp193–6

DfE (2012) *Statutory Framework for Foundation Stage.* London: DfE Publications

DfES (2004) *Every Child Matters: Change for Children.* London: The Stationery Office

DfES (2007) *Early Years Foundation Stage. Statutory Framework and Guidance.* Nottingham: DfES Publications

Dahlberg, G. and Moss, P. (2005) *Ethics and Politics in Early Childhood Education.* London: Routledge

Desforges, C. and Abouchaar, A. (2003) *The Impact of Parental Involvement, Parental Support and Family Education on Pupil Achievement and Adjustment. A Literature Review*. DFES Research Report 433. London: DfES

Draper, L. and Duffy, B. (2006) Working with parents, in Pugh, G. and Duffy, B. *Contemporary Issues in the Early Years* (3rd edition). London: Sage

Evangelou, M., Sylva, K., Edwards, A and Smith, T. (2008) *Supporting Parents in Promoting Early Learning The Evaluation of the Early Learning Partnership Project*. DCSF-RR039 **http://www.education. gov.uk/research/data/uploadfiles/DCSF-RR039.pdf** accessed 2 November 2010

Feinstein, L. (2003) Inequality in the early cognitive development of British children in the 1970 cohort. *Economica*, 70: 73–97

Feinstein, L. (2004) Mobility in pupils' cognitive attainment during school life. *Oxford Review of Economic Policy*, 20(2): 213–29

Gabriel, N. (2010) Adults' concepts of childhood, in Parker-Rees, R., Leeson, C., Willan, J. and Savage, J. *Early Childhood Studies* (3rd edition). Exeter: Learning Matters, pp137–51

Garrison, J. (2008) Ethical obligation in caring for the Other: Reflections on Levinas. In *Levinas and Education*. (edition D. Egea-Kuehne). Oxford: Routledge

Glenny, G. and Roaf, C. (2008) *Multiprofessional Communication*. Maidenhead: Open University Press

Gregory, E. (2005) Playful talk: The interspaces between home and school discourses. *Early Years*, 25(3): 223–35

http://www.dcsf.gov.uk/everychildmatters/publications/0/1904/ Parents as Partners in Early Learning (PPEL) Project Parental Involvement – a snapshot of policy and practice PPEL Project Phase 1 Report accessed 3 November 2010

Johnstone, J. and Nahmad-Williams, L. (2009) *Early Childhood Studies*. London: Pearson Longman

Kirkpatrick, S, Barlow, J. Stewart-Brown, S. and Davis, H. (2007) Working in partnership: User perceptions of intensive home visiting. *Child Abuse Review,* 16: 32–46. John Wiley and Sons Ltd

Loreman, T. (2009) *Respecting Childhood*. London: Continuum

Melhuish, E.C., Mai, B., Phan, M.P., Sylva, K., Sammons, P., Siraj-Blatchford, I. and Taggart, B. (2008) Effects of the home learning environment and preschool center experience upon literacy and numeracy development in early primary school. *Journal of Social Issues,* 64(1): 95–114

Morrow, V. (1998) *Understanding Families: Children's perspectives*. London: National Children's Bureau/ Joseph Rowntree Foundation

Needham, M. and Jackson, D. (2012) Stay and play or play and chat; comparing roles and purposes in case studies of English and Australian supported playgroups. *European Early Childhood Education Research Journal,* 20(2) June: 163–76 Routledge: Taylor and Francis Group

Noddings, N. (1984) *Caring: A feminine approach to ethics and moral education.* Berkeley, CA: University of California Press

Noddings, N. (1992) *The Challenge to Care in Schools – An alternative approach to education.* New York: Teachers College Press

Noddings, N. (2010) Care ethics in education, in *Educating the Young: The Ethics of Care. New International Studies in Applied Ethics,* 4, ed. J.A. Kentel, pp7–19. Bern, Switzerland: Peter Lang AG International Academic Publishers

ONS (2011) Households and families, Social Trends 41. **www.ons.gov.uk/ons/rel/social-trends-rd/ social-trends/social-trends-41/index.html** accessed 9 August 2012

Parents Early Education Partnership (PEEP) **www.peep.org.uk** (accessed 25 September 2012)

Parents, Early Years and Learning (PEAL) **www.peal.org.uk/** (accessed 25 September 2012)

Pen Green Centre **www.pengreen.org/** (accessed 25 September 2012)

Robson, S. (2006) Parent perspectives on services and relationships in two English Early Years centres. *Early Child Development and Care,* 176(5): 443–60

Rogoff, B. (1990) *Apprenticeship in Thinking*. Oxford: Oxford University Press

Rogoff, B. (2003) *The Cultural Nature of Human Development*. Oxford: Oxford University Press

Rogoff, B. Mistry, J. Göncü, and Mosier, C. (1993) Guided participation in cultural activity by toddlers and caregivers. *Monographs of the Society for Research in Child Development* serial nos 236, 58(8): 5–6

Sameroff, A. (1975) *Transactional models in early social relationships. Human Development,* 18: 65–79

Sammons, P., Sylva, K., Melhuish, E., Siraj-Blatchford, I. Taggart, B., Grabbe, Y. and Barreau, S. (2007) *The Effective Provision of Pre-School Education (EPPE) Project: Summary Report Influences*

on *Children's Attainment and Progress in Key Stage 2: Cognitive Outcomes in Year 5.* London: DfES/Institute of Education, University of London

Schaffer, H.R. (2004) *Child Psychology.* Oxford: Blackwell Publishing

Sheldon, S.B. and Epstein, J.L. (2005) Involvement counts: Family and community partnerships and mathematics achievement. *Journal of Educational Research,* 98(4); 196–206

Shonkoff, J. and Phillips, D. (2000) *From Neurons to Neighbourhoods.* Washington, DC: National Academy Press

Smart, Neale, B. and Wade, A.C. (2001) *The Changing Experience of Childhood.* Cambridge: Polity Press

Smit, F., Driessen, G., Sleegers, P. and Teelken, C. (2008) Scrutinising the balance: Parental care versus educational responsibilities in a changing society. *Early Child Development and Care,* 178(1): 65–80

Vandenbroeck, M., Roets, G. and Snoeck, A. (2009) Immigrant mothers crossing borders: Nomadic identities and multiple belongings in early childhood education. *European Early Childhood Education Research Journal,* 17(2): 203–216. Routledge: Taylor and Francis Group

Vygotsky, L.S. (1978) *Mind in Society: The development of higher psychological processes.* Cambridge, MA: Harvard University Press

White, D. and Woollett, A. (1992) *Families: A Context for Development.* Brighton. Falmer Press

FURTHER READING

Brooker, L. (2010) Constructing the triangle of care: Power and professionalism in practitioner/parent relationships. *British Journal of Educational Studies,* 58(2): 183, 184

Cox, M.J. and Paley, B. (2003) Understanding families as systems. *Current Directions in Psychological Science.* American Psychological society. pp193–6

Noddings, N. (2010) Care ethics in education, in Educating the young: The ethics of care. *New International Studies in Applied Ethics,* 4 (edition J.A. Kentel), pp7–19. Bern, Switzerland: Peter Lang AG. International Academic Publishers

Rogoff, B. (2003) *The Cultural Nature of Human Development.* Oxford: Oxford University Press

WEBSITES

http://peal.org.uk

www.peep.org.uk

www.pengreen.org/pengreencenter.php

http://zerosei.comune.re.it/inter/nidiescuole.htm

ONS (2011) Households and Families, Social Trends 41. **www.ons.gov.uk/ons/rel/social-trends-rd/social-trends/social-trends-41/index.html** accessed 9 August 2012

8 Professionalism – Raising the stakes in the Early Years: 'She's only going to work with little children'

Helena Mitchell and Ingram Lloyd

Over recent years there have been considerable changes in the way that the workforce in the Early Years sector is configured in England. Sources as diverse as the Select Committee report in 2000, the OECD, academics such as Moss (2007), Osgood (2006), the new Labour government between 1997–2010, and the recently published Nutbrown Review (2012) have contributed to a changing view of what it means to be a professional working with young children.

By the end of this chapter you should have:

- considered the meaning of professionalism and what it means in Early Years contexts;
- engaged with the arguments about the motives for professionalising the Early Years workforce;
- understood the history of the ways in which the workforce is being professionalised;
- reflected upon the impact that the changes have had, and may have in the future on those who work with our youngest children.

Introduction

Since 1997 there has been an increasingly urgent debate about what it means to be a professional working with young children. For too long, working with young children has been perceived to be a Cinderella role, one which has low status and low pay. Such perceptions are all important because they have impacted upon the sector's attractiveness to potential staff as well as on salaries and professional expectations. Low levels of pay continue to affect people's perception of the worth of the job and even the worth of the people involved. This was clearly illustrated during a Parliamentary Select Committee when the Commons met to discuss Early Years Education. Barry Sheerman, the chair of the Education subcommittee made the now-infamous statement that:

Most people in this country would not get someone who is unqualified and untrained to fix an appliance such as a washing machine or dishwasher, even if the person were recommended or appeared in the Yellow Pages. However, many people leave their children in the care of unqualified people who are paid the minimum wage, or sometimes less when the rules are bent...

In terms of quality of training, the pre-school care system in Denmark, which covers up to age seven, was astonishing. All staff are graduates and properly trained, and on average they earn only about 10 per cent less than qualified teachers. According to evidence given to our Committee, pay and training in this country are worst in respect of the ages of nought to three, five and eight – probably the most sensitive period in a child's development.

(Hansard, 18 Oct 2001: Column 310WH)

The importance of ensuring that those who work with young children have appropriate training and qualifications has been increasingly recognised as a goal which should be pursued by every nation in the twenty-first century. By comparison to some other nations, such as New Zealand and Denmark, England has been lagging behind. See, for example, OECD (2006) and Smith and May (2006). But the debate is complex. It is underpinned by a number of questions.

- What does professionalism mean in the Early Years sector?

- What kind of role is appropriate for those working with young children? Should it be a qualified teacher, or someone who has gained the status of Early Years Professional? Should the role be reconfigured as that of a pedagogue, in which the practitioner contributes elements of care, education and social engagement? What qualification levels are appropriate for those working with young children? Should this be level three (equivalent to A level standard) or degree level?

- What about pay and conditions? Staff in Early Years settings have tended to be poorly paid, certainly in comparison to those in other sectors of education. What are the implications of raising qualification levels? Will the sector be able to afford higher rates of pay and improved conditions?

- How is this all likely to impact upon the children at the heart of the debate?

- Can or should parents afford higher fees (as Early Years workers gain higher qualifications) or should there be more government subsidy?

This chapter will address these questions in the context of recent and current developments, drawing upon a range of relevant evidence. For some staff who have been working with young children for some years, changes to the Early Years workforce have often seemed to be challenges to the work in which they have engaged. As Osgood (2006) points out, practitioners find it difficult to resist changes in Early Years qualification requirements even though they may not believe in their validity or effectiveness.

Childcare has traditionally been viewed as an occupation suited to women, and indeed, the majority of the workforce is female. Yet the notion that working with young children requires qualities which are allied to motherliness, and that possessing such qualities prevents engagement with a professional role, must be challenged. It also has negative connotations for those men who choose to work in Early Years settings.

Rabe-Kleberg raises a relevant question: *Does ... motherliness prevent or obstruct a woman from pursuing professional development and a career?* (2009, p214).

Surely possessing qualities which enable a worker to relate to young children and build effective relationships should be celebrated rather than used as a reason to inhibit professional recognition for such a role? Yet it is a construct which seems to militate against recognising staff as being career orientated at the same time as possessing a quality which is recognised as important in an Early Years setting. While acknowledging that few policy makers would openly subscribe to the view that Early Years workers need maternal qualities but little in the way of qualifications, Moss (2006) acknowledges that an important element of Early Years settings involves a homely environment, and that such an environment is often sought out by parents and carers.

Professionalism

The need for professionalism in the Early Years sector has become an issue for debate, which Brock (2006) identifies as being a contemporary question. For those outside the Early Years sector professionalism is a long and well established tradition. In the medical, legal and teaching professions there are clear entry criteria and subsequent training and career paths exist. Arguably those people who have particular skills acquired through specific training which could have included apprenticeships – electricians, plumbers where a clear level of expertise is recognised by others, in all these cases the workers have joined a profession but are they demonstrating 'professionalism'? What exactly does professionalism mean?

Moss (2006) defines Early Years workers as technicians or researchers and in illustrating the difficulties of defining professionalism within the sector he raises the question of the roles that the adults take. Are they technicians where low levels of qualifications are the norm? Or are they researchers where the adult is a learner themselves and a reflective and discursive practitioner who actively engages and understands children's thought processes and development? Moss supports Oberhuemer's (2004) view of professionalism, as change from technician to researcher occurs when there is the ability to gain extra qualifications, and to effect a change in working conditions and status. On the other hand, being in a profession must by definition exclude others who are not part of this exclusive group. In addition, being part of the group and engaging in reflection and review of practice enhances the development of the professional persona and the view of oneself as a proactive and competent member of a profession. In the context of these ideas, how do you view your role? Do you see yourself as a practitioner technician or a practitioner researcher? It may be that you feel that neither of these categories is appropriate given the variations in your role.

For those working in the Early Years sector the idea of being a professional or demonstrating professionalism is multifaceted. For many of those outside the sector it appears there is little comprehension of how or why the person working with young children should be regarded as a professional. Indeed, even those working in the sector struggle with the notion of their role as professionals (Hargreaves and Hopper, 2006), a challenge noted previously in the Rumbold report in 1990, paragraph 150:

> *adults working with the under fives have traditionally enjoyed less esteem than those working with children of statutory school age, outside and even within the ranks of the professions themselves. This is reflected, in substantial measure, in levels of pay.*

Osgood (2004, p13) cites a childminder's view that public perception of their work was poor and *the enormity of the task we have taken on ... (as presented by the media) ... implies that working in child care is merely fun is undervaluing our work and legitimising the low pay.*

The Nutbrown Review, entitled *Foundation for Quality* (2012) emphasises that *A new long term vision is needed for the Early Years workforce, with a reformed system of qualifications to help achieve this* (2012, p5).

The proposals, which draw upon a wealth of evidence from a wide range of respondents, represent the most coherent attempt to provide a clear and carefully structured framework which can be a blueprint for a future Early Years profession. Whether the current government will implement the 19 recommendations remains, at the time of writing, to be decided. Nevertheless, there are a number of different potential models for the professionals working with young children, specifically those drawn from other countries which have been more successful in developing their early childhood services, and two of these will be examined below. Before you read the first extract, take time to reflect on these questions.

- What essential qualities do you think the adults working with young children should possess? Why do you think these are important?

- What qualification levels are appropriate for these workers? Why? How might qualifications impact on the experience of young children in an Early Years setting?

- Should all those working with young children aspire to being viewed as professionals in the same way that teachers and doctors are viewed as professionals?

- If so, what might be the implications of this?

EXTRACT 1

Organisation for Economic Co-operation and Development (OECD) (2006) *Starting Strong II*, pp166–7. OECD Publishing

- *The pedagogue model* favoured by the report is the graduate social pedagogue. This professional is the main worker in early childhood settings in Denmark and other countries, but works also in out-of-school provision, youth work, residential and foster care for children, with the elderly and in services for persons with severe disabilities. Pedagogues, however, are not teachers but have a distinctive identity: their approach to children is through the concept of pedagogy in which care, upbringing and learning have equal shares. For them, the early childhood centre is not a junior school, but a socio-educational centre, a site for human relationships and for learning that springs

continued

from social interaction. A central understanding is that the early childhood institution should contribute, alongside the parents, to the individual child's development and well-being, which is generally interpreted as learning to live in society and sharing a society's fundamental values, including respect for autonomy and independence. It is an approach prompted more by family and social life than by education (Lund, 2005). According to Boddy et al. (2005), social pedagogy 'provides a strong basis for an approach to both children and young people that embodies ideals of active citizenship, rights and participation, and for working with the whole child and her family'.

- *The 'new teacher' or 'early childhood specialist' model*, also uses the 'pedagogy' approach (care, upbringing and learning) with children. In Sweden, following the integration of early childhood services into education in 1996, the profession of pedagogue continued until reform in 2001 when it was combined with free-time pedagogues and primary school teachers into a unified profession 'teacher'. These branches of the same profession receive common core training for 18 months at tertiary level. Then, for a further two years, teachers in each branch specialise intensively in their own field. This constitutes an obvious strength of this particular profile – intensive training in child development and pedagogy, which pre-primary teachers in the United Kingdom and other countries often lack. After graduation, all three branches work together in teams in the pre-schools, on school sites in the pre-school classes, in the primary school classes, and in free-time services, each branch taking the lead whenever it is appropriate. This integration of training is intended to serve the interests of children – integrating the child's journey through education, with care at all levels of the system, all taking place in the same setting and with staff working in teams right across the system from 1 to 16 years. The child's day is integrated through having the same teams of teachers (pre-school, primary teachers and leisure-time staff) working together daily within the same setting, and through following a unified curriculum from kindergarten into secondary school. It is too early yet, to assess the effects of this innovation.

The Children's Workforce Development Strategy, created by the New Labour government in the early years of the twenty-first century, considered radical new proposals for the Early Years workforce. The strategy included the introduction of Foundation degrees, two- or three-year work-based routes for practitioners, sanctioned by employers, and forming part of a 'climbing frame' to enable childcare workers to move from the more usual National Professional Qualifications (NVQs) through to a full honours degree and the status of Early Years professional, or even on to a PGCE course. The intention of these routes was initially to upgrade the qualification levels of practitioners but in many cases it led to better-qualified staff moving into areas of better provision for which they were now qualified. It is difficult to know whether the pedagogue role was ever really under serious consideration. Yet in the context of Early Excellence Centres and the Sure Start Local Programme, in which a more holistic approach to children and families was implicit, such a role might have been ideal.

- *Why do you think there are so many challenges in establishing Early Years workers as professionals?*

- *What do you think might be the benefits for young children and their families of the pedagogue model?*

- *What disadvantages might result from such a model?*

- *What are the economic implications?*

- *Integrated training would bring together aspiring Early Years workers with those who wish to work with children in mainstream education. How might this impact upon practice?*

The issues about the Early Years workforce have been recognised for many years by those working in the sector. The contrast between the qualifications, training and status of those working with children in the UK and in certain European countries is very marked. The drive towards integrated services in Sweden, for example, has been well ahead of that in England and Scotland (Cohen et al., 2004). One way that this has been addressed in the UK has been through the development and growth of undergraduate courses in childhood and early childhood studies, introduced in universities and colleges since the mid-1990s with some of the first being led by social policy. The introduction of the degrees was driven academically by the recognition that too many of those working with young children lacked in-depth knowledge about child development, and that the development of academic courses in childhood would enable the development of a new breed of professionals working with children, one which would be able to raise quality and would be entitled to better pay (Calder, 2006). Better quality would only be achieved by a better qualified but also more settled workforce.

One of the major challenges for the Early Years private and voluntary sector is the high rates of staff turnover, and the need to use agency staff. Qualification levels have risen but, according to the Brind Report (2010), only 14 per cent of paid staff across all aspects of the childcare sector are qualified to level six (degree level). And although pay levels rose between 2009 and 2010, most staff are paid less than £14.43, which also according to Brind is the national hourly wage for UK employees.

Early Years Professional Status and Qualified Teacher Status

The debate about the suggested models is still ongoing, although the publication of the final report of the Nutbrown Review in June 2012 has set out clear proposals for a career structure. Since 2006, and the publication of the OECD report, there has been the successful development of a new professional career path for those working with young children, Early Years Professional Status, which underwent a national evaluation in 2011

(Hadfield et al., 2011). The establishment of the EYP route, vaunted by the Labour government as *equivalent to Qualified Teacher Status* (QTS), required workers to have, or gain at least an ordinary degree, to have at least English and maths GCSE at grade C or above, and to demonstrate that they could meet the 39 standards for EYPS through a complex paper-driven exercise and a five and a half hour visit to the prospective EYP's setting to assess how far their claim could be verified. The model for this assessment, very different from the model for achieving QTS, was in fact predicated on a previous model for achieving the status of Higher Level Teaching Assistant. Using such a model could be seen as undermining government rhetoric about equivalence to QTS. In addition, the entry requirements for QTS remained higher than EYPS, where a grade C science GCSE as well as maths and English is also necessary for those who wished to become a qualified teacher. So although the level of qualification within the workforce was improving, the notion of having joined a 'profession' was denied due to the bar for entry into the teaching profession being higher. Nevertheless, the first National Survey of Practitioners with EYPS (2011) provided positive feedback about the impact of the status on practitioner perceptions and practice:

> *Just over three-quarters of practitioners (76 per cent) felt obtaining EYPS had improved their sense of professional status and 80 per cent felt it had increased their confidence as a practitioner.*

> (Hadfield et al., 2011, p6)

Lumsden (2012) notes that the EYP and EY teacher are *complementary but essentially different* because the teacher has an education focus while the role of the EYPs is more holistic and requires advocacy for young children. This difference has not generally been acknowledged, however, although it offers a real and coherent perspective on the synergies and disparities between the two. Despite the identification of EYPS as equivalent to QTS, it is clear that there are considerable barriers to realising this aspiration. What do you think are the main impediments? How can these be overcome?

Perhaps very importantly, those gaining EYPS have had no bargaining power over rates of pay or conditions as there has been no universally recognised pay scale or a real professional body to act on their behalf, although there have been links with the Aspect trade union. As McGillivray notes (2007), both these factors have only added to the frustration and confusion of those in the sector who have questioned what the real benefits of gaining EYPS might be, given that neither colleagues nor parents have a clear understanding of this new status or what differences will be made. Nutbrown (2012) has recognised these dilemmas in her review, and indeed in her report for the Early Years workforce she sets out the following vision:

> *Early Years staff have a strong professional identity, take pride in their work, and are recognised and valued by parents, other professionals and society as a whole.*

> (2012, p10)

Such a vision is much closer to the suggested models which were highlighted in the extract from the OECD report above. How far do you agree with Nutbrown's vision of identity and the bringing together of EYPS with a newly identified Early Years teacher? At the time of writing the coalition government has not responded to Nutbrown's report, and it remains to be seen as to whether her vision and 19 recommendations will be implemented even in part.

Nevertheless, as noted above, gaining EYPS has had a positive impact on many of those Early Years practitioners who have gained the status in the past five years. Success has led to a growth in self-confidence and self-esteem. Eraut (2008) found that gaining a qualification represented a recognised competence in a profession and a significant change in career terms. Hallet's (2008) interviews with foundation degree graduates included responses such as *I seem to walk taller. I know what I am doing and am not afraid to say so*, emphasising the benefits of undertaking a foundation degree where theoretical knowledge underpinned by good practice and reflection are brought together.

It could be that practitioners who have enhanced their qualifications by completing a foundation degree may well be more articulate and able to demonstrate their knowledge and expertise to a wider public than before. This confidence is part of professionalism – where a practitioner can explain philosophy and practice. The vocational and work-based learning that Hallet describes is very supportive and to some extent provides opportunities for individualised learning and matches QAA requirements in the qualifications benchmark for foundation degree (QAA, 2004).

A similar sentiment was expressed by respondents in Wild and Mitchell's (2010) study of 17 recent EYPS graduates who were asked how the experience had impacted upon them. One respondent noted:

> The whole thing right from Foundation degree was an absolute roller coaster. I don't know how I got on it and stayed with it in the first year. But EYPS it brought out the professional in me.

Another explained the way it had impacted upon her as:

> The way I've changed as a person, not just educationally, generally, confidence has just rocketed. I've found my voice.

So despite the many frustrations of recognition and pay barriers, it was the impact on their view of themselves and the growth of confidence which was most powerful, and which, in enabling the linking of theory and practice led to a renewed confidence in professional knowledge and a recognition of a changed identity, linking in with the work of Eraut (2009) and Polyani (1958) in making the tacit overt.

Professionals in Different Early Years Contexts

EXTRACT 2

Moss, P. (2007) Structures, understandings and discourses: Possibilities for re-envisioning the early childhood worker. *Contemporary Issues in Early Childhood*, 7(1): pp31–4

continued

The move to an integrated workforce accompanied by a highly qualified 'core' worker has significant financial implications – it does not come cheap. Staffing accounts for most of the cost of early childhood services, about 80% in most countries (OECD, 2001). A split early years workforce, with a highly qualified minority of teachers and a lower qualified majority of childcare workers, enables and legitimises a low cost workforce: the majority have substantially inferior material conditions because they are less educated which, in turn, is rationalised by 'childcare services' requiring less well-qualified workers. But replace a split system and a split workforce with an integrated system and workforce, with a new core graduate occupation that accounts for at least half the workforce, and costs increase substantially. Pedagogues and early childhood teachers in the Nordic countries are paid only slightly less than school teachers, while in New Zealand the principle of pay parity between pre-school and primary school teachers has been agreed.

But who pays? In a market system where many early years services are treated as private commodities for parents to purchase as consumers (the prevailing model in most of the English-language world), an integrated workforce based on pay parity with school teachers cannot be funded from parental fees: most parents could not afford the cost, even with some element of fee subsidy for lower income parents. Even where publicly funded services are more common, many countries would baulk at the public expenditure implications. Apart from New Zealand, which is an outlier here, only the Nordic countries have been prepared to make the shift to a higher qualified, higher paid workforce and this shift is supported through high levels of tax based public funding. Thus, public expenditure on early childhood services in Sweden and Denmark is equivalent to about 2% of GDP (OECD, 2001), more than three times the level in the United Kingdom even after nearly a decade of increased public spending in this area; while in 2000, taxes in the three countries accounted for 54, 49 and 37 percent of GDP respectively (OECD, 2003, pp. 38–39).

It is possible, therefore, to point to some important national examples of structural workforce change, at least with respect to organisation and material conditions. The same, however, cannot be said of the third structural dimension, the composition of the workforce, in particular its gendered nature. Even in Nordic countries where early childhood work has been restructured and revalued, the work is still done largely by women. In Denmark, for example, though up to a quarter of pedagogue students are men, the proportion of men working in early childhood services is low: just 2% of staff in nurseries (taking children under three years), 6% in kindergartens (for children from three to six years) and 9% in age-integrated institutions (taking children under and over three). But the proportion rises to 24% in free-time services (school-age childcare) and 41% in youth clubs (Jensen & Hansen, 2002). So, with a wide range of work possibilities open to them, male pedagogues largely opt to work with older children, young people and adults.

This suggests that the gendering of the workforce cannot be explained in terms of low pay. More likely is a combination of how the work is understood in society – as essentially 'womens work' (discussed further below) – and of how education and employment are structured in ways that reproduce gendered workforces. Thus, local initiatives in various

European countries that have had some success in drawing men into education and employment for early childhood work have been based on changes to practice that make education and employment more attractive and welcoming to men as well as expressing a strong commitment to diversity (see, for example, Meleady & Broadhead, 2002; Peeters & Vandenhroeck, 2003; Wohlgemuth, 2003; Hansen et al, 2004).

Two linked questions hang over early childhood services that are split, underresourced and rely on a workforce that has low levels of qualification and pay and is highly gendered. Is this desirable, for children, parents or workers themselves? Arguably not, with these conditions devaluing and exploiting the workforce and not being conducive to good practice. Is it sustainable, can things carry on like this? There are a number of reasons to doubt they can. Demand for workers is increasing as services expand, while the supply source, the pool of younger and less educated women, is shrinking as the level of women's education increases and as those with lower education have increased employment opportunities elsewhere in the service sector. Coomans (2002) describes the projected fall over the next decade in the numbers of women in Europe with low educational qualifications and spells out the likely consequences in stark terms: 'Wherever the present standard for any category of job is "low qualified women around the age of 30", there will unmistakably be a strong need to improve the quality of job so it will be acceptable to people with higher educational attainments. And if no improved professionalisation of the job is achieved then it will rapidly end up in a severe labour supply shortage' (p. 8).

POINTS TO CONSIDER

- *The essentially gendered nature of the Early Years workforce is found in many countries. Male pedagogues in Denmark usually choose to work with older children and adults. Should this issue be seen as a challenge which needs to be addressed, and if so, how?*

- *Moss emphasises the economic arguments which impact upon any vision and plans for Early Years workers, and the ways in which those countries which have substantially invested in Early Years have chosen to do so. How far do you agree that financial investment is crucial if there is really to be a substantial change in the configuration of the Early Years workforce?*

- *If investment is important, who should provide the finance?*

It is illuminating to consider how other countries resource their educational systems, and how they view the content and structure of Early Years education. Although international comparisons are very helpful, it is also necessary to treat them with some caution. In studying the approaches taken in different countries it is important to respect and value the ways in which countries establish, develop and review their systems. A study of similarities and differences between systems is instructive in that it offers alternative approaches which can enable us to reflect upon and review our own. There are many comparative studies which provide views of different systems of early education and care. Some such as the work of Reggio Emilia are well known internationally, and are sometimes held up as examplars of excellent practice. Other studies, such as that of Woodhead (2009), are perhaps less so. In an exploration of early childhood education in Ethiopia, India and Peru, Woodhead highlights very different systems with far less economic resource. The work of Tobin et al., initially in 1989, and then later in 2009, draws comparisons between pre-schools in China, Japan and the USA. In each of these the role of the practitioner differs in terms of the practitioner's training, expectations and responsibilities. The nature of early childhood education in different countries is inextricably linked to culture, society and to economic considerations. So although these comparisons are helpful, and often fascinating, they cannot be transferred to other systems, although they can offer opportunities to reflect upon our own practice and to consider different ways of approaching provision.

Financial issues in professionalising the workforce

A critical aspect which Moss raises is that of finance. How can an effective Early Years provision be funded? In countries such as Sweden taxation is high to pay for high-quality provision. It is an economic and political decision to put resources into early education, spending money on comprehensive and high-quality training and provision. In England the question of funding has to some extent been bypassed, although the new Labour governments of the early twenty-first century viewed improving qualification levels of practitioners working with young children as a priority, and directed funding towards the Early Years Sector Endorsed Foundation Degree and the EYPS programme. What they did not do was to resolve the issue of funding for EYPS, if indeed it was the equivalent of QTS. Despite the many requests for clarification of this issue it remained unresolved. Those practitioners gaining EYPS were not eligible for any specific pay scale, and this issue has continued to undermine the validity and recognition of the status. However, many EYPs are employed in private or voluntary settings which have very limited budgets and would not be able to fund payment of a graduate salary. Teachers working in such settings often take reduced salaries too. The real issue is that there has been no agreed salary scale. Lumsden (2012) acknowledges the difficulties which some settings would face if they were to pay a graduate salary, but suggests that if a small number of such settings were to work together, they could each contribute towards the financing of an EYPS salary, and then each benefit from some dedicated support from the EYP. This idea is a novel but innovative suggestion. A survey of Early Years professionals commissioned by the Children's Workforce Development Council (now absorbed into the new Teaching Agency) reported that

> *60 per cent of respondents earned under £24,000 per annum (full-time), and many earned significantly less, particularly if they worked in the PVI sector, or as childminders.*

(CWDC, 2010, p6)

As to government funding to enable EYPs to have salary scales equivalent to teachers, that seems increasingly unlikely given the current financial constraints. The new career routes suggested by the Nutbrown (2012) Review have similar financial challenges, but could be affordable because they would build upon the current system of Early Childhood Studies degrees and teacher training provision. In terms of employment in private and voluntary settings though, the issue of salaries will still be a challenge.

Young children's learning and development

One of the most important reasons for improving the qualification levels of those practitioners who work with young children must be that staff with higher qualification levels are able to deliver higher-quality provision. A range of evidence now supports this hypothesis. It is necessary to define what is meant by higher-quality provision.

The longitudinal EPPE study (Sylva et al., 2003–8), with its allied study of researching effective pedagogy (REPEY) (2002), provided clear evidence of what constituted high-quality provision. The data for the study was drawn from more than 3000 settings across the range of provision including day nurseries, nursery classes and nursery schools and children's centres. High-quality provision was characterised by behaviours such as open-ended questioning and sustained shared thinking, and staff having a good understanding of appropriate pedagogical content. Among other criteria shared by high-quality provision was that the manager was a qualified teacher, and some of the staff were also graduates, often also qualified teachers (Siraj-Blatchford, 2008). Findings from the EPPE study have been very powerful in emphasising that high-quality Early Years education leads to improved outcomes for children and that this effect is long-lasting, echoing the findings of the US-based Weikart Perry Pre-school study in the 1960s and 1970s.

Although the findings from the EPPE (2008) study emphasised that trained teachers were instrumental in delivering high-quality provision, the more recent Graduate Leader Fund (previously the Transformation Fund) evaluation (2011) also highlighted that those settings which had appointed *a graduate leader with EYPS made significant improvements in quality for pre-school children (30 months to five years) as compared with settings which did not* (2011, p2). The difference related to the quality of interactions with children and with other practitioners, and the ways in which the EYPs were able to support learning, develop communication and lead practice. In both the Graduate Leader Fund Evaluation and the CWDC National Survey of EYPS practitioners, most of those surveyed were in leadership and management roles where they were able to direct, support and influence practice. Such evidence supports the impact that professionalising the workforce is beginning to have on Early Years provision, although as EYP status is relatively new, the evidence must be viewed with some caution. The Department of Education Business Plan (May, 2011) states that the coalition government is committed to improving the quality of the Early Years workforce.

However, uncertainty over the future of both EYPS and the Nutbrown Review's recommendations could further unsettle those practitioners who have gained the status. This is unfortunate because many EYPs perceive their status as beneficial, emphasising increased credibility with their colleagues, and the majority (80 per cent) reporting increased confidence in their ability to practise (Hadfield et al., 2010). Furthermore, the majority had engaged with their own future continuing professional development (CPD) needs, an important marker of professionalism. Mathers et al. (2011) also emphasise the importance of ongoing CPD, as such programmes are vital to supporting EYPs as *change agents and leaders of learning* (2011, p7). Yet national awareness of the Early Years Professional Status is limited. It may be too soon to expect there to be national awareness of EYPS because it is still relatively new.

CHAPTER SUMMARY

In the eleven years since Barry Sheerman compared the pay and status of those working with young children unfavourably with washing machine mechanics, there has been a considerable amount of investment in the training and development of practitioners. The numbers of practitioners qualified to at least level 3 (A level equivalent) and level 6 (Graduate level/EYPS) has risen since 2006. According to the Brind report (2010), the highest qualification levels for those staff in full daycare settings were held by those in children's centres, of whom 19 per cent were qualified to this level. This is an increase of 9 per cent since 2006.

Qualification levels across the sector vary of course. Provision is variable, and there is a plethora of qualifications which can be difficult to understand. The Nutbrown Review's attempt to provide a clear and coherent framework for qualifications is both welcome and timely, building upon much that has been achieved in the past few years.

The focus on qualification levels for Early Years workers has helped to raise awareness across the sector, and to improve practice and provision, as well as providing those who have taken up the challenge with increased self-esteem and confidence, if not more pay. A continuing commitment to growing the workforce is essential for the benefit of the sector, but most importantly for the children who attend the many Early Years settings.

References

Brind, R., Norden, O., McGinigal, S., Oseman, D. and Simon, A. (2010) Childcare and Early Years providers survey. DfE http://media.education.gov.uk/assets/files/pdf/o/sfr%20main%20text%20osr172011.pdf accessed 19 April 2012

Brock, A. (2006) Dimensions of Early Years professionalism – attitudes versus competences? **http://www.tactyc.org.uk/reflections-papers.asp** accessed 14 April 2012

Calder, P. (2006) History and background of the Early Childhood Studies Degree Network. Unpublished paper produced for Early Childhood Studies Degree Network Conference, Research into Reality, Woburn House, London, 14 March 2006

Cohen, B., Moss, P., Petrie, P. and Wallace, J. (2004) *A New Deal for Children?* University of Bristol: The Policy Press

Danish Federation of Early Childhood Teacher and Youth Educator (BUPL) (2009) *Integrating Leadership and Pedagogy in Early Childhood Institutions.* Copenhagen: BUPL

Department for Education and Skills (2005) *Ten Year Strategy.* London: Stationery Office

Eraut, M. (2008) How Professionals Learn through Work. Draft report. SCEPTrE Report **http://surreyprofessionaltraining.pbworks.com/f/How+Professionals+Learn+through+Work.pdf** accessed 17 April 2012

Hadfield, M., Jopling, M., Royle, K. and Waller, T. (2011) *First National Survey of Practitioners with Early Years Professional Status.* CeDare, University of Wolverhampton

Hallet, E. (2008) I seem to walk taller: the impact of work-based learning and reflective practice upon Foundation degree graduates' professional practice. Proceedings from the Work-based Learning. II Futures Conference. Middlesex, May 2008. **http://213.5.176.40/~uvacacuk/wp-content/uploads/2010/08/WBLFII-FINAL.pdf** accessed 17 April 2012

Hansard (2001) *Select Committee Report*, 310WH

Lumsden, E. (2012) *The Early Years Professional: A New Professional or a Missed Opportunity?* Research Overview, University of Northampton

Mathers, S., Moody, A., Karemaker, A., Graham, J., Sylva, K., Siraj-Blatchford, I., Hall, J., Clemens, S., Newmark, T. Rahim, L. and Penfold, C. (2011) *Evaluation of the Graduate Leader Fund Final Report*, DFE-RB144

McGillivray, G. (2007) *Mirror, Mirror On The Wall: Reflections of the Early Years Professional.* CECDE 2007 International Conference. Dublin

Moss, P. (2007) Structures, understandings and discourses: Possibilities for re-envisioning the early childhood worker. *Contemporary Issues in Early Childhood* 7(1): 30–41

Nutbrown, C. (2012) Foundations for Quality, Review of Early Education and Childcare Qualifications: Final Report **https://http://media.education.gov.uk/MediaFiles/A/0/9/%7BA098ADE7-BA9A-4E18-8802-D8D4B060858D%7DNUTBROWN%20FINAL%20REPORT%20-%20final.pdf** accessed 9 August 2012

OECD (2006) Starting Strong 2. Early childhood education and care. Ch 7, pp166–7: Appropriate training and working conditions for early childhood education and care staff

Osgood, J. (2004) Time to get down to business?: The responses of Early Years practitioners to entrepreneurial approaches to professionalism. *Journal of Early Childhood Research*, 2(1)

Osgood, J. (2006) Rethinking Professionalism in the Early Years: Perspectives from the United Kingdom. *Contemporary Issues in Early Childhood*, 7(1): 1–4

Osgood, J. (2006) Deconstructing professionalism in early childhood education: Resisting the regulatory gaze. *Contemporary Issues in Early Childhood*, 7(1): 5–14

Polanyi, M. (1958) *Personal Knowledge: Towards a post-critical philosophy*. London: Routledge and Kegan Paul

QAA (2004) Benchmarks for Foundation Degree

Rabe-Kleberg, U., (2009) Maternalism and Truncated Professionalism – Historical Perspectives on Kindergarten Teachers, in Scheiwe, K. and Willekens, H., *Childcare and Preschool Development in Europe*, London: Palgrave Macmillan

Rumbold Report (1990) Starting with quality. DfES London: Her Majesty's Stationery Office **http://www.educationengland.org.uk/documents/rumbold/rumbold01.html** accessed 18 April 2012 **http://www.educationengland.org.uk/documents/rumbold/rumbold02.html** accessed 18 April 2012

Siraj-Blatchford, I., Taggart, B., Sylva, K , Sammons, P. and Melhuish, E. (2008) Towards the transformation of practice in early childhood education: The effective provision of pre-school education (EPPE) project. *Cambridge Journal of Education*, 38(1): 23–36

Siraj-Blatchford, I., Sylva, K., Muttock, S., Gilden, R. and Bell, D. (2002) Researching effective pedagogy in the Early Years. Research Report 356, DfES

Smith, A.B. and May, H. (2006) Early childhood care and education in Aotearoa-New Zealand, in Melhuish, E. and Petrogiannis, K. (2006) *Early Childhood Care and Education, International Perspectives.* Abingdon: Routledge

Sylva, K., Melhuish, E., Sammons, P., Siraj-Blatchford, I. and Taggart, B. (2003–2008) Effective Pre-School and Primary Education. 3-11 Project (EPPE 3-11). A longitudinal study funded by the DfES, formerly The Effective Provision of Pre-School Education. (EPPE) Project (1997–2003). **http://eppe.ioe. ac.uk/eppe/eppepdfs/beraglamorgan05.pdf** accessed 17 April 2012

Tobin, J.J. (2009) *Preschool in three cultures revisited: China, Japan and the United States.* Chicago, London: University of Chicago Press

Weikart, D. http://www.high-scope.org.uk/About+Us/History accessed 2 August 2012

Wild, M. and Mitchell, H. (2010) Listening to and learning from the voices of professionals in the Early Years. Unpublished paper presented at EECERA Conference, September 2010

Woodhead, M., (2009*)* Pathways through Early Childhood Education in Ethiopia, India and Peru: Rights, Equity and Diversity. Young Lives Working Paper 54 **http://www.publications.parliament. uk/pa/cm200102/cmhansrd/vo011018/halltext/11018h01.htm** accessed 19 April 2012

Brock, A. and Rankin, C. (2011) *Professionalism in the Interdisciplinary Early Years Team: Supporting young children and their families.* London: Continuum

Cable, C. and Miller, L. (2008) *Professionalism in the Early Years.* London: Hodder Education

Eraut, M. (2008) How professionals learn through work. Draft report. SCEPTrE Report **http://surrey-professionaltraining.pbworks.com/f/How+Professionals+Learn+through+Work.pdf**

Miller, L. and Cable, C. (2011) *Professionalization, Leadership and Management in the Early Years.* London: SAGE

www.education.gov.uk/childrenandyoungpeople/earlylearningandchildcare

www.education.gov.uk/nationalcollege/index/support-for-schools/childrens-centre-system-leaders.htm

www.education.gov.uk/childrenandyoungpeople/earlylearningandchildcare/delivery/ b00201345/graduate-leaders

9 Multi-professional working in the Early Years

Helena Mitchell

The importance of professionals working together to ensure that children and families are given the best possible service has increased in priority in the past few years. Children's centres in England bring together many different professionals, and offer an ideal opportunity for working across professional boundaries. This chapter considers some of the elements of effective multi-professional working, drawing on a range of evidence from relevant studies. The rapid development of Sure Start children's centres, which is the context for much multi-professional early years working, is examined prior to considering the ways in which professional communities define themselves before being able to engage in working across professional boundaries. Finally the chapter examines the need for effective leadership and clear communication strategies in effective multi-professional working.

By the end of this chapter you should have:

- considered the ways in which multi-professional working has grown in Early Years contexts and the ways in which it can support children and families;
- considered how the community of practice to which the Early Years workforce belongs relates to other professional communities in multi-professional working, and the challenges that may result;
- considered the importance of shared aims, clear leadership and strong communication strategies in effective multi-professional working.

Introduction

The terminology around multi-professional working varies. Some authors refer to multi-professional working and others to inter-professional working or inter-agency working. These different labels may include differences of interpretation and practice. It appears that the term multi-professional working covers a wide range of different models of working, and the term itself has been chosen for use in this chapter because it relates to the workforce involved rather than to the agencies concerned. It is the professionals who form the workforce and who are required to work together. Ways in which the overarching government vision is translated into local versions of multi-professional working are varied, and may not necessarily build upon already established partnerships in localities.

Being able to be work in a multi-professional team involves having a level of professional expertise and identity. Issues around the development of professionalism for Early Years practitioners were examined in Chapter 8, and for those working in Early Years environments, the definitions of professional identity and community are an important prior requirement to being able to engage in a multi-professional team.

Work with young children and families has involved professionals from different agencies for many years, but these professionals have not necessarily worked in concert. The birth of a baby automatically involves healthcare professionals, while social services may become involved at any time in a child's life. Until the early part of the twenty-first century, the education service had not been involved with most children and families before children approached the age of five years, the statutory school starting age in England. But with an increasing number of children attending nursery education, children beginning schooling from the age of four years in some areas, and the growth of private and voluntary daycare providers, the overlap between different services has increased. There has been a move towards multi-professional working in children's services for some time, which can been seen in the establishment of the Early Excellence Centres in the late 1990s, charged with bringing together a range of provision for young children and families on one site. In actuality, many of the Early Excellence Centres were multi-sited, but they did succeed in bringing together elements of health, education and social work so that they were more accessible to families within local communities (Bertram et al., 2002). Despite the apparent initial success of the Early Excellence Centres, they were overtaken by a further interagency initiative, Sure Start, and have now become Sure Start children's centres.

The background to and history of multi-professional working in the Early Years

The notion of children's centres only really came into existence through the new Labour government in the early years of the twenty-first century, and the personal commitment of Gordon Brown, then Chancellor of the Exchequer, to pursue potential policy options to tackle issues of child poverty and social exclusion (Johnson, 2011, p2). In following up this directive Norman Glass, a senior economist, was responsible for developing the focus on young children and families, and looking for ways in which there could be greater co-ordination between services. These services were to be cross-generational (thus for children and their families), but also locally driven and responsive to the needs of the relevant areas.

So the growth in children's centres across the country focused initially on areas considered to be most in need of high-quality integrated services. These were mostly inner-city areas in large urban conurbations, and the focus was on families with children up to the age of four years. As the programme was rolled out, however, all areas were required to manage the development locally. In total in summer 2012 there were around 3,600 Sure Start children's centres across the country (Direct Gov, 2012a). Thus all children and families should have access to social work, education and health which is local, accessible and located on one site where possible. For such services to be available to all families in their locality there was a need for many professionals to relocate to the new children's centres. For some professionals, it meant working at a number of such centres because professional specialism was needed at a number of different centres at different times each week. For professionals such as health workers, location in a range of different settings was not unusual, but the requirement for multi-professional working necessitated building new and more in-depth relationships with the other professionals in each centre. It involved the breaking down of professional barriers, and transcending professional identities, never an easy option.

Every Child Matters

The changes bringing together different agencies were underpinned by the five outcomes of Every Child Matters, which became law through the Children Act of 2004, and impacted at that time not only on the professionals working with children and families but also on local and central government itself. The introduction of Every Child Matters is often cited as a response to the Laming Report on the death of Victoria Climbié in London in 2000, which in part it was. But it was also a fundamental part of the policy developments championed by the New Labour government since 1997, strengthening the provision for children and families through integrated working.

According to Moss (2006a), the need for a pedagogical approach is clear. In drawing comparisons with the children's workforce in other countries, it appears that the notion of *shared orientations and values* for the workforce from the beginning of their training is fundamental to success. Bringing together already established services with the difficulties of ensuring that all professionals have shared values and beliefs and appreciate each other's viewpoints is far more of a challenge. Values and beliefs are deeply rooted and personal for each individual and therefore, how far should professionals working together be expected to have shared values and beliefs? How far is the leadership of an integrated centre responsible for building a shared vision including values and beliefs? What is the role of in-service training in this context?

Shared values and beliefs

Establishing shared values and beliefs in a workforce where there are many different qualifications and in which staff come from many different backgrounds does present a challenge. The splintered nature of the Early Years workforce, with its varied range of qualifications and differing experiences, together with pay and conditions which lack uniformity, forms perhaps one of the major barriers to effective multi-professional working. These differences can engender a sense of unfairness, and despite having been identified as an issue early on in the establishment of children's centres, they have not been resolved in any satisfactory manner despite attempts by individual centres and local authorities (Cottle, 2011). Focusing parity on job titles is important, but pay and conditions are an enduring source of concern, and the gendered nature of the workforce, which is predominantly female, emphasises the way that *the work is understood in society* (Moss, 2006, p34). Even in countries where working with young children is more highly valued, such as Denmark, a gendered workforce is widespread.

During the early part of the twenty-first century, a massive building programme was implemented in England to update facilities and professionals were relocated to enable easier and more effective multi-professional working. As the initiative progressed the age range for the programme was extended to include a focus on young children up to the age of five years. In addition the Extended School initiative was created involving schools developing a core offer of services including wrap around care and specialist services (Direct Gov, 2012b).

Sure Start

Overall, the creation of Sure Start began to transform the ways in which early childcare and education were delivered. The increase in children's centres across England was rapid between the years of 2002 and 2010. The vision was of a centre in each community, and 3,500 children's centres by 2010. An in-depth study by Weinberger et al., (2005) which focused on two local Sure Start programmes provided a fascinating range of evidence about many aspects of the programme.

The background to the establishment of children's centres has been examined in other publications, for example Anning and Ball (2008), DCSF (2008). As Sure Start programmes have grown they have been the subject of a series of evaluations designed to provide clear evidence for further development, highlighting aspects of strength and areas needing reassessment (NESS, 2012).

The name Sure Start is reminiscent of the Head Start Programme in the USA, and has similarities in that it is aimed at improving the social and cognitive development of children in low socio-economic status (SES) areas (NHSA, 2012). But perhaps the most important recent research to underpin Sure Start is the Effective Provision of Pre-School Practice (EPPE), a longitudinal study which has examined the quality of provision for early education. One of EPPE's key findings was that quality was higher overall in integrated settings, nursery schools and nursery classes. Furthermore, Eisenstadt (2011), the first national director of Sure Start, also emphasises the findings of NESS and the evidence from EPPE supporting the effectiveness of children's centre working especially for children from disadvantaged backgrounds.

Sure Start was the epitome of the new Labour government's ambitions for multi-professional working, and it retains a leading role in the coalition government's policy for children and families. In line with coalition government policy, there is a new focus upon voluntary and community involvement, drawing upon organisations that have had previous involvement with families to be more involved with children's centres. Funding reviews focus on accountability and transparency, and any interventions must be drawn from those with a proven evidence base.

Funding has always been a challenge in the centres, especially with the diversity and complexity of their offer, and the individual nature of each centre. Government changes to funding have emphasised local priorities (although localism was always a feature of Sure Start), removing ring-fenced funding, and focusing on core purpose rather than core offer (DfE, 2012a). It is interesting to examine the localism agenda a little further. One of the drivers for Sure Start was increasing the educational attainment of disadvantaged children, through engaging their families in a community support service. The name Sure Start, derived in some measure from Head Start (see above), offers a very different programme, however. It is clearly directive, highly structured (and very successful). The very success of Head Start has been attributed to its structure. The localism agenda for Sure Start children's centres meant that all programmes were individual not devised centrally, so the very tenet on which educational disadvantage was perceived to have been addressed in Head Start was missing from Sure Start. Johnson (2011) cites Melhuish and Hall's comment on the individuality of the Sure Start programmes, highlighted in the first tranche of evaluation evidence published in 2001. Melhuish also repeated these comments to a Commons Committee in 2009 (also cited in Johnson, 2011, p11).

Nevertheless, the Sure Start children's centres have continued to flourish, primarily because of the evidence from EPPE that emphasises the effectiveness of integrated centres in enabling young children's achievement. A further factor though is that the centres are well liked by families, and there is now evidence that they are reaching the most disadvantaged families who were the original target group and:

> *are well-placed to provide improved integrated services that will help support the most disadvantaged children and families and in a way that can contribute to narrowing the gap between the children of disadvantaged and more advantaged families.*

(NESS, 2012, Executive Summary)

The challenges of multi-professional working

To return to the question posed at the beginning of this chapter, what is the meaning we ascribe to multi-professional working? According to Atkinson et al. (2005) there are a number of different models which may include co-location of staff groups, the creation of new and separate structures, and the establishment of steering groups which drive forward change but possess no actual resources. Decisions are driven through the participants' organisations. Local area working is very important with parents and carers involved throughout so that services are responsive to local needs. In a well-argued text which draws upon recent and relevant experience of multi-professional working, Davis and Smith address the reader directly thus:

> *It is important for you to realise that the reason it is difficult to define integrated working (their term) is because there is no single way to do it.*

(2012, p102)

They further discuss the complexity of different models and the range of complexity which may present itself in different models and at different levels. Such an approach reflects the challenges and is a refreshing change from the many directive texts which while not lacking commitment and beliefs, espouse a rather directive approach to those who find themselves implementing or even inventing the models.

Indeed, the development of multi-professional working may go through a number of stages, and Frost (2005) describes different levels of working, ranging from level one, which involves co-operation, through to level four, where there is total integration. Rowe (2005) discusses some of the challenges in a local Sure Start programme. The challenge of bringing together different services effectively is certainly a mammoth one, and issues of attitudes of the professionals involved are crucial to successful implementation. In addition, the need for effective communication by all participants has been identified by Glenny (2006), Glenny and Roaf (2008) and Alexander and Macdonald (2001).

A further range of models are provided by a recent report on leadership in children's centres (Sharp et al., 2012) published on the NCSL website, which also provides a useful glossary of relevant terminology.

The previous chapter discussed notions of professionalism, and considered how far practitioners in early childhood settings have been able to build a professional identity. The increased drive towards a professional workforce, with practitioners working for higher qualification levels and engaging in CPD, can be identified as markers of professionalism, although these initiatives have been directed by government initiatives rather than arising from the workforce. Nevertheless, a percentage of those in the workforce have responded and qualification levels across the sector have risen. In considering working across professions and agencies, it is essential to begin from the starting point of how those engaging in such working define their professional knowledge and community.

POINTS TO CONSIDER

- *Consider the different terminology used to define multi-professional working. What does this mean to you?*

- *Which models of multi-professional working have you encountered?*

- *What were their key features?*

The work of Wenger (1998) is instructive in identifying and helping to define the ways in which workers build their own community, which he labels a *community of practice*. A group of practitioners working together have specific routines and behaviours, ways of identifying and judging competence, and to some extent mutual accountability for the success of the enterprise. Yet the individual within the community still plays a vital role.

EXTRACT 1

Wenger, E. (1998) *Communities of Practice Learning, Meaning and Identity.* **Cambridge: Cambridge University Press, pp252–3**

By keeping the tension between experience and competence alive communities of practice create a dynamic form of continuity that preserves knowledge while keeping it current. They can take care of problems before they are recognized institutionally. It is communities of practice, therefore, that can take responsibility for the preservation of old competencies and the development of new ones, for the continued relevance of artifacts, stories, and routines, for the renewal of concepts and techniques, and for the fine tuning of enterprises to new circumstances.

- *Spreading of information*. The mutual accountability derived from pursuing a joint enterprise and the interpersonal relations built over time together make the sharing of information necessary, relevant, and tailored. As a result, a new piece of information acquired by one member can quickly become everyone's. In communities of practice, information entails communication because it is part of an on-going process of negotiating meaning. Information travels through a community of practice at a rate, for reasons, and with effects that reflect this process. Communities of practice are thus nodes for the dissemination, interpretation, and use of information. They are nodes of communication. It is therefore often useful to have communities of practice that cut across other types of locality, such as product lines or specific functions, so that knowledge travels naturally across the landscape. For instance, I noted the usefulness of simultaneous membership in communities of practice of coworkers and peers – with complementary and overlapping forms of competence, respectively (Chapter 2). This idea requires multimembership to be elevated to an organizational principle.

- *Home for identities*. A focus on communities of practice does not entail paying less attention to individuals. On the contrary, it places a very specific focus on people, but not people in the abstract. It is commonplace to say that it is people who make the difference in an organization, but it is less commonplace to understand this truism in terms of focusing on what makes us human, on what enables us to make a difference – on the work of negotiating identities inherent in knowledgeability. What we learn with the greatest investment is what enables participation in the communities with which we identify. We function best when the depth of our knowing is steeped in identity of participation, that is, when we can contribute to shaping the communities that define us as knowers.

  Aligning learning with the goal of an organization depends critically on the allegiance of participants. This allegiance in turn depends on the communities of practice in which their engagement and their identities constitute each other. Indeed, the kind of personal investment and social energy required for creative work are not a matter of institutionalized compliance or abstract affiliation; they are a matter of engaging the identities of participants. Because developing an organizational competence has to do with practice, it has to do with communities and identities. In this regard, treating people as members of communities of practice does not mean stereotyping them, but rather honoring the meaningfulness of their participation and valuing their membership as a key to their ability to contribute to the competence of the organization. By offering an institutional home to the communities of practice that are key to its competence, an organization helps sustain the kinds of identity that allow participants to take active responsibility for some aspect of organizational learning.

Communities of practice are organizational assets because they are the social fabric of the learning of organizations. Not being formal entities, however, they are a resource that is easily overlooked.

Communities of practice

It can be too easy to overlook the individual's view of themselves as a professional, and the implications this has for the way that they define themselves and their role. The importance of recognising that individual practitioners are part of a community of practice, and that the community has ways of organising, relating and demonstrating competence is crucial. Reflecting on practice of the community can enable identification of its critical features, and acknowledging its norms, boundaries and ways of working has to be recognised and valued before the individuals will be able to engage fully in a multi-professional team in which their ways of working may be challenged.

Legacy of professionalism

Hudson (2007) discusses the challenges which arise from what he terms the *legacy of professionalism* (2007, 21(1)3), and outlines two models of interprofessional working, which he terms pessimistic and optimistic models. In many ways the pessimistic model reflects the ways in which professional boundaries inhibit working across those boundaries, while the optimistic model, which he defines as the *new professionalism* can be indicative of new, more open ways of working based on teamwork and reflective practice. In working across professional boundaries, practitioners may be defined as creating a new community of practice, one in which they have to adjust to shared ways of working and more effective communication to meet the needs of those using the services.

Participant allegiance

Wenger also raises the important issue of participant allegiance, and the need for the goals of the organisation to be aligned to those of the participants. Without this participant allegiance the opportunity to work effectively both within professional boundaries and across them will be sorely tested. Any organisation needs to build upon the skills and knowledge of its workforce rather than to impose a top-down approach.

Yet effectively, the top-down approach has been the driver for multi-professional working, with the previous new Labour governments of the late 1990s and first decade of the twenty-first century imposing the change. Garrett (2009), in his analysis of the reform agenda, particularly highlights the ways in which the rhetoric employed in government documentation focused on the role and responsibility of the individual worker in achieving the collective vision. There is no doubt that there are many laudable elements of such a vision, but the need to ensure that those enacting the vision are empowered to develop it needs to be acknowledged. Cottle (2011), writing about an ESRC project which aimed to understand practitioners' perspectives on what constitutes quality in Sure Start children's centres, exposes many of the inherent tensions in a complex and multi-layered system. Despite their commitment, practitioners often struggle to balance policy requirements with their own view of their role in their particular context. This struggle may lead to creative approaches towards their roles, including the multi-professional aspect, but it is dependent on the individual centre, context and local challenges as to its success.

As Leadbetter et al. state:

> *How professional identity is maintained while divisions of labour are renegotiated and role boundaries are blurred or redefined is a complex and multifaceted problem.*

(2007, p96)

A confident belief in one's professional identity is an essential prerequisite for working across professional boundaries. How many Early Years' practitioners truly possess that confidence? How can children's centre leaders promote it? Issues of leadership and clear communication are paramount.

The role of leadership in delivering multi-professional working

The vision of the UK coalition government established in 2010 for children's centres appears to focus upon developing strong leadership, building upon the National Professional Qualification in Integrated Centre Leadership (NPQICL), and emphasising the responsibility which children's centre leaders have for the success of their centre, and the range of work which their centre hosts. The challenges which the Centres face are considerable, but there seems to be greater self-confidence amongst Sure Start leaders. This is mirrored in the publication of Sharp and Lord's (2012) detailed report on leadership in children's centres. The emphasis on leadership includes a reference to *multi agency* working, but does not prioritise this. Indeed, the main challenges are summarised as:

- leading in a time of intense change;
- maintaining high-quality services in the face of uncertainty and funding cuts;
- maintaining staff morale and motivation;
- keeping an appropriate balance between universal and targeted services;
- dealing with increasing numbers of vulnerable families, combined with fewer sources of support;
- managing limitations in the understanding by other agencies of the contribution made by children's centres, combined with a perceived low status of Early Years' professionals (2012, p2).

The emphasis is clearly on ensuring that leaders have their own networks of support, and are reflective of the actions required for them to lead successfully. How does this impact upon multi-professional working? Rostron (2012), writing in a publication for local children's centres leaders, states the following:

> *I recognise a frequent disconnection between service delivery and the perceptions and experiences of families. Looking at statistical data in isolation, organisations and services fail to connect with their communities or develop an understanding of the community cultures within them.*

I feel the same can be said of working across professional boundaries. We tend to connect well with the organisations and services we know and understand, while disregarding those who may not cross our path or are less familiar.

(2012, p8)

POINTS TO CONSIDER

- *Can you identify particular ways of working which might be specific markers of a professional community?*

- *What are the challenges for delivering effective multi-professional working in children's centres?*

- *As there is a multiplicity of children's centre models, how can leaders draw on the most effective approaches to promote multi-professional working?*

- *How can leaders decide on priorities in a time of reduced funding?*

Effective communication

EXTRACT 2

Glenny, G. and Roaf, C. (2008) *Multiprofessional Communication: Making systems work for children*, **pp95–97. Maidenhead: Open University Press**

In particular, we found that when the communication systems were going well we did not pick up evidence of the tensions between professionals of different disciplines that were very evident in the contexts where the communication systems were problematic. Most significantly, this was true even in the urban study where the personnel were the same people who had been interviewed 18 months earlier.

When professionals have good relationships, they are more likely to make the space and time to have the quality dialogue that allows them to bring their different expertise to the table. Similarly, when field workers have opportunities for quality dialogue the relationships are more likely to be good. Huxham and Vangen (2005: 154) argue that the building of trust in relationships is crucial to this understanding of the relationship being 'good'. Thus:

> ... trust building must be a cyclic process within which positive outcomes form the basis for trust development. With each consecutive positive outcome trust builds upon itself incrementally over time, in a virtuous circle. Each time partners act together, they take a risk and form expectations about the intended outcomes and the way others will contribute to achieving it. Each time an outcome meets expectations, trusting attitudes are reinforced. The outcome becomes part of the history of the relationship so increasing the chance that partners will have positive expectations about joint actions in the future ...

Anning et al. (2006) also found that joint client focused activities provided power-ful opportunities for developing shared understandings. Huxham and Vangen refine the nature of these activities further in that they argue that small scale, low risk activities are much more likely to meet mutual expectations, so that, 'there is a strong case for initiat-ing collaboration through modest, low risk initiatives ...' (Huxham and Vangen 2005: 154).

Huxham and Vangen also note how vulnerable such trust cycles are to unequal power relations and the perceived need of partner organizations to protect their own interests through the manipulation and control of collaborative agendas. Again we see why, with apologies to Schumacher (1974), 'smallish is beautiful'. The local communication systems were able to produce environments where these kinds of trust cycles were starting to thrive, away from the necessarily more complex and politically weighted agendas of ser-vice managers.

The implications of this are not just that the foundations of trust building are to actively engage with others in small projects, but also that the whole process of trust building takes time.

The need to establish systems of communication which work effectively for those involved in working together in any organisation is paramount. It is not necessarily an easy system to establish, especially in a large and complex organisation. Smaller organisations should present fewer problems, but communication in multi-professional contexts offers fresh challenges. Glenny and Roaf emphasise the importance of building good-quality relation-ships, opportunities for quality dialogue, and the building of trust. All of this takes time and opportunity. For staff working in a multi-site children's centre, the opportunities for such shared working may occur less often, simply because the geographical location oper-ates as a constraint. Anning et al. (2006) discuss the context for such conversations which may well take place informally rather than formally, and in fact, informal situations offer the best prospect for the building up of relationships and getting to know other staff. It is clear that there is a need for commitment to shared working on the part of all those involved in multi-professional contexts, but strong leadership (Chandler, 2006) with a shared vision and values is also essential.

How far does the leadership need to facilitate an understanding of the roles of the dif-ferent professionals, and engender opportunities for developing professional respect? Do those working together need to be able to take on different professional roles to some extent? It is clear that they need to have an understanding of each other's roles in order to support and work with each other effectively, and understanding involves knowing the different procedures which are in place in different professions, and appreciating why these may be different.

A recent case study available on the Department for Education website (DfE, 2012b) writ-ten by a children's centre leader, acknowledges the problems of implementing successful multi-professional working on a split site and emphasises the need for effective planning.

Leadership

Ensuring time for the team to work together regularly each week, appropriate training in which the whole group participates, and shared spaces such as a staff room, which can help to contribute to the building of the informal relationships, are all useful strategies. The need for clear unequivocal leadership in establishing these parameters is apparent.

However, that leadership may be distributed across the team, offering greater engagement with the vision and day-to-day working practices and supporting clear communication. The vision needs to be one which is shared by all participants, and one to which all have been able to make a contribution. This is in direct contrast to the target-driven approaches common in public services in recent years in which staff have been required to deliver externally determined outputs. Such approaches, often described as *command and control* systems (Davis and Smith, 2012), can create further barriers to communication and effective working, especially in complex environments which involve multi-professional working. Staff are likely to focus on their own targets rather than to engage with the shared enterprise of working across professional barriers in order to achieve the common good.

Universal language

One way of developing an integrated workforce is to create training courses which have common elements for all those who are intended to become part of the children's workforce. Implementing a common curriculum, for example, as happens in the training of pedagogues in Denmark, enables the growth of a workforce with a broader conception of their role and identity and a broader understanding of the roles of the other professionals with whom they work. This approach can also establish a universal language, and facilitate communication. It is possible to establish parameters and universal understandings for all staff working in a profession. In the UK, there are courses which support established professionals in the ways in which they can work together but this is of course a top-down rather than bottom-up approach.

CHAPTER SUMMARY

The introduction of multi-professional working was intended to radically transform the ways in which professionals worked together, and the services they offer to children and families. Although there are many potential benefits resulting from this requirement, it offers many challenges for the professionals involved, not least an understanding of their own professional identity and role as well as that of others with whom they work in this brave new society. This is not a step which can be implemented overnight because it requires a radical change in many elements of work. To work with others effectively requires a confidence in one's own identity as a professional and, for many of those working in the new children's centres, professional identity is still in the process of being built.

> **CHAPTER SUMMARY** *continued*
>
> *In order to ensure effective multi-professional working, clear lines of communication are essential, but in complex and individual organisations such as children's centres, these lines depend on building trust through strong relationships. In addition staff need to be confident in their own identity and role, to understand the roles of other professionals and to have a shared understanding of the ways in which they work together. All of this also rests on strong leadership and shared vision. Thus the vision for multi-professional working may be an idea which is enshrined in principle, but difficult to implement in practice. It is still a work in progress.*

References

Alexander, H. and Macdonald, E. (2001) The art of integrated multi-disciplinary partnership working: are there people who just don't want to play? Paper presented at Scottish Evaluation Society conference

Anning, A. and Ball, M. (2008) *Improving Services for Young Children*, London: Sage

Anning, A., Cottrell, D., Frost, N., Green, J. and Robinson, M. (2006) *Developing Multi-professional Teamwork for Integrated Children's Services*. Maidenhead: Open University Press

Atkinson, M., Doherty, P. and Kinder, K. (2005) Multi-agency working. *Journal of Early Childhood Research*, Sage Publications, 3(1): 7–17

Bertram, T., Pascal, C., Bokhari, S., Gasper, M. and Holterman, S. (2002) Early Excellence Centre Pilot Programme Second Evaluation Report 2000–2001, Research Report 361, DfES

Chandler, T. (2006) Working in multidisciplinary teams, in Pugh B. and Duffy, 2006 (4th edition). *Contemporary Issues in the Early Years*. London: SAGE

Cohen, B., Moss, P., Petrie, P. and Wallace, J. (2004) *A New Deal for Children?* University of Bristol, The Policy Press

Cottle, M. (2011) Understanding and achieving quality in Sure Start children's centres: Practitioners' perspectives. *International Journal of Early Years Education*, 19(3–4): 249–65

Davis, J.M. and Smith, M. (2012) *Working in Multi-professional Contexts: A practical guide for professionals in children's services*. London: SAGE

DCSF (2008) *The Sure Start Journey: A summary of evidence*. Nottingham: DCSF

DfE (2012a) The impact of Sure Start Local Programmes on seven year olds and their families. The National Evaluation of Sure Start (NESS) Team Institute for the Study of Children, Families and Social Issues, Birkbeck, University of London

DfE (2012b) Multi Agency Working **www.education.gov.uk/childrenandyoungpeople/ strategy/integratedworking/a0069013/multi-agency-working**, (Direct Gov, 2012a) accessed 16 November 2012

Eisenstadt, N. (2011) *Providing a Sure Start*. Bristol: Policy Press

Frost, N. (2005) *Professionalism, Partnership and Joined-up Thinking*. Dartington: Research in Practice

Garrett, P.M. (2009) *'Transforming' Children's Services? Social Work, Neoliberalism and the 'Modern' World*. Maidenhead, Open University Press

Gasper, M. (2010) *Multi-agency Working in the Early Years: Challenges and opportunities*. London: SAGE

Glenny, G. (2005) Riding the dragon: Exploring the principles that underpin effective interagency networking. *Support for Learning*, 20(4): 167–75, November 2005

Glenny, G. and Roaf, C. (2008) Multiprofessional Communication, Maidenhead, Open University Press

Hudson, B. (2007) Pessimism and optimism in inter-professional working: The Sedgefield Integrated Team. *Journal of Interprofessional Care*, January 2007, 21(1): 3–15

Johnson, S. (2011) Impact of Social Science on Policy: Sure Start Case Study, Report to ESRC, University of Hull

Leadbetter, J., Daniels, H., Edwards, A., Martin, D., Middleton, D., Popova, A., Warmington, P., Apostolov, A. and Brown, S. (2007) Professional learning within multi-agency children's services: Researching into practice. *Educational Research*, 49(1): 83–98

Moss, P. (2004) Why we need a well qualified early childhood workforce, Paper presented at The Early Years Workforce: A Graduate Future, Early Childhood Studies Degrees Network Conference, Regent's College, London, March 16 2004

Moss, P. (2006a) Farewell to childcare? *National Institute Economic Review*, N.195, January 2006

Moss, P. (2006b) Structures, understandings and discourses: Possibilities for re-envisioning the early childhood worker. *Contemporary Issues in Early Childhood*, 7(1): 30–41

NESS (2012) National Evaluation of Sure Start **www.ness.bbk.ac.uk/** accessed 16 November 2012

NHSA (2012) National Head Start Association **www.nhsa.org/** accessed 16 November 2012

Rostron, M., (2012) *Leading Across Professional Boundaries*, **content.yudu.com/Library/A1xpeu/CCLRJuly2012/resources/7.htm** accessed 16 November 2012

Rowe, A. (2005) The impact of Sure Start on health visiting, in Weinberger, J., Pickstone, C. and Hannon, P. *Learning from Sure Start*, Maidenhead: Open University Press

Sharp, C., Lord, P., Handscomb, G., Macleod, S., Southcott, C., George, N. and Jeffes, J. (2012) *Highly Effective Leadership in Children's Centres*. Nottingham: National College for School Leadership

Weinberger, J., Pickstone, C. and Hannon, P. (2005) *Learning from Sure Start*, Maidenhead: Open University Press

Wenger, E. (1998) *Communities of Practice, Learning, Meaning and Identity*. Cambridge: Cambridge University Press

Cheminais, R. (2010) *Developing and Evaluating Multi-agency Partnerships: A practical toolkit for school and children's centre managers*. London: Routledge

Glenny, G. and Roaf, C. (2008) *Multiprofessional Communication*. Maidenhead: Open University Press

Needham, M., Siraj-Blatchford, I. and Clarke, K. (2007) *The Team Around the Child: Multi-agency working in the early years*. Stoke on Trent: Trentham Books

Walker, G. (2008) *Working Together for Children: A critical introduction to multi-agency working*. London: Continuum

WEBSITES

www.education.gov.uk/childrenandyoungpeople

www.education.gov.uk/childrenandyoungpeople/strategy/integratedworking/a0069013/multi-agency-working

www.education.gov.uk/childrenandyoungpeople/earlylearningandchildcare/delivery/surestart/a0076712/www.nationalcollege.org.uk/togetherforchildren

www.nationalcollege.org.uk/docinfo?id=179254&filename=highly-effective-leadership-in-childrens-centres.pdf

www.ness.bbk.ac.uk/

www.nhsa.org/

Index